STANLEY *COMPLETE*

PLUMBING

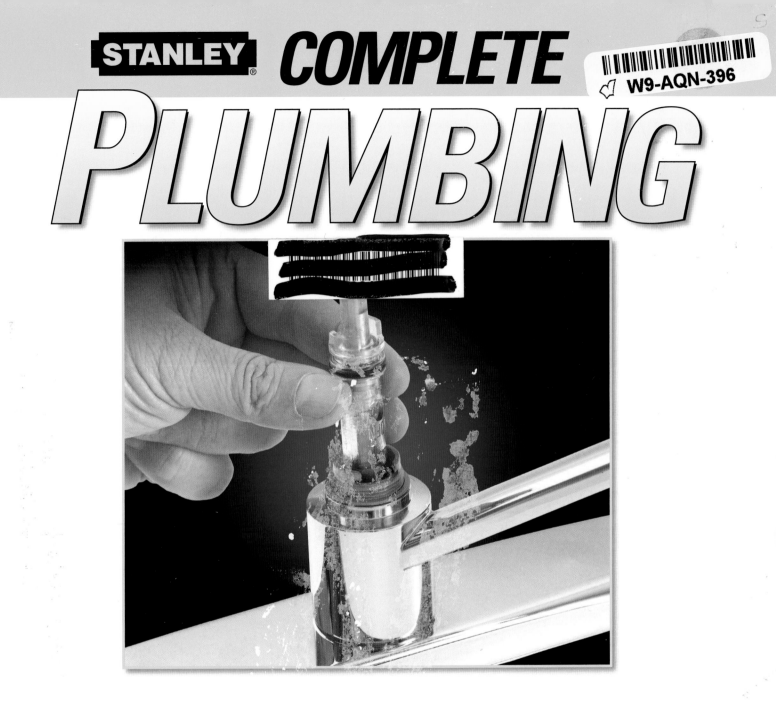

Meredith® Books
Des Moines, Iowa

CONTENTS

Stanley Complete Plumbing
Editor: Larry Johnston
Copy Chief: Terri Frederickson
Copy Editor: Kevin Cox
Publishing Operations Manager: Karen Schirm
Senior Editor, Asset and Information Management: Phillip Morgan
Edit and Design Production Coordinator: Mary Lee Gavin
Art and Editorial Sourcing Coordinator: Jackie Swartz
Book Production Managers: Pam Kvitne,
    Marjorie J. Schenkelberg, Mark Weaver
Imaging Center Operator: Tony Goforth
Technical Editor, The Stanley Works: Mike Maznio
Contributing Copy Editor: Susie Fagan
Contributing Proofreaders: Andrea Kline, Cheri Madison,
    Gary Webster
Other Contributors: Janet Anderson

**Additonal Editorial Contributions from
Abramowitz Creative Studios**
Publishing Director/Designer: Tim Abramowitz
Designers: Kelly Bailey, Joel Wires, Adam White
Writer: Martin Miller
Illustration: Art Rep Services, Inc.
    Director: Chip Nadeau
    Illustrator: Dave Brandon
Photography: Image Studios
    Account Executive: Lisa Egan
    Photographers: Bill Rein, Bill Kapinski,
        Shane Van Boxel, John Von Dorn
    Technical Advisor: Rick Nadke

Meredith® Books
Editor in Chief: Gregory H. Kayko
Executive Director, Design: Matt Strelecki
Managing Editor: Amy Tincher-Durik
Executive Editor/Group Manager: Benjamin W. Allen
Senior Associate Design Director: Tom Wegner
Marketing Product Manager: Brent Wiersma

Executive Director, Marketing and New Business: Kevin Kacere
Director, Marketing and Publicity: Amy Nichols
Executive Director, Sales: Ken Zagor
Director, Operations: George A. Susral
Director, Production: Douglas M. Johnston
Business Director: Jim Leonard

Senior Vice President: Karla Jeffries
Vice President and General Manager: Douglas J. Guendel

Meredith Publishing Group
President: Jack Griffin
Executive Vice President: Doug Olson

Meredith Corporation
Chairman of the Board: William T. Kerr
President and Chief Executive Officer: Stephen M. Lacy

In Memoriam: E. T. Meredith III (1933–2003)

Photography Courtesy of:
(Photographers credited may retain copyright © to the listed
  photographs:

ClimateMaster, Inc.
www.climatemaster.com
Page 275 B

Kohler, Inc.
www.kohler.com
Page 200 BR, 201 BR, 278 B

RenewABILITY Energy, Inc.
www.renewability.com
Page 240 B

L = Left, R = Right, C = Center, B = Bottom, T = Top

All of us at Meredith® Books are dedicated to providing you with the
information and ideas you need to enhance your home and garden.
We welcome your comments and suggestions about this book. Write
to us at:

Meredith Corporation
Meredith Books
1716 Locust St.
Des Moines, IA 50309-3203

If you would like more information on other Stanley products, call
1-800-STANLEY or visit us at: www.stanleyworks.com
Stanley® and the notched rectangle around the Stanley name are
registered trademarks of The Stanley Works and subsidiaries.

Note to the Readers: Due to differing conditions, tools, and
individual skills, Meredith Corporation assumes no responsibility
for any damages, injuries suffered, or losses incurred as a
result of following the information published in this book.
Before beginning any project, review the instructions carefully,
and if any doubts or questions remain, consult local experts
or authorities. Because codes and regulations vary greatly,
you always should check with authorities to ensure that your
project complies with all applicable local codes and regulations.
Always read and observe all of the safety precautions provided
by manufacturers of any tools, equipment, or supplies, and
follow all accepted safety procedures.

KNOWING YOUR LIMITS

If you are handy and able to work methodically, most of the projects in this book are within your reach. However, some are time-consuming and involve skills beyond plumbing. Understanding your limits and the constraints of time can assure an enjoyable, safe project.

Plan your time carefully; your family will not be able to use a plumbing fixture until you have finished the repair or installation. The "Prestart Checklist" at the beginning of each project will help you gather the needed tools and estimate the time needed to complete the project.

Even a well planned project can run into unforeseen problems. You may find yourself in need of tools or parts, so do your work while the stores are open.

Working safely and comfortably
Before attempting any project, turn off the water. Then turn on a faucet to make sure the water supply is off.

Take care not to touch nearby electrical outlets, especially if you are wet.

Plumbing can be physically demanding, not because of heavy lifting but because you often have to work in cramped areas. Make the work site comfortable. Spread towels as cushions, use a drop cloth to catch water and grime, and illuminate the area with a stand-up flashlight (page 22).

Hiring a pro
Even if you believe you are competent to do the work, you may not have the time. Rather than forcing your family to live in a work site for months, it may be worth the extra money to hire someone who can get the job done quickly. More importantly, local codes may require that only licensed contractors perform certain types of work. Some types of work call for the expertise of a qualified plumbing contractor.

Choosing a plumber
For a major job, obtain quotes from two or three plumbers. Ask for references and talk to former customers to see if they were satisfied. Make sure the plumbing contractor is licensed and bonded to work in your area and has liability and worker's compensation insurance so you will be protected in case of a mishap.

Levels of plumber involvement
Most professional plumbers would rather do all the work themselves. However, if you feel confident that you can work on a project and need only a bit of reassurance that you're installing things correctly, a plumber may agree to work as a consultant. Often an hour spent with a pro can save you plenty in materials and labor.

You might hire a plumber to do only the rough-in work of running supply and DWV (drain-waste-vent) pipes. Once the rough plumbing is installed, have a local inspector approve it before you finish paying the plumber. Then you can close up the walls and install the fixtures.

Working with a plumber
Once the work has begun, use this book to see how the job ought to be done. If you are dissatisfied, or if you do not understand what the plumber is doing, don't hesitate to ask questions.

Be firm but polite. Whenever possible, save all your questions for the end of the day, so you won't be a nuisance. However, if you feel the work is shoddy or the plumber is shrugging off your concerns, make it clear that you will not pay until you are satisfied. Have all work inspected.

Calling in a pro

Finding a quality plumbing contractor begins with a phone call, but requires follow-up with references, assurance of proper licensing and insurance, and a clear understanding of what, how, and when the work will be performed.

GETTING READY

Some homeowners avoid plumbing chores because they see them as difficult and messy. As a result they call in a plumber for minor problems they could easily handle themselves. Others tackle the most complex plumbing projects, often with disastrous results.

Armed with this book you can determine which projects you are comfortable with doing yourself and which are best left to pros. The complete step-by-step instructions will help you satisfactorily complete those projects you choose to do.

Scoping out the job

Typically any plumbing that is exposed (not hidden in walls) is easy to work on for a handy person with no special knowledge or skills. Faucets and traps can be dismantled, unclogged, and repaired or replaced using inexpensive tools. Trips to the hardware store for replacement parts are usually more time-consuming than the chore itself.

The work becomes more challenging when the fixtures get heftier and more complex. You can replace a bathroom sink quickly but a kitchen sink, with its mass of plumbing underneath, is a bigger job. Plumbing and fittings that are partially hidden, such as a shower faucet and its supply lines, may require carpentry, tiling, and other skills.

Anytime you install a plumbing fixture where there was none before—in other words whenever you need to run new pipes—you enter a new arena. New plumbing must conform to codes and must be inspected by a local building department.

Getting the work done

Often the most difficult part of a job is not the actual plumbing but dealing with obstacles. You may have to squeeze into cramped quarters. Use a kneeling pad, a drop cloth, or even an old pillow to make the worksite as comfortable as possible. Position a flashlight or work light so you can see clearly.

There is one basic rule for most plumbing projects: **Shut off the water and test to make sure the water is off.** Keep a bucket and some old towels handy to catch the small amounts of water that may dribble out of pipes.

Before tackling a project understand plumbing in general and your home's system in particular.

CHAPTER PREVIEW

     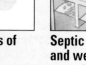

Shutting off the water
page 8

Drain-waste-vent system
page 10

Supply system
page 12

Principles of venting
page 14

Septic systems and wells
page 16

Organize tools
Use separate buckets for different categories of tools. One bucket can hold general carpentry tools, while another can hold tools for cutting and joining pipe.

Give yourself room
Because most of a plumbing system is behind walls and ceilings, demolition is one of several carpentry skills needed in a plumbing project. Allow plenty of working space when opening a wall—making a large patch takes only slightly more time than a small patch.

SHUTTING OFF THE WATER

There is one basic prerequisite for most plumbing projects: Shut off the water to the work area, then test to make sure the water supply is shut off. Failing to shut off the water can lead to a mess, with water spraying all over the place.

Every adult family member should know how to shut off the water, both at the fixtures and to the entire house.

Fixture shutoffs

Most homes built in the past 40 years have a separate stop valve (also called a fixture shutoff valve) for each faucet, toilet, and fixture. A supply tube (sometimes called a riser) runs from the stop valve to the fixture. (A faucet has two stop valves, one for hot water and one for cold; a toilet needs only a cold-water shutoff.) If a fixture does not have a stop valve, you will have to shut off water to part or all of the house before

working. It's a good idea to install a stop valve so you can stop the flow quickly in case of emergency (pages 118–119).

A stop valve typically has a body with a chrome finish and an oval handle. In an older home it may be shaped like a house valve with a round or decorative ceramic handle.

Most stop valves are made for light duty because they are used only for emergencies or repairs. That means they might not shut off the water completely. Do not crank down on its handle with pliers; you may break the valve. Some close in only a quarter turn. See pages 116–117 to repair a faulty stop valve or supply tube.

Main shutoffs

Every home has at least one main shutoff, which controls water flowing to the entire

house. Often there is one main shutoff inside the house and another outside.

An inside main shutoff is usually located near the point where water enters the house. Often it is near the water meter. There may be two valves, one on each side of the meter. If your home has no meter (some homes don't), look for a large pipe that enters the house, often through a basement floor or at the bottom of a crawlspace. The shutoff should be somewhere along the run of that pipe.

In regions where winters are mild, the main shutoff valve may be outside the house.

An outside shutoff valve is near the point where a pipe branches off from the utility's main line to bring water to your home. If you have a parkway—a narrow strip of land between the sidewalk and the street—the outside shutoff will likely be there. If you

Stop valves

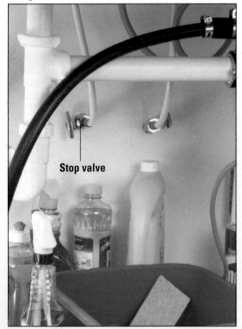

Kitchen sink stop valves often are hidden amid pipes and tubes under the sink. Stop valves allow you to shut off water to the kitchen faucet. There may be a separate stop valve for the dishwasher.

Stop valve

A saddle tee-valve tied into a supply pipe runs cold water to a refrigerator's icemaker. Although a saddle tee is a handy way to tap into a line, some municipalities forbid its use. Check local building codes.

Hot shutoff   Cold shutoff

In-faucet stop valves are found on some tub/shower faucets. Use a large slot screwdriver to turn water on and off.

cannot find yours, ask your water utility department where to find it.

In temperate regions an outside shutoff is usually housed in a plastic or concrete underground container, sometimes called a Buffalo box (below). Usually the box lid can be pried up, but you may need to dig away vegetation to free it.

In colder regions the shutoff will be below the frost line, typically at the bottom of a tube covered with a cast-iron cover. You may need a key, a long-handle wrench, to be able to reach down to the valve and turn the water on and off. Keys are usually the same size and type throughout a neighborhood. Often your water utility department will loan you a key for your shutoff.

Intermediate shutoffs

You may find other shutoff valves on exposed supply pipes in a basement, crawlspace, utility room, or access panel behind a bathtub (page 12). These will probably be in pairs, one for hot and one for cold water. (If the water has been running recently, you can tell which pipe is hot by feeling them with your hand.) These are probably intermediate shutoffs, meaning they control water supply to a portion of a house.

To find out what a shutoff valve controls, close it and go through the house turning on faucets and flushing toilets. Remember that a toilet with a tank will flush once after the water is off; listen or look for water refilling the tank after the flush.

If you have hot-water heat in your home, there will be shutoff valves near the boiler. These have nothing to do with the supply pipes for your plumbing fixtures.

Water meters

To keep track of water usage or to check that the utility is charging correctly, read your water meter. If your meter has a series of dials, each is labeled for the number of cubic feet it measures. It may be that some dials turn counterclockwise while others turn clockwise. A meter with a digital readout simply displays the amount of cubic feet of water used. Note the number at the start of the month or billing period, then read it again at the end and subtract the first number to calculate your use.

Shutoff valves

An in-house main shutoff, a fairly large valve found near the point where water enters the house, shuts off water for the entire house. As shown above, the shutoff valve is often next to the water meter.

A Buffalo box is another type of whole-house shutoff. Common in the South and Southwest, this buried box can be found outdoors. Pry off the lid. Inside you'll find a standard valve that you can turn with your hands or one that requires a special key.

Intermediate shutoff valves control water flow to part of the house. There will be two or more pairs of these.

DRAIN-WASTE-VENT SYSTEM

Drain-waste-vent (DWV) pipes carry waste and water out of the house without gurgles or fumes. Never install or replace a DWV pipe without consulting a building inspector. These pipes must be installed according to precise specifications.

Drainpipes

The centerpiece of a DWV system is the **main stack,** usually a pipe 3 or 4 inches in diameter, that runs straight up through the roof. A **secondary stack,** perhaps 2 or 3 inches in diameter, serves a branch of the system.

Branch drainpipes of smaller diameter—typically 1½ or 2 inches—carry water from specific fixtures to a stack.

Drain stacks in older homes are often made of cast iron, which rusts through after 80 years or so. In older homes the branch drains typically are made of galvanized steel, which is much more likely to rust and corrode shut. In newer homes plastic pipe is used for stacks and branch drains. The first plastic pipe to be used was ABS, which is black. Since the 1970s ABS has generally been replaced by white- or cream-colored PVC pipe. In rare cases drainpipes are made of copper.

Drainpipes must be sloped, usually about ¼ inch per foot, so water runs freely through them. Codes require special fittings make sweeping turns rather than abrupt turns, so waste does not get trapped in the pipes.

Drainpipes often have **cleanouts**—places where a plug can be temporarily removed—so the pipes can be augered to clear a clog.

The main drain line

Water travels downward through the stacks to the main drain line, which leads to the municipal sewage system or to a septic system. In older homes the main drain may be made of clay pipe or other porous material. Tree roots sometimes work their way into the main line, causing wastewater to back up into the house. The solution is to call a company that specializes in augering main lines.

Vent pipes

For water to flow smoothly without gurgling, there must be an air passageway behind the water (below). Vent pipes extend from the drainpipes up through the roof to provide that passage. Vent pipes also carry odors out of the house.

The drainpipe for each plumbing fixture must be connected to a vent that supplies the pipe with air from the outside. In some cases the drainpipe is connected directly to a main or secondary stack pipe, which travels straight up through the roof. More often a drainpipe is connected to a **revent** pipe that reaches up and over to tie into the main vent stack. Plumbing codes strictly prescribe where vent pipes can connect to the stack and how far they should travel. In most cases a "wet" section of pipe—the part that carries wastewater—cannot be used as a vent, even if it is usually dry. Examine the illustration on the opposite page, and you'll see that all the vent pipes lead to sections of a stack that never carries running water.

If your drainpipes gurgle when you run water in a sink or flush a toilet, call a professional plumber for an inspection. A vent may be stopped up and need clearing. Or the plumbing may be incorrect, and you may need a new vent line.

In some cases local codes allow for other venting strategies. For instance a basement sink might be vented with a special wall vent, which simply runs out the wall. Or a cheater vent, a small device that draws air from the room rather than outside, may be allowed.

Why venting is necessary

Try to quickly empty a bottle with a narrow mouth; it will gurgle and glug as it slowly empties. Open the vent cap on a plastic gas container and it flows smoothly. That's because the vent hole allows air to enter behind the flowing liquid, producing a quick, glug-free flow. Vent stacks in a household plumbing system work the same way.

Air trapped

Vent open

Irregular flow

Smooth flow

FIXTURE TRAPS

Fumes and gas

Trapped water

The drain water for every fixture must run through a trap—a section of pipe shaped like a sideways P or an S. Because of its shape a trap holds water, creating a seal that keeps fumes and gases from entering the house. A toilet has a built-in trap. Sink traps are made of chrome-plated brass or plastic with joints that can easily be taken apart.

DWV System

Main stack

Secondary stack

Revent

Tub trap

Main soil stack

Branch drainpipe

Vent

Waste

Main cleanout

Branch drainpipes lead from fixture traps to a stack, which carries water out of the house. Vent pipes allow fumes to escape and provide an air passageway behind the drained water.

SUPPLY SYSTEM

Pipes that carry water into the house are less complicated than the drain-waste-vent (DWV) pipes. Typically a single pipe runs to the water heater, where it divides into cold and hot pipes that supply faucets, fixtures, and toilets. Shutoff and stop valves make it possible to turn off the water along the supply system (pages 8–9).

Water purity
If the water comes from a utility company, it is tested regularly to ensure it is safe to drink. If you have a private well, testing for purity is your responsibility. If your water tastes bad or produces stains, running the main supply line through a water softener and/or a water filter may help.

Water meter
If your water bill is the same from month to month, you probably have unmetered water. If you have a water meter, the bill reflects how much water enters your house. A water meter may be found inside the house, or it may be in the Buffalo box outside.

Water heater
Near the water heater one pipe branches off to supply cold water throughout the house, and another enters a gas or electric water heater, which typically holds and heats 30 to 50 gallons of water. A supply pipe exits the heater to deliver hot water throughout the house. If you often run out of hot water while bathing, consider buying a water heater with a larger capacity.

Supply pipes
Supply pipes run in pairs throughout the house. Vertical pipes are called risers.

Supply pipes may be copper, galvanized steel, or plastic. Galvanized steel pipes rust and corrode over time, causing leaks that lower water pressure. Plastic PVC supply pipes have been banned by most communities for interior use because the joints may become loose. Newer plastic pipes, made of rigid CPVC or flexible polyethylene (PE), are more reliable and are permitted in many areas. Copper is the material of choice in most areas. It is long-lasting and its smooth surface does not collect deposits that slow the flow of water. A properly soldered joint, using lead-free solder, is as strong as the pipe itself.

A nail or screw can easily pierce a copper or plastic supply pipe, so plumbing codes prescribe measures to keep supply pipes out of harm's way. Pipes within walls should be placed in the center of studs so that nails cannot reach them. Protective metal plates may also be required.

Pipe sizes and water pressure
The larger a pipe's inside diameter, the greater the water pressure. If water pressure is too low, the problem may be the supply pipes.

The inside diameter of the pipe bringing water into a house is typically 1 inch or 1¼ inches. Soon after entering the house, the pipe size changes to ¾ inch. Pipes that carry water from room to room may be ¾ or ½ inch; the larger size is preferable. Pipes that supply water to specific fixtures are usually ½ inch to the stop, then ⅜ or ¼ inch.

A bathtub access panel

Bathtub plumbing is complicated, so many homes have an access panel to allow you to reach it. To find an access panel, look in the adjacent room or closet, on the wall directly behind the tub faucet.

Locating supply lines

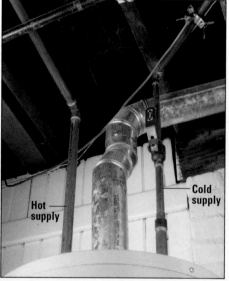

Hot supply

Cold supply

Near the water heater supply lines branch into cold and hot pipes—an excellent place to start tracing your supply system. Most water heaters have "hot" and "cold" stamped on the top of the metal housing.

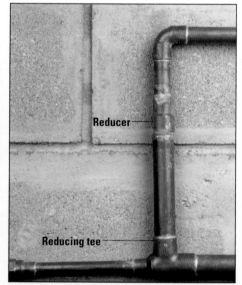

Reducer

Reducing tee

Some lines reduce in dimension along their run. Here a pipe steps down in size from ¾ inch to ½ inch.

Hammer arrester

Shutoff

Shutoff

Cold supply for toilet

Water heater

Water softener

Hot water supply

Hammer arrester

Cold supply for toilet

Cold water supply

Main shutoff

Water meter

Unsoftened water

Cold, softened water

Hot, softened water

Supply pipes usually run in pairs that carry hot and cold water. Various shutoff valves allow you to turn off water for a single fixture, a room, or the entire house.

PRINCIPLES OF VENTING

How will the drain be vented? That's the first question to answer as you plan for plumbing a new appliance or an addition to your system. When developing a plumbing system plan, you may choose from several venting types; each option may present problems or complications. Before finalizing a plan have the venting scheme approved by the local plumbing inspector.

Vent types

A true vent is a vertical pipe attached to a drain line that travels through the roof with no water running through it. If a fixture is close to the stack and on the top floor, the upper part of the stack serves nicely as a vent (as is the case for the toilet shown below). Many fixtures are not so conveniently located, however, and other solutions must be found.

A revent pipe, also called an auxiliary vent, attaches to the drain line near the fixture and runs up and over to the main vent.

It may attach directly behind the fixture (sink, below) or to the horizontal drain line (revent alternative, opposite).

If two fixtures are on opposite sides of a wall, they may tie into the stack with a sanitary cross; this is called a common vent (back-to-back sinks, opposite).

When a fixture is close enough to a stack, a wet vent (tub, below) may be allowed by code. In this case the tub's drain empties into a pipe that also serves as a vent.

For a freestanding sink code may allow a loop vent (opposite). If reventing is difficult and wet-venting isn't allowed, you may have to install a separate vent pipe through the roof (see page 181).

An air admittance valve (AAV) opens to let air in when waste drains, then gravity closes it to keep sewer gases from escaping back into the room. Codes in many localities allow these relatively new devices to take the place of vent lines. Depending on the size of the unit and any code restrictions, AAVs can be used to vent multiple fixtures. Check codes to make sure they permit AAVs.

TYPICAL VENTING ALTERNATIVES

Revent

True vent

Wet vent

Main vent (stack)

A true vent pipe must remain dry while water runs down the drain. A wet vent also serves as a drain line but is large enough that it is never actually filled with water.

VENTING WITH AN AIR ADMITTANCE VALVE (AAV)

Window framing in wall prevents installation of vent line

AAV

The critical distance

When you're remodeling your plumbing system, can you install a wet vent, or do you have to install a revent or a separate vent? Finding the answer can involve complicated calculations, based on formulas that can vary from one locale to another. The size of the pipe that codes require, the type of fixture you want to install, and the number of fixtures that are already wet-vented on the same line are three factors that determine the critical distance—how far the fixture can be from the vent pipe. Measure the length of the pipes carefully and consult a plumbing inspector to determine whether wet-venting is possible.

Installing vent pipes

Vent pipes, often narrower than drainpipes, need not slope like drainpipes. Normally they run level or plumb, unless there is an obstacle to work around.

Vents must be installed so they stay dry. This means that they should emerge from the top of the drainpipe, either straight vertically or at no less than a 45-degree angle from horizontal, so that water cannot back up into the vent.

The horizontal portion of a revent pipe must be at least 6 inches above the fixture's flood level—the highest point to which water can rise. (On a sink the flood level is the sink rim or overflow hole.)

The main drain

Plan drain lines to minimize the possibility of clogs. The general rule is that smaller drain pipes—1¼ inches for bathroom sinks and 1½ inches for kitchen sinks, for instance—lead to larger branch drains. These in turn lead to the main stack, which is the largest pipe of all—typically 4 inches. Because the main stack is also vertical, it will rarely clog.

The main stack leads down into the ground and then out toward the municipal sewer. The underground horizontal pipe, or main drain, that runs toward the sewer line can sometimes get clogged, especially if it is an old drain made of clay pipe. (For how to clear a clogged main, see pages 56–57).

OTHER VENTING OPTIONS

Loop vent

At least 6" above flood level

Here are other common ways to tie vents into a stack. Check local codes to see which methods are accepted in your area, then choose the method that requires the least number of holes or notches in studs.

Revent alternative

Common vent

Sanitary cross

Catch basin

Many people pour grease down a kitchen sink, which can lead to clogged drain lines. In some older homes the kitchen sink has its own stack and the drain line runs out to a catch basin—a container that traps grease. Occasionally the grease must be removed from the catch basin. A catch basin typically is behind the house and has a large metal cover. In many cases, however, the catch basin has been bypassed and is no longer in use. There may also be a rectangular grease trap under the kitchen sink. This needs to be cleaned regularly.

SEPTIC SYSTEMS AND WELLS

f your home is outside a city or suburb, it probably has its own septic system rather than a municipal sewage system. Or if your home was built before municipal sewer lines were run, there may be an old, inactive septic system in your yard; you probably don't need to remove it.

How it works

In a typical septic system, wastewater flows from the house downhill to the septic tank, which may be made of concrete or plastic. Solid sludge sinks to the bottom of the tank and scum rises to the top. Baffles trap the scum so only liquid effluent leaves the tank. Bacteria slowly break down solid waste. Not all of the solids can be broken down in the tank. The gradual buildup must be pumped out.

Effluent flows out from a pipe into a distribution box. From there it flows into perforated pipes made of clay or plastic. The pipes run through a leach field. As effluent leaches into the soil, it is further broken down by microbes in the soil. Some of the effluent evaporates, and the rest provides nutrient-rich liquid that nourishes plants.

Avoiding septic system problems

If too much water runs into the tank, waste may be pushed out before it completely breaks down. To avoid problems fix dripping faucets and encourage family members to use minimal water. Use plain white toilet paper that is approved for septic systems. Avoid flushing bulky, inorganic items that could clog the system.

Be careful what you pour down the drain. Products that can inhibit the breakdown of waste include bleach, drain cleaners, paint thinner, motor oil, and any hazardous liquid.

A garbage disposer produces sludge that can clog a septic system. Using one is forbidden by many local codes. Do not drive a car or heavy machinery over the leach field; you could damage the pipes.

Additional tanks

To reduce the volume of waste flowing into a septic system, a kitchen sink's drain may run directly into a catch basin, which captures cooking grease. A catch basin (also called a grease trap) must be serviced separately from the septic tank (page 15).

In some systems water from the washing machine runs into a seepage pit, which is either a hole filled with rocks or a pit lined with unmortared concrete blocks. If you have a seepage pit, be sure to use environmentally safe detergent.

Aerobic systems

Most septic systems are anaerobic (without oxygen), meaning that wastewater stays underground. In areas with poor soil drainage, an aerobic lagoon is sometimes used. In this system waste runs into a small pond (which should be fenced) where it is digested by both bacteria and algae.

Other areas may require an aerobic tank system, which must be pumped regularly.

HOW SEPTIC SYSTEMS WORK

Access hatch

Septic tanks vary according to local codes and practices, but all have one common purpose: They collect solids and hold them before wastewater flows into a leach field. This example has two compartments for capturing solids. In the tanks microbes break down the waste materials. Finally wastewater is dispersed through perforated drainpipes.

Wastewater from house

Baffle

Baffle

Opening between tanks

Primary tank collects most solids

Secondary tank collects remaining solids

Wastewater flows to leach field

Distribution box

Perforated drainpipe

Regular maintenance

If the septic system is large enough and properly installed, it will require only occasional attention.

■ Once a year use a sludge pole to check the sludge level. If the tank is almost half full, have it pumped. Usually a tank must be pumped every three or four years.

■ If the leach field starts to smell or if water backs up out of drains, contact a septic company immediately. There may be a clog that can be cleared if dealt with quickly.

■ Ensure that the leach field does not become saturated with water in the spring or during rainy times; a soaked field will not absorb effluent. You may need to redirect a gutter downspout, for instance.

■ Usually bacteria remain in the tank and continue to work. However if you suspect that the bacteria have been killed (by dumping chemicals down the drain, for example), you can buy an enzyme additive that will colonize the tank with microbes; just pour it down a drain.

Is the system large enough?

Codes determine how large a system must be—both the tank and the field—based on the number of people in the household. However if the toilets and faucets will be in constant use, you may need a system larger than what is required. Adding plumbing may require a larger septic system. If water backs up during wet periods, even when the tank is not full, the leach field may be too small. Consult a septic service firm to see if you need a larger tank or field.

Graywater irrigation

Some homes in areas with dry climates have a system that directs graywater—waste from clothes washers, bathtubs, and sinks—to an irrigation system that waters the lawn or specific plants. This system usually has only a very basic filter to keep out lint and hair. Be sure you use detergents that will not harm plants and do not pour chemicals down the drains.

UNDERSTANDING A WELL SYSTEM

Pump control box

Power source

Pressure tank

Well cap

Tank valve

Submersible pump

Depending on local conditions a private well may be hundreds of feet deep, reaching far enough to provide safe drinking water even during dry spells. Have the water tested regularly for contaminants, especially if you detect a change in smell or taste.

The most common system uses a submersible pump. The pump sends water into a pressure tank, which maintains an even water pressure for household use. The tank must have air trapped inside. If there is too little air, it becomes waterlogged and will switch on and off frequently. If there is too much air, bursts of air may occasionally cough out of faucets. The solution for either problem is the same: Shut off power to the pump and drain the tank until there is no more pressure. Open a faucet in the house to drain all the water. Then close the faucet and turn the pump back on. A tank that leaks must be replaced.

PLUMBING TOOLS

For a modest amount of money—probably less than the cost of a single visit from a plumber—you can assemble a tool kit that will tackle most plumbing jobs in your house. Invest in quality tools. They will stand up to tough tasks and be more comfortable to use.

General plumbing tools
These tools are useful no matter what kind of pipe you work with. An **adjustable wrench** adjusts to grab nuts and bolts. A **locking adjustable wrench** is a handy variation that quickly tightens or releases nuts and bolts. A pair of **groove-joint pliers** is useful for tightening and loosening joints. A **14-inch pipe wrench** is the ideal size for most projects. (To add to the wrench's persuasive force, slip a 1¼-inch steel pipe over the handle to increase the leverage.) If you will be working on steel pipe, buy a pair of pipe wrenches (add an 18-inch size).

To clear clogs in sinks, toilets, and tubs, first try a **flanged plunger**, whose funnellike flange extends to fit snugly into a toilet.

To plunge a sink or tub, fold up the flange. A **pressure plunger**, which expels a burst of water, sometimes can clear clogs standard plungers can't. If the clog is in a sink trap, you can often pull the hair and gunk out with a **ribbed plastic declogger.**

When those measures do not clear a clog, use a **hand-crank auger**, also called a snake. A **toilet auger** has a sleeve to protect the toilet bowl's porcelain finish.

A **putty knife** scrapes away old putty and other types of hardened debris. You'll need

Adjustable wrench

Putty knife

Pressure plunger

Locking adjustable wrench

Pipe wrench

Flanged plunger

Groove-joint pliers

Ribbed plastic declogger

Hand-crank auger

Toilet auger

both **phillips** and **slot screwdrivers** to disassemble fixtures and fittings—a **4-in-1** combines both types. Use a **wire brush** to clean parts and encrusted pipe threads. A **strainer wrench** helps you twist out the upper part of the drain assembly in a sink or tub. To remove a large nut like that beneath a kitchen sink basket strainer, a **lock-nut wrench** is easier to use than groove-joint pliers. When repairing a faucet you may need to get at the seat, a small part inside the faucet body. Use a **seat wrench.**

A **basin wrench** reaches into small spaces to loosen or tighten hold-down nuts. Without this tool removing a kitchen or bathroom faucet is nearly impossible.

Tools for plastic pipe

You can use just about any saw to cut plastic pipe—a hacksaw, a standard backsaw, an ordinary handsaw, a circular saw, or even a power miter box. However an inexpensive **plastic pipe saw** (also known as a PVC saw) cuts easily and leaves few burrs. Use it with a **miter box** to ensure straight cuts. After

cutting, burrs must be removed completely; a **deburring tool** does the job better and more quickly than a utility knife. To cut supply pipe (1 inch and smaller), you also can use a scissors-type **plastic pipe cutter.** Be sure to get a heavy-duty model made for PVC pipe. For PEX and other flexible tubing, a **plastic tubing cutter** makes a quick, clean cut.

Slot screwdriver

Wire brush

Basin wrench

4-in-1 screwdriver

Seat wrench

Strainer wrench

Lock-nut wrench

STANLEY
MADE IN U.S.A.

Plastic tubing cutter

Miter box

Deburring tool

Plastic pipe cutter

Plastic pipe saw

Tools for copper pipe

A **tubing cutter** cuts copper pipe cleanly, quickly, and without bending the pipe out of round. For working in tight spots, you might need a **small tubing cutter** as well. (A hacksaw can cut copper pipe, but a dull blade may cause you to dent the pipe, making it difficult to add fittings.)

To bend flexible pipe without crimping, use a **tubing bender.** Choose the size that tightly slips onto the pipe. A **flaring tool** may be needed for certain types of compression fittings, particularly in outdoor installations. A **handle puller** smoothly detaches faucet handles without strain or damage.

To sweat copper pipe and fittings, buy a **propane torch.** A model with an **electric igniter** is easiest—and safest—to use. To protect flammable surfaces from the propane torch flame, use a **fiber shield** or prop an old cookie sheet behind the joint being heated.

The ends of copper pipe and the insides of fittings must be burnished before soldering. A **multiuse wire brush** does both jobs. Or buy a **reamer brush** for the fittings and a roll of **plumber's emery cloth** for the pipe ends. Before joining pipes paint **flux** on the pipes using a **flux brush.**

Reamer brush

Tubing benders

Small tubing cutter

Multiuse wire brush

Plumber's emery cloth

Tubing cutter

Flux

Flux brush

Flaring tool

Handle puller

Fiber shield

Propane torch with electric igniter

Standard propane torch

CARPENTRY TOOLS

When running new plumbing lines, much of your time will be spent cutting and drilling to clear a path for the pipes. This work must be done with precision so the house's framing will not be compromised.

In addition to plumbing tools, have on hand a set of general carpentry tools, including a **hammer** and **tape measure.**

A **flat pry bar** will enable you to disassemble most nailed-together framing members. Occasionally you may need a longer pry bar.

Demolition chores may require small or large **sledgehammers.** Horizontal drainpipes must slope slightly. To check the slope use a **carpenter's level** for long sections of pipe and a **torpedo level** for short sections.

Use a standard ⅜-inch **drill** to bore holes in 2× lumber. For installing screws buy a **magnetic sleeve** and several screw heads. If you have to drill more than 10 holes, consider renting or buying a heavy-duty, ½-inch drill. Buy several **spade bits**—they wear out quickly. Attach spade bits to a **bit**

extender when extra reach is needed.

A **quick-change sleeve** speeds switching **twist bits.** Make finder holes with a **long bit.** For cutting holes larger than 1 inch in diameter, buy a **hole saw.** A **right-angle drill** makes it possible to drill straight holes in tight places—handy when running pipe.

If you need to cut away a small amount of concrete or masonry, a hammer and **cold chisel** may be all you need. Renting or buying a **hammer drill** will speed tough-to-bore holes in concrete.

Torpedo level

Carpenter's level

Bit extender

Long bit

Flat pry bar

Magnetic sleeve

Hole saw

Spade bits

Twist bits

Drill

Hammer

Quick-change sleeve

Tape measure

Sledgehammer

Right-angle drill

Hammer drill with masonry bit

Cold chisel

CARPENTRY TOOLS _continued_

To get to pipes inside a wall, you'll need to cut through drywall or plaster. For small jobs a **drywall saw** is adequate. A full-size **hacksaw** is useful for cutting steel and copper pipes and for removing rusted fittings and old sections of pipe. Have a **close-work hacksaw** for working in tight areas. Full-size hacksaw blades as well as shorter metal cutting blades are most commonly used. A **stand-up flashlight** makes it easier to work in cramped, dark quarters.

For cutting access panels and opening areas of flooring, use a **jigsaw.** It can also be used for cutting holes in subflooring for drains and close bends. A **handsaw** is useful for altering framing or cutting access holes.

To chisel a large area, rent an **electric jackhammer,** also known as a chipper. You can choose from several types of **jackhammer chisels** to suit the job at hand.

Should your project call for cutting through subflooring or notching framing members,

a **reciprocating saw** is indispensable. It reaches to cut boards in tight and awkward spots and can even slice through nails and screws. You can also use it to cut into galvanized steel drain and supply lines. Several types of blades are available, including metal-cutting blades. Buy several; they often bend or break.

Drywall saw

Handsaw

Close-work hacksaw

Utility knife

Hacksaw

Jigsaw

Reciprocating saw

Jackhammer chisel

Stand-up flashlight

Electric jackhammer

Use a **circular saw** for notching studs and, with a metal-cutting blade, for cutting cast-iron pipe. You'll also need it if you revise existing framing to suit a new installation.

For large projects a **power miter box** (or chopsaw) with a fine-cutting blade does a quick and precise job of cutting PVC pipe. Make sure long pipes are supported to make a square cut and avoid binding.

Power miter box

Circular saw

SAFETY FIRST
Tools that protect

Whenever you're doing work that creates sparks or flying debris, wear **safety goggles.** Preserve your hearing when using power tools—or even a simple hammer—with **ear protectors.**

Protect your hands with **leather gloves** when working with rough framing or cut pipes. When clearing clogs you may get spattered with caustic chemicals; wear long clothes and **heavy-duty rubber gloves.**

Plug power tools into a **GFCI-protected extension cord,** which will shut off the moment it senses danger from exposure to water. (Cordless tools are safest.) When you're sweating joints have a **fire extinguisher** nearby.

GFCI-protected extension cord

Fire extinguisher

Safety goggles

Ear protectors

Leather gloves

Heavy-duty rubber gloves

PIPES

The new pipes you install will probably be either copper supplies or PVC drainpipes. However it's also likely that you'll encounter other types of pipe, such as galvanized steel and even cast iron. If you have only a short run to make, you may choose the original material type. However most inspectors would prefer that you use copper or PVC, which are less expensive and easier to install.

Cast iron

Most homes built before the 1960s have **cast-iron** vertical stacks and perhaps cast-iron horizontal drainpipes as well.

This material is strong and usually durable; a pipe in good condition can be expected to last for decades. However it can rust. It's not unusual for one or two sections to rust through while the rest of the pipe remains in good shape. Sections of cast-iron pipe can be replaced with plastic pipe by using transition fittings.

In older cast-iron installations, each pipe has a bell-shaped hub at one end (below) into which the next pipe's straight end fits. The joint is sealed by packing it with oakum—a kind of oily fiber—and then pouring in molten lead. Newer cast-iron pipe is joined with no-hub fittings, consisting of neoprene sleeves tightened with stainless-steel clamps.

Plastic

Plastic pipe is inexpensive and easy to use. Joints are glued together using primer and cement made for the particular type of plastic (page 34).

Black **ABS** (acrylonitrile-butadiene-styrene) pipe was the first plastic pipe to be used in homes. It is no longer permitted in many areas because its joints occasionally come loose, but normally it can be expected to last. (For how to install or add on to ABS, see page 129.)

White or cream-colored **PVC** (polyvinyl-chloride) pipe is now the most common choice for drainpipes. It lasts nearly forever, is strong, and is impervious to most chemicals. Stamped printing on the pipe tells the pipe size, as well as its "schedule," an indication of strength. Schedule 40 is considered strong enough for most residential drain lines.

Schedule 80 PVC is sometimes used for cold-water supply lines, though many inspectors disapprove of it. It definitely should not be used for hot-water supply because it shrinks and expands with changing temperature. **CPVC** (chlorinated

Hub

Cast iron

PVC

ABS

0 ASTM D-2665 [NSF-dwv] [⊗] ▪ PVC 1120 PR 330 PSI @ 23c ASTM D-1785 [NSF-pw] [⊗] ▪ CP110P

Pipe sizes

Material	Outside circumference	Inside diameter
Copper		
	2"	½"
	2¾"	¾"
	3½"	1"
Steel (galvanized or black)		
	2"	⅜"
	2⅜"	½"
	3⅛"	¾"
	4"	1"
	4¾"	1¼"
	5½"	1½"
	7"	2"
Plastic (PVC, CPVC, or ABS)		
	2¾"	½"
	3½"	¾"
	4¼"	1"
	5⅛"	1¼"
	6"	1½"
	7½"	2"
	10½"	3"
	14"	4"
Cast iron		
	7"	2"
	10⅛"	3"
	13⅜"	4"

polyvinyl-chloride) pipe has the strength of PVC and is heat resistant, so many codes allow its use for interior supply lines (pages 130–131).

New **PEX** supply pipe has a hoselike flexibility and joins with compression fittings, making it easy to install (pages 132–133). However it is expensive and is not allowed by many codes.

Steel pipe

Many older homes have **galvanized steel** pipe for supply lines and possibly for branch drain lines. It is a dull gray when old and slightly shiny when new.

Galvanized pipe is strong—it's difficult to drive a nail through it—but don't expect it to last more than 50 years. Joints develop rust and, even worse, the insides can become clogged with mineral deposits, causing low water pressure.

Black steel pipe is used for gas lines only. It should not be used for water supply because it rusts more quickly than galvanized steel. (An exception: In some areas black steel is used for water supply lines leading into a boiler, steam lines, and air lines.)

Steel pipe is joined to fittings by first wrapping the threads with pipe-thread tape or covering them with pipe joint compound (which may be gray or white) and then tightening. The joints must be very tight; inadequately tightened joints eventually may leak.

Copper

Copper pipe is extremely long-lasting and resists corrosion, making it ideal for supply pipes. It is more expensive than plastic but still reasonably priced.

Rigid copper pipe comes in three thicknesses: The thinnest, rated "M," is usually considered strong enough for most residential applications. Thicker pipes, rated "L" or "K," are used outdoors and for drains.

Rigid copper pipe is joined to fittings by "sweating"—soldering the pieces together. A well-soldered joint should be wiped smooth; if there is a visible drip, the joint may not be strong (pages 126–127).

Flexible copper tubing is often used to supply an icemaker, dishwasher, or other appliance. It is easily bent to make fairly tight turns. If it gets kinked, however, there's no way to fix it; the piece must be replaced. It is joined to fittings and valves using compression fittings (page 111) or soldered.

CPVC

PEX tubing

Galvanized steel

Black steel gas pipe

Rigid copper

Flexible copper tubing

STANLEY PRO TIP

Finding the inside diameter

To determine a pipe's inside diameter (ID), wrap a piece of tape or a strip of paper around the pipe, then make a mark to indicate the outside circumference of the pipe. Use the pipe sizes chart opposite to find the inside diameter of the pipe.

SUPPLY PIPE FITTINGS

Whatever the material most fittings fall into one of four categories: couplings, which join pipes in a straight line; elbows, which turn corners; tees, Ys, and crosses, which allow pipes to branch out into new lines; and caps, which seal the ends of pipes between rough-in and the final installation of fixtures and appliances.

Always buy more fittings than you think you need—they're inexpensive, and it's easy to undercount while planning. You'll save yourself extra trips to the home center.

Copper fittings

A **brass drop-ear elbow**, or **stub out**, has two wings that can be attached to a stud or wall. Some can be sweated; some are **threaded**. Copper supply elbows (also called ells) are available in 90- and 45-degree angles. A **standard elbow** has two female openings of the same size; a **street elbow** has one female and one male end and is useful in tight spots. A **reducer elbow** makes the transition between one pipe size and another. A **cap** closes a pipe end; it is often installed to keep dirt out when fixtures will be installed later.

A **straight tee** fitting has three openings all the same size. A **reducer tee** has one smaller opening to accommodate a smaller pipe. Usually the two openings opposite each other are larger, and the perpendicular one is smaller.

Couplings simply join pipes in a straight line. A copper or plastic slip coupling, also known as a repair coupling, has no central indentation and can slide all the way onto one pipe, allowing you to join two pipes that are rigidly held in place. A **reducer coupling** makes a transition to a smaller pipe size.

Brass drop-ear elbow, sweatable

Cap

Reducer coupling

Standard 90° elbow

45° elbow

Brass drop-ear elbow, threaded

Reducer elbow

Coupling

45° street elbow

Straight tee

Selecting supply lines

To connect a faucet or toilet to a stop valve, choose among several types of supply tubes. **Plastic** tubes are inexpensive, but their thickness may restrict water flow.

A solid **copper** or chrome tube, hollow or PEX-lined, must be cut to fit.

A **braided stainless steel** or **braided plastic** supply tube is flexible and forgiving with respect to length.

When buying a supply tube, be sure that one end will fit the stop valve, which has a ⅜- or ½-inch opening. The other end is sized to fit

a faucet or a toilet inlet tube. Buy a longer tube than you think is needed and cut or bend it to fit. Use pipe-thread tape when joining.

Plastic

Copper

Lined chrome

Braided stainless steel

Braided plastic

Steel fittings

Threaded steel pipe (both galvanized and black gas pipe) can be assembled moving in one direction only because all the threads are clockwise. Threaded steel fittings cover the same range of types as copper fittings: **caps, couplings, elbows**, and **tees**. Threaded drop-ear elbows are fastened to framing to support a stop valve and supply tube.

To break into a line, use a special coupling called a **union**, which has three parts. It allows you to dismantle and join pipes from either side.

When changing pipe material be sure to use the correct transition fitting. Use a dielectric fitting (page 28) when joining copper to steel. It has a plastic seal that stops the ionization process that would otherwise corrode the joint. Plastic-to-steel and plastic-to-copper transition fittings are also available. Always use pipe-thread tape (page 134) when joining steel pipe. White tape is rated for water pipes, yellow for gas.

Other pipe materials

Flexible supply pipe is an increasingly accepted alternative to copper and steel. Using nylon and brass compression fittings, it is ideal for remodeling and installs much more quickly than traditional supply pipes (pages 132–133).

Galvanized cap

Coupling

Reducer coupling

Tee

90° elbow

Reducer elbow

45° elbow

Galvanized cross

Union

Choosing plastic or copper/chrome traps

Most traps are made of thinner-gauge tubular pipe. The parts join with slip nuts and washers so the trap can be easily taken apart for cleaning. A bathroom sink uses a 1¼-inch trap; a kitchen sink uses a 1½-inch trap.

A plastic trap will last nearly forever but is sometimes considered unsightly. When buying a chrome-plated copper trap, spend a bit more for one made of 17-gauge metal; thinner tubing may corrode within a couple of years.

PEX fittings

Cross-linked polyethylene, or PEX, is an extruded plastic pipe approved by codes in most localities for use as supply pipe. It is the easiest supply-pipe material to install, cutting more quickly than PVC, iron, or copper, taking turns and corners without crimping, and relying on quick and easy attachment to fittings with one of several systems that employ crimp rings.

Most fittings for PEX piping come in brass, although some manufacturers make bronze, copper, and engineered plastic fittings. You'll find PEX fittings configured to do the same jobs as fittings for other kinds of pipe. **PEX unions** join two lengths of piping, **elbows** turn corners, **T-fittings** provide a flow in two directions from a central source, and **drop-ear elbows** mount to vertical surfaces for the attachment of fixtures. Like fittings for other supply-line materials, PEX fittings are made in reducer models to join pipes of different diameters.

The chief difference between various manufacturers' PEX systems is not in the quality of the piping but in the method used to install the fittings to the pipe. Some manufacturers rely on crimped copper rings (using the same tools developed for earlier polybutylene piping). Others have developed stainless-steel rings that require proprietary tools (but allow complete visibility of the crimping process, which helps you avoid off-kilter rings and the subsequent leaky joints).

Union

90° elbow

T-fitting

Drop-ear elbow

PEX fittings—brass or plastic?

Choosing brass or plastic PEX fittings means knowing what type of water the pipes will carry. Both materials are equally strong when it comes to making watertight joints. However certain water sources contain substances, such as minerals and chlorine, that have a corrosive effect on copper or brass. In these cases use plastic fittings. This medical-grade product can tolerate just about anything.

PEX transition fittings

PEX to CPVC — PEX to iron — PEX to copper

PEX manufacturers make fittings especially designed to accomplish the transition between their polyethylene tubing and other materials. Shown (l-r) are PEX-to-CPVC, PEX-to-copper, and PEX-to-iron piping.

STANLEY PRO TIP

Use a dielectric union to join dissimilar metals

Dielectric union — Brass fitting — Galvanized iron

When two dissimilar metals come into contact with each other, they generate a small electric current. The current will ultimately corrode the materials at their juncture, a process often accelerated by water and the minerals it can contain. The result is a slow but sure progression toward a leaky joint. A dielectric union is made expressly for the purpose of eliminating the electric current and its corrosive effects.

Another company employs an expansion tool that increases the diameter of the PEX pipe to allow insertion of expansion fittings around which the plastic shrinks. Then the joint is sealed with a pressed plastic ring.

Supply-line valves

Numerous styles of supply-line valves are made to control the flow of water into your house or to fixtures. **Gate valves** and **ball valves** are often found on the main water lines of a house. A **fixture shutoff valve** allows you to shut off water to a fixture to repair it. **Vacuum breakers** keep potentially contaminated water from siphoning back into the water line.

Compression fittings

Compression fittings form a watertight joint by using a soft metal band that fits tightly around the pipe. When the nuts of the fitting are tightened, the soft metal band is pushed into and expands to conform to the recesses inside the fitting, making a watertight seal.

Supporting hardware

Because no piping material is intended to be self-supporting, the industry has developed specialized hardware to keep piping immobilized so the joints at the fittings don't crack and leak. **Plastic pipe hangers** are made to cradle PVC and other plastic materials. **J-hooks** and **pipe straps** attach to wood framing or masonry surfaces. **Wire hangers** support lengths of iron piping at a fixed distance, and **strapping** allows cut-to-fit support for angled piping.

Gate valve   Ball valve   Fixture shutoff valve   Vacuum breaker

Compression fitting: supply valve

Shutoff valve
Compression ring
Compression nut

Compression union

Compression nut
Compression ring
Union

Plastic pipe hangers   J-hooks   Wire hangers

Pipe straps   Strapping

To avoid the corrosion that occurs at junctures of dissimilar materials, always use hardware made from the same materials as the pipe it supports. Use plastic on plastic, copper on copper, steel on steel.

DRAIN AND VENT FITTINGS

A plumbing inspector will pay close attention to DWV fittings, so be sure to list them in detail in your plan. Drain fittings make gradual turns to reduce the chance of clogs; vent fittings can make sharper turns. The dimensions of the drains and vents vary according to use. A toilet typically requires 3-inch drain fittings and 2-inch vent fittings, while a sink will use a 2-inch drain with a 2- or 1½-inch vent. On the other hand an upflush toilet (pages 249–251) uses a 2-inch drain but needs a 3-inch vent because the force of expelling water upward requires a lot of compensating air. Here are some of the common drain and vent fittings your project may call for.

A **waste cross** (sometimes called a "sanitary cross") and a **double-Y** have two branch openings. A **reducer** or a **reducer bushing** connects different size pipes.

A **90-degree drain elbow** is called a sweep or a quarter bend. **Quarter bends** are available in short, medium, or long radii; when in doubt use the **long radius elbow** if you have the room.

When working in a tight place, you can choose among a number of elbows, including a 60-degree, a 45-degree (or eighth bend), and a 22½-degree (or sixteenth bend).

When running a line for a toilet, be sure to use a special **closet bend**. Its large end accepts a toilet flange, installed after the finished floor surface is completed.

Reducer bushing

Waste cross

Closet bend

Double-Y

Long-radius elbow

Reducer

When coming out of the wall for a sink drain, use a **trap adapter**; the trap can be screwed directly onto it.

Tees and **single-Ys** of all sizes are available. The two openings opposite each other in a straight line are called the run openings; the other opening is the branch opening. When describing a tee the run size is given first, then the branch size. For instance a **2×2×1½ tee** has two 2-inch run openings and one 1½-inch branch opening. Always buy a **waste tee** (sometimes called a "sanitary tee"), which has a curved rather than an abrupt bend.

Codes require drain lines to have cleanouts at regular intervals. Install a Y with a **cleanout** plug or attach a cleanout plug to the end of a pipe.

To make a transition from galvanized steel to plastic drainpipe, use a plastic **male-to-threaded PVC coupling**.

To join plastic to cast iron, use a special adapter fitting with a **neoprene sleeve**. Reinforced with a stainless-steel sheath, it tightens around both types of pipes to make a permanent joint.

An **air admittance valve** can act as a vent for single or multiple fixtures whose location prohibits running a separate vent through the house roof. National codes allow them, but some local codes do not. Be sure to check your codes before installing one.

Single-Y

45° street elbow

Male-to-threaded PVC coupling

Waste tee

Neoprene sleeve (with stainless-steel sheath)

45° elbow

90° drain elbow (quarter bend)

Coupling

Cleanout

Trap adapter

2×2×1½ waste tee

Air admittance valve

MAPPING A HOME SYSTEM

Before attempting a major plumbing project, know your home's system. It may first appear to be a tangled web of hidden pipes, but you can soon learn where all the pipes go and what they do. Start by consulting the illustrations on pages 11 and 13, which have an overview of how plumbing systems work.

If you have architectural drawings of your house that include the plumbing, the job may be done. However plumbers often deviate from plans, so take some time to compare the plans with the actual pipes.

If you have architectural drawings that do not show plumbing, make several copies and sketch in the existing plumbing. If you have no drawings, sketch your own. Later turn rough sketches into orderly drawings (pages 40–41).

Tips for finding pipes

If you still can't find all the pipes after following the guidelines at right, try these methods:

■ If an interior wall is thicker than the other walls (the usual thickness is 4 to 4½ inches), chances are good that it is a wet wall through which the main stack runs.

■ To find pipes in walls, turn on water and hold a stethoscope or a drinking glass against the wall surface. Supply pipes will hiss, and drainpipes will gurgle.

■ Turn off any intermediate shutoff valves and test to see which rooms they control.

■ If it is safe climb onto your roof and run a hand-crank auger down through a vent pipe. Have a helper listen as you wiggle the auger. In this way you can map both the main and secondary vents.

■ If you have hot water heat, map heating pipes separately. In older homes radiator pipes are usually larger than supply pipes, though they may resemble drainpipes.

■ In a newer home, copper heat pipes (which carry water to convectors or to radiant-heat lines) may be ½- or ¾-inch copper and look just like supply pipes.

DWV map

Locate the main stack, which is the largest-diameter pipe in a home. It should have a cleanout (near the floor in older homes, about 42 inches up in newer), which you can use to clean out the main drain line. The stack usually runs straight up to the roof, but it may have an offset.

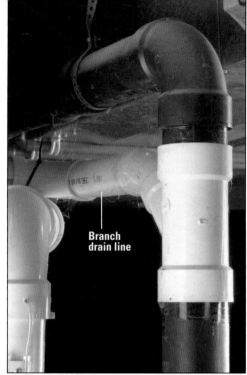

A secondary stack is a feature of most homes and often serves the kitchen. It also extends up through the roof, and it should have a cleanout. From a basement or crawlspace, you may be able to look up and see branch drain lines entering the stack.

The main stack in an older home is a thick cast-iron pipe. It almost certainly travels straight up to the roof. It may have a cleanout plug like the one shown, or there may be a cleanout hub on the floor.

A secondary stack in an older home is cast iron. Unlike the main stack, it may go around obstacles. Belowground it may join directly with the main drain or it may run to a common catch basin (page 15).

To follow the course of the supply lines, start where the main line enters the house and find the main shutoff (pages 8–9). Near the water heater note where the single pipe branches off into hot and cold and how the hot/cold pairs branch off to supply different areas of the house.

To trace the supply pipes further, determine where they enter the floor above. A supply pipe may run vertically with the wall (the pipe is called a riser). However it's normal for the supply pipe to turn and run horizontally. Supply pipes end near drainpipes.

You'll likely find an access panel in the wall directly behind a shower (shown) or bathtub faucet. Remove the panel to expose the plumbing—it will provide valuable clues about how supply lines are routed.

Older supply pipes are made of galvanized steel. If you see extensive rust at the joints, plan to replace the pipes. If water pressure is low in all or part of the house, mineral buildup may be the problem.

Take note of pipe sizes. Risers should be ¾ inch, but in many old homes they are only ½ inch, which can lead to low water pressure, especially if the pipes are galvanized steel.

You may find an access panel in a place other than behind a tub. Chances are good that such a panel was installed when a plumber had to make a repair.

PLUMBING CODES

Plumbing is the most complicated aspect of most bathroom and kitchen remodeling projects. Plumbing must conform to building codes to prevent dangerous and unhealthy conditions.

The National Uniform Plumbing Code applies generally to the entire country. You must also follow local codes, which may be more stringent. When planning your project request information about local plumbing codes from your local building department. Have the plans approved before starting work and perform all work to the satisfaction of the inspector (opposite). Draw a detailed plan (pages 40–41) that includes a list of all materials.

Common codes
The first priority is venting. Drainpipes that are not properly vented will run sluggishly and may release noxious fumes into the house. See pages 14–15 for solutions to most venting problems. Here are some other important code considerations:
■ Fixtures must not be placed too close together. This is critical in a bathroom, where space may be at a premium. See page 172 for clearances.
■ Determine the correct pipe sizes for drains, vents, and supply lines (page 37).
■ Most inspectors will accept rigid copper pipe for supplies and PVC for drains.
■ To ensure adequate water pressure, you may need to replace an existing globe shutoff valve with a full-bore ball or gate valve (page 36), which does not impede the flow of water. If pressure is very low, you may need a booster pump. Where pressure is too high, you may need a pressure-reducing valve.
■ The installation of plumbing must not weaken the structure of a house. The inspector may require that you reinforce joists that have been cut to accommodate pipes. Other requirements include the use of fire caulking around pipes and placement of protective plates over pipes.

Use purple primer when joining PVC pipes so the inspector can quickly tell that the pipes have been primed. Pipes that are glued without primer will eventually leak.

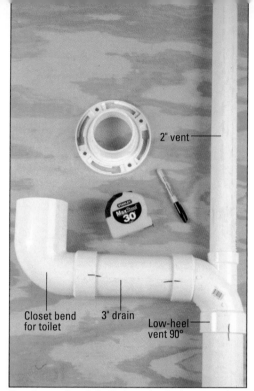

Purchase the right fittings by listing them in detail on your plan. Be sure to use special drain fittings (like the closet bend shown) so wastewater can flow smoothly. Inspectors will have specific fitting requirements for different fixtures.

CORRECT SLOPE FOR DRAINPIPE

Slope ¼" per 1'

In most cases drainpipes must slope at least ¼ inch per running foot. Running a drain across a room that does not have a basement or crawlspace may call for careful calculations. Codes may require that vent pipes slope ⅛ inch per foot. Some codes allow level vents.

Cutting a notch in a joist greatly weakens it. So whenever possible bore holes through joists instead. This calls for careful work; holes for drainpipe must be at slightly different levels so the pipe will slope. Whether notched or bored long spans may need doubled joists (shown).

Codes call for cleanouts at various points so drains can be easily augered in case of a clog. To be safe install a cleanout whenever you tap into a drain line unless there is already one nearby.

Once the drain lines are assembled, an inspector will probably test to make sure they do not leak. Some inspectors will simply pour water through the pipes. Other inspectors require that the line be plugged with an inflatable drain plug (shown) and the system filled with water.

STANLEY PRO TIP: **Working with the building department**

Working with the municipal building department and inspectors ensures safe and reliable plumbing. Work done without inspection may not meet code requirements.

Building departments usually work with professional plumbers and may be skeptical of a homeowner's ability to tackle plumbing tasks. Some departments require a licensed plumber to run new lines and some may require a homeowner to pass a written or oral test before doing certain types of work.

Here are some tips for working effectively with a building inspector:

■ The inspector's job is to assess work that has been done, not to manage a project. An inspector may be willing to offer advice but usually isn't obligated to do so. Instead of asking, "What should I do?" propose a plan and present it for feedback.

■ Draw up professional-quality plans, along with a complete list of materials (pages 40–41). Make an appointment with the inspector to go over your plans. Listen carefully and take notes. Be polite and respectful but don't be afraid to ask questions.

■ Schedule inspections and be prepared for them. There will probably be two: one for the rough plumbing and one for the installation of fixtures. Make an appointment only after the work is done—inspectors dislike coming back for a reinspection.

Do not cover up any rough plumbing until the inspector has signed off on it. Doing so runs the risk of having to tear out brand-new walls so the inspector can see the plumbing.

Do you have a septic system?

If you live in a rural area, wastewater may drain into a septic system in the yard rather than flowing into a municipal sewage system. A typical septic system has three parts. Water flows first into a watertight septic tank, which retains the larger solids. Liquid with suspended smaller particles travels to a distribution box, which in turn sends the waste out to a series of perforated pipes. Waste liquid percolates through the pipes and into the ground.

If the system backs up, the tank may need to be pumped by a special service. Be sure you know where the tank is; its lid may be buried.

If grass becomes very lush near the tank, the tank has probably cracked and needs to be replaced.

Ball valve

Valves, fixture controls, cleanouts, and compression pipe fittings must not be covered by a wall or floor surface. In case you need to work on the plumbing in the future, install an access panel. The most common location is behind a tub or shower (page 33).

When changing pipe materials use the correct transition fitting. Without a dielectric union (shown), the joint between galvanized and copper pipe would quickly corrode. Use the approved fitting when changing from plastic to copper, cast iron to plastic, and ABS to PVC.

Old plumbing usually can remain; however new plumbing needs to meet code. If old galvanized pipes and gate valves cause low water pressure, you may need to change them in order to supply the new pipes with enough pressure. As shown, a ball valve has replaced a gate valve.

Hammer arrester

Steel hanger

Copper hanger

Perforated strap

Plastic clamp

Copper clamp

Steel clamp

Water hammer arresters may be required for appliances such as a washing machine (shown) and other locations. Supply pipes may need to be cushioned wherever they run through or against a framing member.

In addition to the main shutoff valve for a house, codes may require shutoff valves that control a portion of the house. A hose bib should have an interior shutoff valve. All faucets and toilets must have individual stop valves (page 8). This corroded old valve will need replacement or repacking.

Use approved clamps or straps to secure pipes. According to most codes copper supply pipe must be supported every 6 feet, galvanized or black steel pipe every 12 feet, PVC or ABS drainpipe every 4 feet, and cast-iron pipe every 5 feet. To be safe install more supports than are required.

Water distribution pipes

Distribution pipes carry water from the main supply line to the rooms in the house, where they connect to branch lines.

Branch pipes

These pipes run from the distribution pipes to the fixtures. As a general rule you can run ½-inch pipe to most fixtures; run ¾-inch pipe to a hose bib or a water heater.

Different fixtures place different demands on supply pipes. Each fixture has a demand rating based on fixture units (see charts, right).

Supply tubes

These are the flexible lines that run from the stop valve to a faucet, fixture, or appliance.

As a general rule run ½-inch supply lines to all fixtures except toilets and bathroom sinks, which use ⅜-inch tubes.

Determining supply fixture units

Add the total number of fixture units in your house using this chart, then estimate how far the pipes travel inside your house.

FIXTURE	UNITS
Toilet	3
Bathroom sink	1
Tub/shower	2
Dishwasher	2
Kitchen sink	2
Washing machine	2
Hose bib	3

Determining supply size

Once you've totaled your home's fixture units, use this chart to check the minimum required size for the distribution pipes. Note that this chart is for estimating only. Local codes may vary, depending in part on the water pressure supplied by the utility.

SIZE OF PIPE FROM STREET	SIZE OF DISTRIBUTION PIPE	LENGTH OF PIPE RUN/NUMBER OF UNITS			
		40'	60'	80'	100'
1"	1"	36	31	27	25
1"	¾"	33	28	25	23
¾"	1"	29	25	23	21
¾"	¾"	18	16	14	12
¾"	½"	6	5	4	4

Sizing drainpipes

Use the chart at right to count the number of fixture units that will be connected to a drain line, then see the chart at far right for the minimum drainpipe size. NOTE: If a toilet connects to a drainpipe, the pipe must be at least 3 inches. Check local building codes.

Fixture trap size

A bathroom sink uses a 1¼-inch trap. Showers and floor drains use 2-inch traps. All other fixtures and appliances use 1½-inch traps.

Determining drain fixture units

FIXTURE	UNITS
Shower/tub	2
Bathroom sink	1
Toilet	3
Kitchen sink	2
Kitchen sink with disposer	3
Washing machine	2
Laundry sink	2
Floor drain	2

Determining drainpipe size

PIPE SIZE	MAXIMUM UNITS, HORIZONTAL DRAINPIPE	MAXIMUM UNITS, VERTICAL DRAIN STACK
1¼"	1	2
1½"	3	4
2"	6	10
3"	20	30
4"	160	240

ACCESSIBLE INSTALLATIONS

Kitchens and bathrooms often present obstacles to the elderly or people with disabilities. A growing list of plumbing products engineered for easier use plus some simple design changes can create accessible kitchens and baths in any home.

Available resources

The Americans with Disabilities Act (ADA) of 1991 establishes accessibility standards for commercial and public facilities. Some of these regulations pertain directly to plumbing fixtures and the design of bathrooms and kitchens.

The ADA standards are not required for private residences, but they are a valuable guide. Visit the ADA website at www.usdoj.gov/crt/ada/. The local building department can review plans for kitchens and baths to ensure they are universally accessible.

Some plumbing companies carry a line of accessible products. Other companies specialize in ADA-approved sinks and other fixtures, which include those with pedal-operated controls.

Customize your plan

Make sure your layout and fixtures will be useful for everyone in your family for now and in the future. Whenever possible test a product or layout ahead of time to make sure it can be used easily by a person in a wheelchair or walker.

Install grab bars to enable a person to easily enter and exit an area. Locate a grab bar where a person can reach it in case of a slip or fall. Grab bars should be ADA-approved. Be sure to anchor them with screws driven deeply into studs.

Planning an accessible kitchen

ACCESSIBLE SINK SPECS

The top of the sink should be no higher than 34 inches—2 inches lower than a standard countertop. Check for the height that works best; you may go as low as 28 inches.

34" max. to top of sink

Toe clearance 9" min.

Knee clearance 16" min.

27" min.

Provide counterspace for food preparation, with a countertop at the correct height and no cabinet below.

Clear floor space at least 30" wide

Clear floor space at least 48" deep

In front of the sink, provide a clear area 48 inches by 30 inches. Test with a wheelchair to make sure the entry and turnaround area are large enough. Make sure it is possible for a person to wheel up to the sink, operate the handles, and reach the sink's drain plug.

The area under the sink should be free of obstructions such as electrical cables or a garbage disposer.

This sink has a specially designed enclosure below that covers all plumbing, electrical, and mechanical parts. If you install an ADA-approved unit, you will be assured easy access. A typical enclosure is made of vinyl. It is usually not possible to install a garbage disposer inside this type of unit. A one-touch faucet with a pull-out sprayer is often preferred.

Planning an accessible bathroom

A bathroom sink should have the same sort of accessibility as a kitchen sink (opposite).

There should be a space at least 56 inches by 60 inches around a toilet. The space extending in one direction from the center of the toilet should be at least 42 inches.

Grab bar 36" min.

18"

42"

60"

56" min.

Grab bar 42" min.

30×48" clear floor space at lavatory

Clear floor space 48" min.

60"

Provide a stable, ADA-approved seat in a bathtub. Usually it's best to have a detachable handheld shower unit so the person can wash while sitting.

There should be room to wheel into the bathroom and to move easily from one fixture to another. ADA-recommended clearances vary depending on the shape of the bathroom and the position of fixtures; some typical dimensions are shown here.

30"

48"

Seat length 24" min.

36" min. opening

Seat width 16" min.

36"

A shower usually provides easier access than a tub. However the stall must be extra large—at least 36 by 60 inches—and must have a solid seat. A shower curtain is usually easier to operate than a shower door.

The sink shown above has large, easy-to-use handles and roll-under space beneath. The tub and shower unit at right has solid, well-placed grab bars, a stable and slip-resistant seat, and a handheld shower unit.

MAKING DRAWINGS

Professional plumbers usually map a job in painstaking detail to prevent surprises. You should too. Even with a plan changes may be necessary as you work. Framing you find in a wall may be different than you expected or there may be wiring where you want to run pipes.

It's fairly easy to produce plan views and riser drawings that use official plumbing symbols. Making detailed drawings will save time and expense later. Drawing the project helps you think through the job in detail. That may enable you to spot something you might otherwise overlook and avoid a problem. It will almost certainly minimize extra trips to the plumbing supply store. A clear, professional-quality plan also will make your initial meeting with the building department more productive.

Getting started
A plan for new plumbing starts with a map of the existing plumbing (pages 32–33). Use color codes when drawing a plan to indicate the function of each pipe.

If you have architectural drawings, make several photocopies of them. Otherwise make several copies of an accurate scale drawing of the room.

A gridded straightedge like the one shown opposite will help you draw parallel lines. You'll also need colored pencils, an eraser, and a 30-60-90-degree triangle.

Use grid paper and establish a scale, such as ½ inch equals 1 foot. Drawing to scale makes it easy to note any problems with the layout. It also helps in estimating materials.

Final drawings
To make a plan drawing, first draw all fixtures to scale size and make sure they are not too close together (page 172). Put in the drain lines and vents for the fixtures, then add the supply lines. Make riser drawings to show vertical pipe runs as well.

Indicate pipe sizes and the exact type of every fitting so the inspector can approve them. Indicate locations for valves, including stops at fixtures, and specify the type of valve. Make a shopping list of materials based on the drawings.

Show drainpipes with solid lines and supply lines with broken lines. Indicate vertical runs with notes on the overhead view.
Mark hot and cold supply lines with color pencils and color-code drains and vents.
Point to pipe sizes with a curved leader line to avoid mistaking the leader for a pipe. You'll probably draw several versions of the plan before you get all the details right.

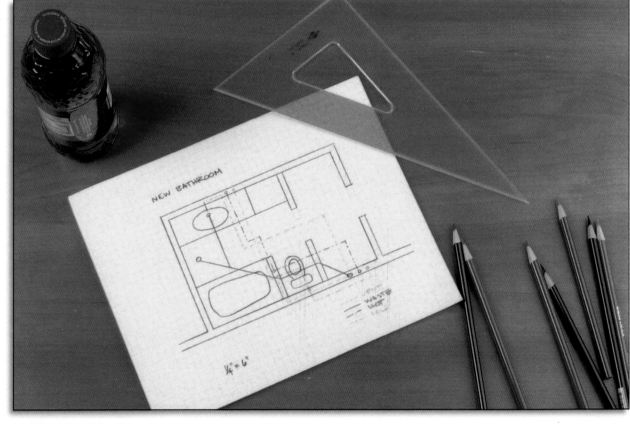

Photocopy the floor plan
For complex projects draw your floor plan and make several photocopies. This allows you to sketch out several trial plans.

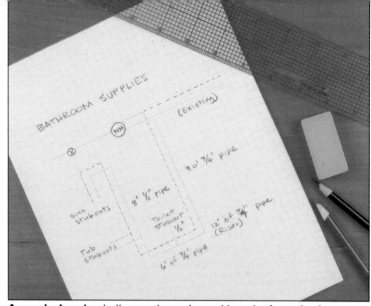

A DWV elevation describes the upward path of the stack, vents, and revents, the length of drainpipe runs, and traps. Its primary purpose is to show how the fixtures will be vented. It doesn't have to be drawn over an architectural drawing.

A supply drawing indicates the estimated length of supply pipes. The main purpose is to determine the minimum size of the pipes (chart, page 37).

Plumbing symbols

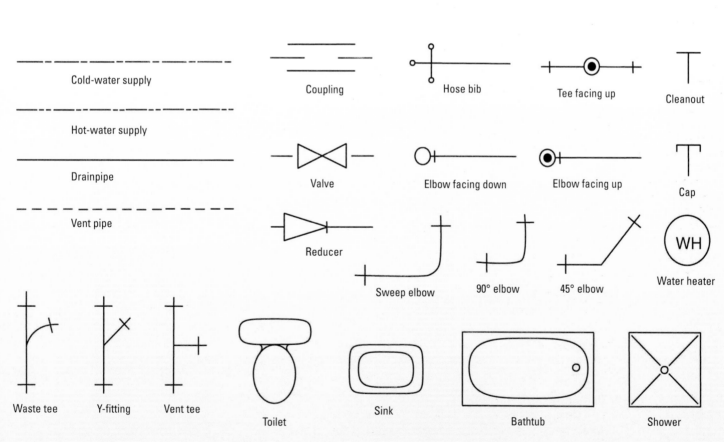

DEALING WITH CLOGGED PIPES

A drain that runs sluggishly or is completely stopped up is usually clogged with grease, soap, hair, or a solid object. The pipes themselves are usually all right.

Preventive measures
Always use the toilet, not a sink, to dispose of semisolid waste. However even a toilet cannot handle large objects.

Equip sinks and tubs with strainers and regularly clear away hair and fibers.

Food that has been ground in a garbage disposer can form a thick paste, especially if grease is part of the mix. Keep grease out of the sink whenever possible. Use cold water when running the disposer, then run hot water for a few seconds to clear the trap.

Diagnosing and unclogging
If only one fixture is sluggish or stopped up, the clog is probably in the fixture's trap or the branch drain line. If more than one fixture is affected, the problem is farther down the line—most likely in a drainpipe or even the stack. If all the fixtures on the first floor are sluggish or stopped, the main drain may need to be augered—a job for professionals.

This chapter describes basic unclogging methods, beginning with the simplest. Start by plunging. If that doesn't work move on to dismantling a trap and possibly replacing the trap. If the problem is farther down the line, use an auger.

Bathtubs, bathroom drains, and kitchen strainers all call for special solutions (pages 50–59).

For low water pressure in a faucet or showerhead, see pages 44–45 for some ways to increase the flow.

Working safely
Chances are you will get splashed while unclogging a drain. If drain cleaner has been poured down the drain, unclogging it can be dangerous (see box opposite). When working with drain cleaner, wear plastic gloves, long sleeves, and safety goggles. Cover the work area with an old rug or a drop cloth before starting work.

Clogged and sluggish pipes can usually be cleared using simple techniques and a few basic tools.

CHAPTER PREVIEW

Clearing aerators and showerheads
page 44

Clearing clogs by plunging
page 46

Dismantling a trap
page 48

Bathroom sink drain
page 50

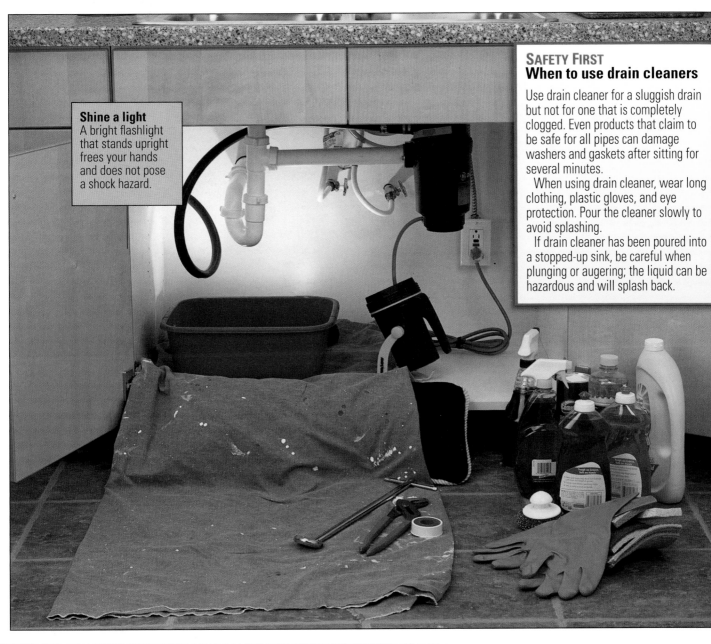

Shine a light
A bright flashlight that stands upright frees your hands and does not pose a shock hazard.

SAFETY FIRST
When to use drain cleaners

Use drain cleaner for a sluggish drain but not for one that is completely clogged. Even products that claim to be safe for all pipes can damage washers and gaskets after sitting for several minutes.

When using drain cleaner, wear long clothing, plastic gloves, and eye protection. Pour the cleaner slowly to avoid splashing.

If drain cleaner has been poured into a stopped-up sink, be careful when plunging or augering; the liquid can be hazardous and will splash back.

Make working under a sink as comfortable as possible by adding a drop cloth, a rug, and even an old pillow, especially where the edge of the cabinet can dig into your back. Place tools so they are easily reached and set up a flashlight.

Kitchen basket strainer
page 52

Sink with disposer
page 54

Clearing drain lines
page 56

Clearing sinks, tubs, or toilets
page 58

CLEARING AERATORS AND SHOWERHEADS

An aerator screws onto the end of a faucet. It mixes water and air for a smooth flow and minimizes splashing.

Tiny particles caught in an aerator's screens reduce the water flow. The solution is usually simple: Unscrew and take apart the aerator, flush the particles out of the screens, reassemble, and screw it back on.

If aerators clog regularly your water system may be at fault. If your home has old galvanized steel pipes, particles are probably flaking off the inside of the pipes and may need to be flushed (page 60). If your home has copper supply pipes, the problem may be that the water delivered by the utility company is impure; try installing a water filter.

If water flows slowly into a washing machine, shut off the stop valves and unscrew the hoses. You'll find a screen at the end of the hose; if it is blocked with particles, clean it out.

Aerators

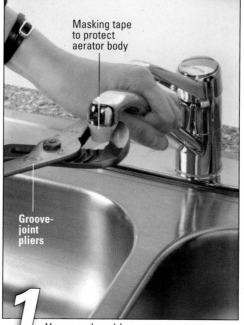

1 You may be able to unscrew an aerator with your fingers. If not, wrap masking tape around the aerator to protect it from scratching and unscrew it with groove-joint pliers. Turn the faucet on and off several times to flush out any debris.

Masking tape to protect aerator body

Groove-joint pliers

2 Disassemble the aerator with your fingers or use a small screwdriver. Note how the pieces go together. If the aerator is damaged, buy a replacement. Clean the screens with a toothbrush and pin, and rinse. If the minerals are caked on, soak them in vinegar overnight and clean again.

Aerator

Disk

Screen

Screen body

Rubber washer

PRESTART CHECKLIST

☐ **TIME**
Just a few minutes to clean out an aerator or showerhead. If mineral deposits are severe, soak the parts overnight.

☐ **TOOLS**
Groove-joint pliers, adjustable wrench, screwdriver, old toothbrush, straight pin

☐ **SKILLS**
No special skills needed

☐ **PREP**
Cover the sink or shower drain so small parts can't slip down

☐ **MATERIALS**
Vinegar, lime-deposit cleaner

AERATOR TYPES

Washer

Disk

Disk body

Screen

Screen body

Aerator body

Washer

Screen

Body with screen

Aerator body

An aerator has two screens, or a perforated disk and a screen. A rubber washer seals it against the spout. Kitchen sprayers have similar configurations. Lay all the parts out in order so you can reassemble them correctly.

Showerheads

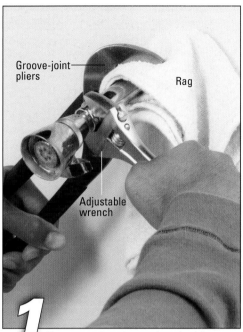

Groove-joint pliers

Rag

Adjustable wrench

1 Unscrew the showerhead with an adjustable wrench. If the shower arm turns while you are doing this, grip it with groove-joint pliers while you unscrew the showerhead. Wrap a cloth around the shower arm to keep from damaging it.

Straight pin

2 Run water backward through the showerhead and poke the spray outlets with a pin or brush to flush out the debris.

3 If the debris does not flush out easily, soak the showerhead overnight in a solution of vinegar and lime-deposit cleaner. Disassemble the showerhead and clean all the parts individually. If the showerhead is damaged, buy a new one.

TWO TYPES OF SHOWERHEADS

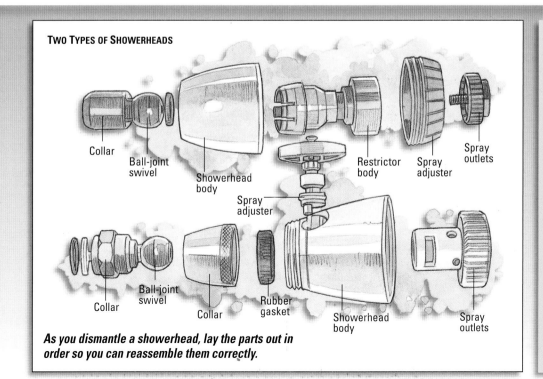

Collar

Ball-joint swivel

Showerhead body

Spray adjuster

Restrictor body

Spray adjuster

Spray outlets

Collar

Ball-joint swivel

Collar

Rubber gasket

Showerhead body

Spray outlets

As you dismantle a showerhead, lay the parts out in order so you can reassemble them correctly.

Check the flow restrictor

Restrictor screen

Restrictor body

To conserve water many showerheads have built-in flow restrictors. If the water pressure in the shower is low, check to see if the restrictor is clogged with mineral deposits. Dismantle the restrictor and soak its parts overnight in lime-deposit cleaner.

CLEARING CLOGS BY PLUNGING

If a sink or tub is sluggish, run hot water through the drain. Check the strainer (if there is one) and clean out any hair or debris that may have collected. If water still drains slowly, the next step is plunging.

To use a flanged plunger on a sink or tub, fold the flange into the body of the plunger. For small sinks you may find that a regular plunger works best.

Plunging works in two ways: by pushing a clog through to the stack, and by pulling debris back up into the sink.

For tough jobs you may want to try a pressure-type plunger, which looks a bit like an accordion (page 95). It generates greater pressure than a standard plunger.

Before plunging make sure the water has only one exit point—through the drain. Plug overflow holes and clamp connecting hoses before you begin.

Sometimes plunging works easily, with little mess. Other times water sprays all over the place. Be prepared to wipe up substantial amounts of water.

PRESTART CHECKLIST

☐ **TIME**
About half an hour to prepare and plunge a sink, tub, or toilet

☐ **TOOLS**
Regular, flanged, or pressure-type plunger

☐ **SKILLS**
No special skills needed

☐ **PREP**
Block any alternate passageways through which plunged water may flow

☐ **MATERIALS**
No special materials needed

1 If a drain is sluggish, wait for most of the water to drain out. If the drain is clogged, bail out the water. For best results there should be about 2 inches of standing water in the sink—just enough to cover the plunger.

2 Often hair and dirt caught on the stopper is the cause of the clog. Remove the stopper and clean it off. (If the stopper does not pull out easily, see page 50.) If the sink still does not drain readily, the real clog is farther down the line.

WHAT IF...
A double-drain sink is clogged?

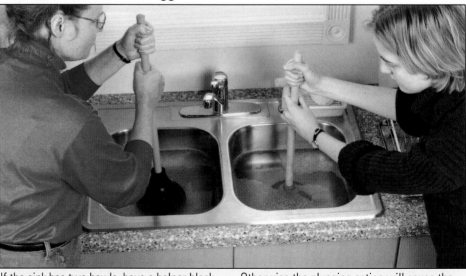

If the sink has two bowls, have a helper block one drain with a second plunger or a rubber sink stopper while you plunge the other.

Otherwise the plunging action will cause the water to spurt up into the other bowl.

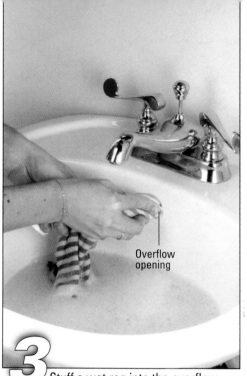

3 Stuff a wet rag into the overflow opening so water cannot spurt through it as you use the plunger. A helper may need to hold the rag in place as you plunge.

Overflow opening

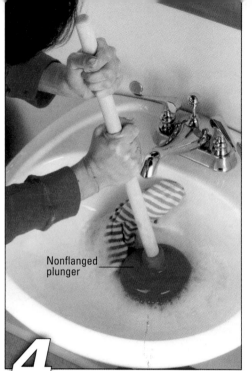

4 Make sure the plunger forms a tight seal around the drain hole. Work the plunger with a steady, firm, up-and-down motion. You'll feel the water pushing and pulling through the drain. If the clog does not clear immediately, don't give up. Make at least several attempts.

Nonflanged plunger

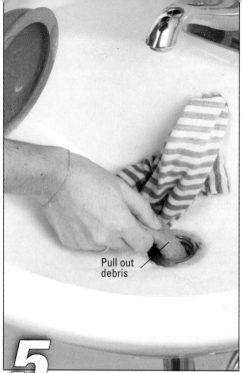

5 If the water suddenly drains out, the clog has passed out of the drainpipe and into the stack, or the plunger has sucked debris back into the sink. If the drain remains clogged after numerous attempts at plunging, move on to dismantling the trap (pages 48–49).

Pull out debris

Plunging a tub

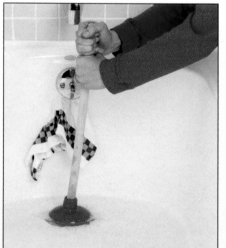

Before plunging a bathtub remove the drain assembly (pages 58–59) and stuff the overflow hole with a wet rag. Remove the strainer and bail or add water until there is just enough water to cover the plunger.

Plunging a toilet

Plunge a toilet with a flanged plunger with the flange pulled out. Fit the flange into the drain hole, seat the plunger firmly around the hole, and push and pull vigorously.

STANLEY PRO TIP

Pushing through with water pressure

An expansion nozzle (also called a balloon or blow bag) can blast a blockage through to the stack. Check your local codes to make sure use of this tool is allowed. Attach the nozzle to a garden hose, insert it into the drain, and turn on the hose. The nozzle will expand to seal the drain. Pressure builds until a valve in the bag releases a burst of water to push the clog through the pipe.

DISMANTLING A TRAP

A trap seals out gases (page 10) and provides a bottleneck that prevents clogs from traveling farther down the line. That's why most clogs are found in a trap bend.

To clear a clog dismantle the trap and clean it out. You'll probably need to replace some rubber washers as they get brittle with age. It's not unusual to find that the entire trap needs replacing. If even one component is leaky, replace the entire trap rather than a single piece—one worn component is likely to mean wear in others. Less expensive chrome-plated traps are notoriously short-lived. They may look OK on the outside but squeeze the bottom of the bend with your fingers to check the trap. If you feel it give, even slightly, the metal is corroded. For durability buy a plastic trap or a chrome-plated trap that is made of heavy-gauge brass.

Bathroom traps are 1¼ inches in diameter; kitchen drains are 1½ inches.

PRESTART CHECKLIST

☐ **TIME**
About an hour to dismantle and reinstall a trap

☐ **TOOLS**
Groove-joint pliers, toothbrush, hacksaw, sandpaper

☐ **SKILLS**
Dismantling and connecting parts with washers and nuts

☐ **PREP**
Prepare a comfortable worksite (page 43); have a bucket or dishpan and a drop cloth in place

☐ **MATERIALS**
Washers, pipe tape, perhaps a new trap

Groove-joint pliers · Trap · Bucket or dishpan

1 Place a bucket under the trap. Loosen the nut on each side of the curved piece with groove-joint pliers. Slide the nuts out of the way and pull the curved piece off.

2 Use a toothbrush to remove hair and other debris that has collected in the trap. If the trap is in good shape, replace the washers and reassemble it. If any parts are damaged, install a new trap (Steps 3–5).

S-TRAP
Tailpiece
Washer
Drain elbow
Trap

P-TRAP
Tailpiece
Nut
Washer
Trap
Drain elbow

An S-trap ends with a vertical rather than horizontal piece; many codes forbid its use. A typical P-trap consists of the tailpiece, curved trap piece, and a drain elbow. The drain elbow slips into a threaded drain pipe or a trap adapter in the wall.

Pipe tape

Tailpiece

Nut

Washer

3 Take the old parts to a home center or hardware store to find replacements. Make sure the new pieces will fit exactly; you may need to cut the tailpiece or drain elbow. Begin assembly by wrapping pipe tape clockwise around the threads of a tailpiece, and screw it onto the drain body.

4 With the tailpiece installed dry-fit all the pieces to make sure they join with ease. If you have to force a connection, it may leak. For each joint slide on the nut, then the washer.

5 Assemble the pieces and hand-tighten all the nuts. Then go back and tighten the nuts with groove-joint pliers. To test the drain for leaks, stop up the sink, fill it with water, and open the stopper. Watch carefully for any leaks as the water flows through. Tighten joints where necessary.

CUT THE TAILPIECE
Cutting trap components

To cut a chrome-plated trap piece, place it in a miter box and cut with a hacksaw. To avoid denting the pipe, exert gentle pressure as you cut. After cutting remove any burrs with sandpaper.

STANLEY PRO TIP

Plastic vs. metal traps

Metal usually is associated with durability, but in the case of sink traps, plastic is the long-lasting choice. Usually you can replace a chrome trap with a plastic one; just make sure it's the right size for the sink and the drainpipe. If appearance is important choose a chrome-plated brass trap.

Trap with a cleanout plug

Cleanout

Some heavy-duty traps are equipped with a cleanout, a plug that can be removed. Place a bucket under the trap, unscrew the plug, and let the water run out. Reach inside with an auger to remove debris.

BATHROOM SINK DRAIN

The pop-up assembly on a bathroom drain has several moving parts that wear out over time. If the unit is made of thin metal or plastic that is easily bent or broken, you may not be able to repair it.

Troubleshooting

If a stopper is loose and won't stay open, tighten the pivot ball retaining nut.

If a stopper is difficult to raise, loosen the pivot ball retaining nut. If that doesn't work remove the pivot rod, clean out the opening in the drain body, and replace worn gaskets or washers.

If the stopper does not seat all the way into the drain body when you pull up on the lift rod, adjust the lift rod.

If a stopper does not hold water, remove it and clean the rubber seal. If there is an O-ring, replace it or the stopper.

If water leaks from the pivot rod, tighten the retaining nut. If it still leaks, remove the pivot rod and replace the gaskets.

PRESTART CHECKLIST

☐ **TIME**
An hour or so for most repairs

☐ **TOOLS**
Long-nose pliers, groove-joint pliers, screwdriver

☐ **SKILLS**
No special skills needed

☐ **PREP**
Make the work area comfortable; place a bucket under the assembly to catch water

☐ **MATERIALS**
Replacement 1¼-inch rubber or plastic washers, perhaps new gaskets, perhaps a new drain assembly, plumber's putty

Adjusting the stopper

1 Some stoppers can be removed simply by pulling up. With others you twist a quarter-turn or so, then lift. A third type has a hole through which the pivot rod passes (shown); remove the pivot rod first. Check the O-ring for damage; replace it if necessary.

2 To adjust a stopper up or down, loosen the lift rod screw with your fingers or with a pair of long-nose pliers if it is corroded. Slide the clevis strap up or down as needed, tighten the nut, and test.

BATHROOM DRAIN ASSEMBLY

A pop-up assembly only looks complicated. A pivot rod, connected to the lift rod with a clevis strap, raises and lowers the stopper.

3 Disconnect the trap (page 48). Slide the clevis strap off the pivot rod, loosen the retaining nut, and remove the pivot rod. Insert a screwdriver into the drain opening in the sink to keep it from turning, and loosen the locknut with pliers.

Locknut

4 Unscrew the locknut. Push down on the sink flange with one hand while you unscrew the drain body with the other.

Sink flange

Locknut

Drain body

5 Buy a new drain assembly with a lift rod that fits through your faucet or buy a new faucet and drain body. Slip the sink flange through the hole in the sink and screw on the drain body. Tighten the locknut, install the pivot rod, attach it to the clevis strap with the spring clip, and adjust.

Spring clip

(page 48)

STANLEY PRO TIP

Easy fix for a leaking drain body

You may need to tighten the retaining nut on a pivot rod from time to time, either to seal a leak or to keep a stopper from falling down when it's supposed to stay up.

REFRESHER COURSE
Dismantling a trap

Loosen the slip nuts on the curved trap piece with a pair of groove-joint pliers. Slide the nuts and rubber washer out of the way and pull the pieces apart. Unless the rubber washers are in pristine condition, replace them. If the trap is damaged, replace it.

WHAT IF ...
There is no rubber gasket?

Rope of putty

A bathroom sink flange may come with a rubber gasket that seals it to the sink. If not, apply a rope of plumber's putty to the underside of the flange before installing it. Excess putty will squeeze out as you tighten the locknut.

KITCHEN BASKET STRAINER

If water is leaking under the sink, the basket strainer may not be tightly sealed. To test, close the stopper, fill the sink with water, and inspect from underneath with a flashlight and a dry rag.

If the strainer leaks try tightening the locknut using groove-joint pliers or a spud wrench (opposite). If that doesn't solve the problem, remove the strainer, following the steps on these pages. Either clean the drain hole and reinstall the strainer or install a new strainer.

A strainer made of thin metal or plastic may soon fail to seal water. A better-quality strainer costs more but will last longer.

Installation is the same for all kinds of sinks: stainless steel, cast iron, or acrylic.

PRESTART CHECKLIST

☐ **TIME**
About 2 hours to remove a basket strainer and install a new one

☐ **TOOLS**
Groove-joint pliers, spud wrench, hammer, plastic putty knife, screwdriver

☐ **SKILLS**
Dismantling and reinstalling a trap (pages 48–49)

☐ **PREP**
Make the worksite under the sink comfortable; position a bucket to catch water

☐ **MATERIALS**
New basket strainer, plumber's putty, replacement 1½-inch rubber or plastic washers

Tailpiece

1 Unscrew the slip nuts at the bottom and top of the tailpiece. Gently pull the tailpiece down from the strainer and remove it. Unless the washers are in very good condition, buy replacement washers. If any part of the trap is damaged, replace it as well.

Locknut

2 Loosen the locknut with groove-joint pliers or a spud wrench (opposite). Remove the nut and pull out the strainer. Scrape the old putty away from around the sink hole and clean with a rag.

KITCHEN SINK STRAINERS

- Strainer
- Basket
- Rubber washer
- Fiber washer
- Locknut
- Strainer
- Basket
- Rubber washer
- Fiber washer
- Metal washer
- Retaining bracket

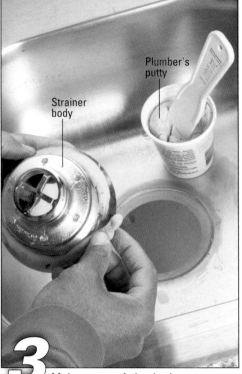

Strainer body

Plumber's putty

3 Make a rope of plumber's putty (do not use putty that has started to dry) and place it around the sink hole or under the lip of the strainer body. Press the strainer body into the hole and center it.

Standard screwdriver

Groove-joint pliers

4 Have a helper hold the strainer in place while you slip on the rubber washer, the fiber washer, and the locknut. To keep the strainer from spinning while you tighten the locknut, insert the handles of a pair of pliers into the holes and brace them with a screwdriver.

Plastic putty knife

5 Tighten the locknut as tight as it will turn. Scrape away the squeezed-out putty with a plastic putty knife to avoid scratching the sink. Reattach the tailpiece. To test for leaks close the stopper, fill the sink, and pull out the stopper.

WHAT IF ...
There is a leak from the garbage disposer?

If water leaks from above the disposer (that is, at the point where the disposer attaches to the sink), tighten the mounting ring screws. If that doesn't solve the problem, remove the disposer, disconnect the flange, clean the hole around the sink, and install a new rope of putty.

If water leaks from the connection where the drain connects to the disposer, tighten the two screws on the drain adapter. You may need to replace the rubber gasket inside. If water seeps from the disposer housing, replace the disposer.

Replacing a disposer?
For instructions on installing a new trap and disposer for a kitchen sink, see pages 220–221.

GET A GRIP WITH A SPUD WRENCH

Tightening and loosening a basket strainer's locknut is difficult because the nut is large and hard to reach. A pair of groove-joint pliers does the trick but may be cumbersome. A spud wrench (below) or a special basket-strainer wrench makes the job easier. If the nut is very tight, place the tip of a screwdriver against one of its lugs and tap with a hammer until it loosens.

SINK WITH DISPOSER

A clogged sink with a disposer presents a couple of problems. To use a plunger you must compress a large volume—the amount in the disposer—and you have to keep the pressure from simply escaping out the dishwasher drain hose. The method shown here will take care of the second problem. You can't remedy the first one.

Clamping the dishwasher hose creates an imperfect seal and can crack the hose. Then you're left with a plugged drain plus the need to replace the hose.

The easiest and least time-consuming method is to remove the P-trap, the probable location of the clog. But removing the trap is a little messy, and the other methods may forestall this necessity. If you don't want to go to the trouble of plugging the dishwasher nipple, go straight to the section about removing the trap.

PRESTART CHECKLIST

☐ **TIME**
About half an hour to disconnect the hose, plug the outlet, plunge the sink, and reassemble

☐ **TOOLS**
Depending on the task: screwdriver, plunger, groove-joint pliers, hand auger, cutoff broomstick section

☐ **SKILLS**
Removing a hose clamp, plunging a sink, removing a sink trap, using a hand auger

☐ **PREP**
Make the working area under the sink comfortable; position a bucket to catch water

☐ **MATERIALS**
Rubber plug, duct tape

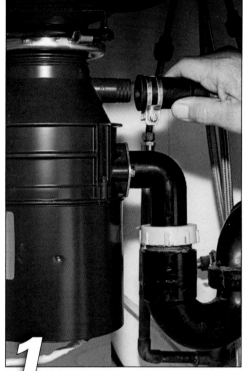

1 Using the appropriate size straight or phillips screwdriver, loosen the dishwasher hose clamp and remove the dishwasher hose. Plug the hose with a rag to absorb the small amount of remaining water it might contain.

2 Insert a ¾-inch cork or rubber plug (from a hardware store) into the dishwasher nipple with enough force to seal it but not so much as to crack it. Secure the plug with a ¾-inch×2-foot length of duct tape to keep it in place when you plunge.

3 Fill each side of a double sink with about 4 inches of water, leaving the drain on the disposal side open and plugging the other drain with the rubber sink stopper. Have a helper hold the rubber stopper firmly in place. Set the plunger on the drain opening at an angle and put pressure on the plunger to expel the air from under it. Keep the plunger flange firmly seated on the drain opening and work the plunger vigorously up and down, pulling the plunger up sharply after several strokes. Repeat until the clog is free or try another method.

Clearing a jammed disposer

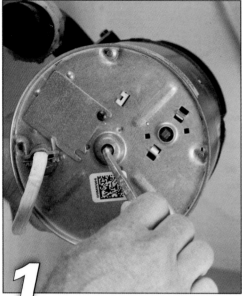

1 A clogged disposer can be made worse by something jammed in the blades. If the disposer hums but won't run, it's jammed. Turn off the power to the unit, insert an impeller wrench into the square hole at the bottom, and work the wrench back and forth to try to dislodge the jammed article.

2 Turn the power on and reset the machine (see Step 3). If the motor still hums, shut the power off and push a piece of old broomstick (about 2 feet long) into the drain until it contacts the bottom of the disposer. Holding the stick against the side of the drain, push it in a circle to turn the impeller.

Reset button

3 If the broomstick spins the impeller, remove the object with tongs, a magnetic wand, or a piece of duct tape stuck in reverse on the end of the stick. Don't try to get the object with your hands. Reset the disposer. If this method doesn't unjam the unit, it's time to call a pro.

WHAT IF ...
The drain is still clogged?

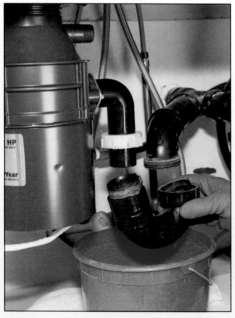

USING A HAND AUGER (OR "SNAKE")

Set screw

Greasy buildup

Clog

Auger cable

Auger tip

If none of your attempts to unclog the drain is successful, set a bucket under the P-trap and remove the trap. Remove the waste clogging the trap and reassemble the trap. If the unit still does not drain freely, remove the trap and extension pipe and try working a hand auger into the clogged area within the pipe in the wall space.

CLEARING DRAIN LINES

Whenen a sink, toilet, or tub becomes clogged, first try plunging. Bail out most of the water but leave a couple of inches so the plunger can seal tightly around the drain opening. Seal any openings—such as the overflow openings of a bathroom sink or a tub—by firmly pressing a wet rag into the opening. When plunging a double-bowl sink, seal the drain hole of the other bowl. If you have a dishwasher, clamp its drain hose tightly before plunging so you won't force water back into the dishwasher.

If plunging doesn't work try using a hand crank auger, dismantling a trap, or forcing pressurized water into the drain.

If more than one drain is stopped or runs slowly, take more aggressive steps. Auger through an intermediate cleanout or trap. If that doesn't solve the problem, you may need to auger the main drain. Call a professional sewer service or rent a power auger and do it yourself.

PRESTART CHECKLIST

☐ **TIME**
With a rented power auger, an hour or two to run it through a main drain

☐ **TOOLS**
Hand-crank or power auger, adjustable wrench, pipe wrench, perhaps a hammer and chisel

☐ **SKILLS**
Identifying and opening traps and cleanouts

☐ **PREP**
Clear the area and gather materials for cleanup afterward

☐ **MATERIALS**
Pipe-thread tape, replacement cleanout plug, bucket

Unclogging a house line

1 Remove a cleanout plug using an adjustable wrench or a pipe wrench. A cleanout usually provides access to the main or secondary stack.

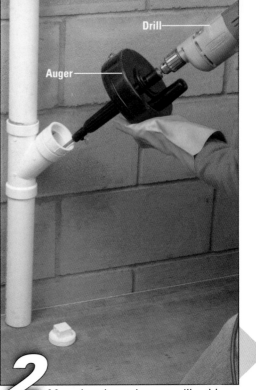

2 Many hand-crank augers like this one have a shaft that attaches to a standard power drill (opposite). The resulting tool is more powerful and easier to use than a basic hand-crank auger (page 55).

TYPES OF TRAPS

A single drain cover on a bathroom floor opens to a drum trap. A house trap typically has two trap covers near each other on the floor. Both can be augered.

Pipe wrench

Cleanout cover

Cable

Power auger

Foot switch

3 The main drain, the line coming from the street to your house, may be clogged by tree roots that have grown into it. (Many old drain lines are made of clay or have permeable joints.) Open the cleanout plug. If you have a metal cleanout plug, you may have to loosen it with a hammer and chisel.

4 Rent a power auger with several bits to handle various obstructions. Rental staff can advise on which bit to use. Select the bit and attach it with the setscrew provided on the cable end. Position the auger close to the pipe to minimize the length of exposed cable. **Make sure cords are not lying in water.** Plug in the auger. Wear heavy rubber gloves. Push the cable into the drain until you hit an obstruction. Switch on the auger and use the foot switch to start the cable rotating. Let it run for a while, then turn off the auger and push the cable in farther.

WHAT IF ...
You have a brass plug?

Almost every cast-iron cleanout has a brass plug, often painted over. Try to remove it with a pipe wrench. (If you reuse the brass plug, first wrap the threads with pipe-thread tape.) If it won't budge try to turn it with a hammer and cold chisel. Install an expandable rubber replacement cleanout.

AUGERING FROM THE ROOF

Handheld power auger

Auger

Vent stack

The easiest way to auger a stack is from the roof, pushing down; that way, you have gravity on your side. Be sure to establish firm footholds before working on a roof.

Some crank augers have a shaft that fits the chuck of a power drill, as well as a hand crank. Use a variable-speed drill only—a single-speed drill turns too quickly, which can jam the auger in the pipe.

CLEARING SINKS, TUBS, OR TOILETS

A hand-crank auger clears most household clogs. It consists of a metal cable with a widened tip that grabs or pushes debris. Power-operated augers work quicker, but a fast-turning auger can get stuck so tightly you cannot extract it.

You can run an auger through the sink and into the trap rather than dismantling the trap. However before doing so on a bathroom sink, you'll need to remove the pivot rod (pages 50–51). It's usually not possible to auger a kitchen sink because of the garbage disposer and because the drain assembly for a double-bowl sink has too many turns.

If a tub drains slowly, hair and soap sludge may be stuck to the drain assembly. A plunger-type assembly (right) is less complicated and less likely to clog than a pop-up assembly (opposite), but both need occasional cleaning.

A toilet auger (opposite) is the solution when plunging fails. Otherwise remove the toilet to auger out the clog (page 95).

PRESTART CHECKLIST

☐ **TIME**
About 2 hours to dismantle a trap and auger a branch line

☐ **TOOLS**
Groove-joint pliers, hand-crank auger

☐ **SKILLS**
Dismantling and reinstalling a trap

☐ **PREP**
Make the worksite comfortable; place a bucket under the trap to catch spills

☐ **MATERIALS**
Replacement washers for the trap

Augering a sink trap

1 Dismantle the trap. Loosen the auger setscrew and pull out about a foot of cable. Push the cable through the pipe until it stops. You've probably run into a bend in the pipe rather than the obstruction. Tighten the setscrew. Crank clockwise until the cable moves forward.

Labels: Drain opening; Hand-crank auger

2 Loosen the setscrew, push the cable until it stops, tighten the setscrew, and crank again. The auger may grab rather than push the obstruction. If so pull out the auger, clean away any hair and gunk, and reinsert the auger to remove more of the obstruction.

WHAT IF …
You must auger a tub?

1 To auger a bathtub, first check to see whether there is a drum trap in the bathroom (pages 56, 162). If so auger from there. Otherwise remove the overflow assembly (pages 162, 166).

Label: Overflow assembly

2 Run the auger down through the overflow, using the techniques shown.

Label: Overflow

Cleaning a pop-up (rocker-arm) type assembly

1 If the tub has a pop-up assembly, flip the trip lever up to raise the stopper. Gently pull the stopper and the rocker arm up and out of the tub. Clean away any debris.

Rocker arm

2 Remove the cover-plate screws and pull out the cover plate with the linkage connected to it. Clean away any hair, coagulated soap, and other debris that might be attached to the linkage.

Linkage

Cover plate

Stopper

3 If the stopper does not seal completely, loosen the locknut and twist the threaded rod so it rises up about ⅛ inch. Tighten the locknut. Reinstall and test.

Locknut

WHAT IF ...
The auger gets stuck?

If you suspect that an auger is in danger of getting stuck, pull it out rather than pushing and turning farther. It may take four or five attempts before the clog is removed or pushed through the pipe.

If an auger does get stuck, tighten the setscrew and turn the crank counterclockwise. This usually frees it. If that doesn't work push and pull rapidly back and forth.

It may take some time, but these measures almost always work. If the auger will not come loose after repeated tries, call a professional plumber for help.

TOILET AUGER

A toilet auger has a rubber sleeve to protect the porcelain from scratches. It's just the right length and shape to get at clogs inside and just beyond a toilet.

Toilet auger

Sleeve

Clog

FAUCETS

A leaky faucet is the most common household plumbing problem. A house call by a professional plumber will cost plenty, so it makes sense to fix it yourself. This chapter explains how to stop sink and bathtub faucets from dripping from the spout or oozing water from the base of the handle.

Shut off the water

The first step is to stop the flow of water to the faucet (pages 8–9). If there are a pair of stop valves under a sink, turn them off. If there are no stop valves, look for intermediate shutoff valves elsewhere in the house. Failing that, you may have to shut off water to the entire house.

Some bathtub faucets have integrated shutoffs. Look for an access panel behind the tub; shutoff valves may be inside. If not you'll need to shut off intermediate valves or water to the whole house.

After shutting off the water, open the faucet and wait for the water to stop running. If the faucet is on the first floor of a multistory house, you may have to wait a minute or so for the water to drain.

If the house has old galvanized pipes, shutting the water off and turning it back on will probably dislodge debris inside the pipes, clogging aerators in faucets and showerheads throughout the house; see pages 44–45 for how to clean them.

Finding the right parts

You may spend more time finding the correct parts than working on the faucet. To prevent multiple shopping trips, remove the worn parts—perhaps even the whole faucet—and take them with you to the store.

The faucets shown in this chapter are the most common types. Chances are good that yours will look and work much like one of them. However hundreds of faucet types have been made, so you could have an unusual model with parts that are hard to find.

A helpful and competent salesperson can save you plenty of time. Some home centers have knowledgeable people. The staff at a local hardware store may have more expertise. Plumbing supply stores, which cater to professionals, can be impatient with do-it-yourselfers, but they have a wide selection of parts as well as knowledgeable personnel.

If your faucet has a brand name inscribed on its body, look for a repair kit to match.

Otherwise dismantle the faucet to find out its type. Read the relevant repair instructions (pages 62–79) to determine which parts need replacement.

In some cases only inexpensive O-rings and washers are needed. Other times a main part—a cartridge, stem, or ball, for instance—needs to be replaced. Usually replacing the inner workings results in a faucet that works as smoothly and is as durable as a new faucet.

Fix or replace?

If parts are hard to find or expensive, or if the faucet is unattractive, you may be better off replacing the whole faucet rather than repairing it; pages 84–91 show how. Depending on the type and age of the faucet, replacing may take less time.

Other leaks

If water leaks below the sink, the problem may be a leaky stop valve or supply tube (pages 116–117). If the leak is at the point where the supply tube enters the faucet, try tightening the nut. If that doesn't solve the problem, replace the supply tube.

If you can find the parts, most faucet repairs are easy. Otherwise consider installing a new unit.

CHAPTER PREVIEW

Sink faucet repairs
page 62

Tub and shower faucet repairs
page 74

Diverters
page 80

Tub spouts
page 81

At a hardware store or home center, you will find a rack of repair kits that cover the most common faucet types. If you don't find the right parts, they probably can be ordered. Failing that, consider replacing the entire faucet set.

Repair kit

Replacement O-ring

Replacement washer

Worn washer

Before installing a new rubber part, check that it is an exact duplicate of the old part. Worn washers (above) or O-rings are the most common cause of run-on faucets. They come in a variety of shapes and sizes, even within the same brand, so always bring the worn part along when shopping for a replacement.

Installing a flex-line shower unit
page 82

Kitchen sprayers
page 83

Installing a kitchen faucet
page 84

Installing a widespread faucet
page 88

Installing a bathroom faucet
page 90

STEM (COMPRESSION) FAUCETS

Most older two-handle faucets have stems that move up and down as the handle is turned. A rubber washer at the bottom of the stem presses against a seat in the faucet body to seal out water. If the washer or the seat becomes worn, water seeps through and drips out of the spout.

If water seeps below the handle or the base of the faucet, an O-ring or the packing probably needs to be replaced.

Getting the parts

All-purpose repair kits for stem faucets contain washers and O-rings of various sizes. To make sure you have a perfect match, take the stem along when buying the repair kit. An older type of faucet may need a packing washer or string packing. If the stem itself is worn, replacing the rubber parts will not solve the problem. You can replace the stem if you can find a new one; replacing the faucet may be the best option.

PRESTART CHECKLIST

- [ ] **TIME**
  Less than an hour for most repairs

- [ ] **TOOLS**
  Screwdrivers; adjustable wrench; perhaps a handle puller, seat wrench, or seat grinder

- [ ] **SKILLS**
  Shutting off water, dismantling a faucet, installing small parts

- [ ] **PREP**
  Shut off the water, close the sink stopper, and place a rag in the sink to catch any parts

- [ ] **MATERIALS**
  Washer, O-rings, silicone grease, packing

1 **Shut off the water** and open both handles until water stops running. Pry off the decorative cap, remove the handle screw, and gently pry off the handle. If the handle is stuck, tap and pry on one side, then the other or use a handle puller (opposite).

Labels: Decorative cap removed; Handle screw

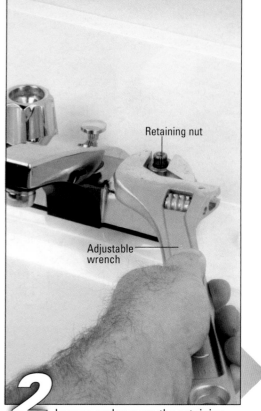

2 Loosen and remove the retaining or packing nut with an adjustable wrench. A sleeve may also cover the stem. Grab the stem with a pair of pliers and pull it out.

Labels: Retaining nut; Adjustable wrench

OLDER AND NEWER MODELS

On older compression faucets (left), string packing or a packing washer keeps water from oozing out the handle. On a newer model (right), an O-ring does the job.

Labels: String packing; Stem; Washer; Seat; O-ring; Stem; Washer; Seat

Washer

O-ring

Seat wrench

Seat

3 If water drips out the spout when the handle is turned off, you probably need to replace a worn washer. Remove the screw and install an exact replacement. If this doesn't solve the problem, or if washers wear out quickly, replace the seat (Step 5).

4 If water seeps out below the handle, replace a worn O-ring or any other rubber part on the stem. Gently pry out the O-ring with a knife or small screwdriver. Rub silicone grease on the replacement O-ring and reinstall it.

5 If the seat is pitted or scratched, remove it using a seat wrench (page 19). Install an exact replacement. If you can't find a new seat, you may be able to grind a worn seat to smooth it.

WHAT IF ...
The handle is stuck?

Handle puller

Handles on older two-handle faucets may be stuck tight. If tapping and prying with moderate pressure does not remove a handle, avoid the temptation to pry hard—you may crack the handle or the faucet body. A handle puller grasps the handle from underneath at two sides and slowly draws the handle off the stem.

STANLEY PRO TIP
Use packing on old stems

String packing

An older faucet may have a rubber packing washer or string packing under a packing nut. If water leaks out the handle, clean out the old packing and install a new packing washer, or wrap string packing around the stem and cram it up into the packing nut.

GRIND A WORN SEAT
Using a seat grinder

Seat grinder

If you cannot obtain a new seat, smooth the existing seat with a seat grinder. Keep the tool stable while you grind; if it wobbles you may make matters worse. The seat should be smooth and even when you're done.

REVERSE-COMPRESSION FAUCETS

This two-handle faucet looks like a stem faucet but operates by opening and closing in the opposite direction. The seat is attached to the bottom of the stem body. The washer attaches to the bottom of the spindle facing up. Opening the faucet moves the spindle downward, allowing flow between the seat and the washer.

Getting the parts

Chicago (shown in Steps 1–5) and Crane (shown on page 65) are among the companies that make this type of faucet. Be sure to get parts made specifically for your model. Washers may be different in shape, so a standard stem washer may appear to fit but will not properly seal. Repair kits typically have O-rings, seats, and washers, so you can replace all the nonmetal parts. Often, however, all you need is the washer.

1 **Shut off the water** and open both handles until water stops flowing. Remove the handle (pages 62–63). Use an adjustable wrench to loosen the hold-down nut. Unscrew and remove the stem.

2 Grasp the stem with groove-joint pliers, using a cloth in the jaws to prevent scratches. Use an adjustable wrench to loosen and remove the nut at the bottom; the seat will not slide out. On models with no bottom nut, twist the seat to remove it.

PRESTART CHECKLIST

☐ **TIME**
Less than an hour for most repairs

☐ **TOOLS**
Screwdrivers, adjustable wrench, groove-joint pliers, perhaps a handle puller

☐ **SKILLS**
Shutting off water, dismantling a faucet, installing small parts

☐ **PREP**
Shut off the water, close the sink stopper, and place a rag in the sink to catch any parts

☐ **MATERIALS**
Seat, washer, and O-rings for your faucet

CHICAGO-TYPE FAUCET

On this faucet the seat is a thin brass cylinder with an integrated rubber gasket, which attaches to the bottom of the stem body. The washer moves up and down to close and open the faucet. An O-ring keeps water from welling up out of the handle.

3 If the seat looks worn, replace it. Depending on the the type of faucet, either slip or twist it into position.

4 Replace the washer. Be sure to install one that is made for your faucet.

5 If water wells up below the handle while water is running, or if an O-ring looks worn, replace it with an exact duplicate.

WHAT IF ...
You have a Crane reverse-compression faucet?

1 One prominent maker of reverse-compression faucets is Crane. Remove a Crane stem as you would a Chicago model. Twist the top portion to unscrew it from the bottom portion.

2 Clean away debris with a toothbrush or soft wire brush. Remove rubber and cork parts. Install exact replacements (the replacement for a cork ring may be made of rubber). Rub silicone grease on the large threads before reassembling.

TWO-HANDLE CARTRIDGE (DISK) AND DIAPHRAGM FAUCETS

Many newer two-handle faucets use individual cartridges or diaphragm stems. Both types are long-lasting and easy to repair.

An individual cartridge is similar to a single-handle cartridge (page 68). It contains a plastic or rubber valve that opens and closes to permit or stop the flow of water.

Fixing a leaky faucet may require replacing the cartridge or replacing O-rings and seals, depending on the manufacturer and model.

PRESTART CHECKLIST

☐ **TIME**
Less than an hour for most repairs

☐ **TOOLS**
Screwdrivers, groove-joint pliers, perhaps a socket wrench, and a handle puller

☐ **SKILLS**
Shutting off water, dismantling a faucet, installing small parts

☐ **PREP**
Shut off the water, close the sink stopper, and place a rag in the sink to catch any parts

☐ **MATERIALS**
Replacement cartridge or O-rings and seals, silicone grease

Cloth

Groove-joint pliers

1 **Shut off the water.** Turn the handles on to drain out any water. The handle may be held with a top screw (page 62), or it may twist off. Wrap the handle with a cloth before twisting it with groove-joint pliers.

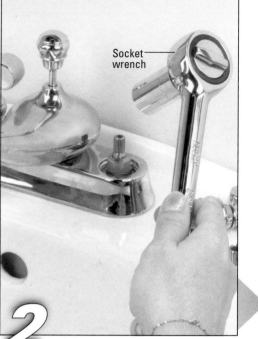

Socket wrench

2 Pull the cartridge up and out. With some types it is important to note which direction the cartridge is facing so you can reinstall it facing the same direction. You may need to use a socket wrench, pliers, or even a special pulling tool made for certain brands of stems (page 73).

PRICE-PFISTER, AND STERLING/ROCKWELL TYPES

O-ring

Cartridge

O-ring

Seat

Body

A cartridge has passageways that can be opened to allow water to pass through to the spout. Companies make cartridges of various shapes and designs.

3 If the cartridge is metal, replacing the rubber parts usually fixes the problem. Pry off the rubber seat at the bottom.

Seat

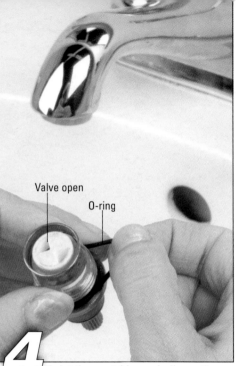

4 Twist the cartridge spindle so the valve opens. Wash out any debris. If the internal parts are worn, replace the cartridge. Replace the rubber seat and any O-rings. Rub the parts with silicone grease.

Valve open

O-ring

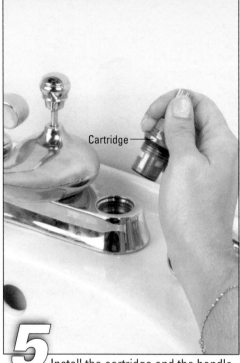

5 Install the cartridge and the handle and test. If you cannot turn the water on or off, remove and reorient the cartridge.

Cartridge

WHAT IF ...
You have a diaphragm faucet?

A diaphragm faucet has two stems similar to those in a standard stem faucet (pages 62–63). However the stem has a neoprene cap, called a diaphragm, at the bottom instead of a washer. Usually you can simply pry off the diaphragm and slip on a new one. If that does not fix a leak, replace the stem or the faucet.

Stem

Diaphragm

Seat

TWO-HANDLE DISK FAUCET

A two-handle disk faucet uses disk assemblies similar to those in a single-handle disk faucet and has springs similar to those in a ball faucet.

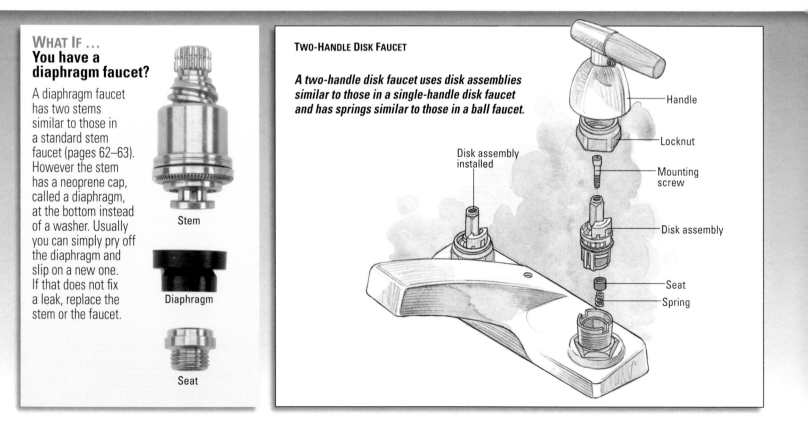

Handle

Locknut

Mounting screw

Disk assembly installed

Disk assembly

Seat

Spring

SINGLE-HANDLE DISK (CERAMIC DISK) FAUCETS

A single-handle disk faucet is made with a pair of ceramic or plastic disks encased in a cylinder. The upper disk rotates when you turn the handle. Water flows when the inlets of the upper and lower disks line up.

Getting the parts

If water wells up around the handle or drips out of the spout, replace the seals with exact duplicates. If that does not solve the problem, replace the entire cylinder—you cannot open it to replace disks. If water flow is slow or erratic, particles of rust and minerals may be clogging the inlets. Cleaning them solves the problem.

PRESTART CHECKLIST

☐ **TIME**
Less than an hour for most repairs

☐ **TOOLS**
Screwdriver, hex wrench, cleaning brush

☐ **SKILLS**
Shutting off water, dismantling a faucet, installing small parts

☐ **PREP**
Shut off the water, close the sink stopper, and place a rag in the sink to catch any parts

☐ **MATERIALS**
Repair kit with seals and O-rings, silicone grease

1 **Shut off the water.** Turn the faucet on until the water stops running. To remove the handle you'll probably need to unscrew a setscrew using a hex wrench or small screwdriver. Lift off the handle and remove the dome housing.

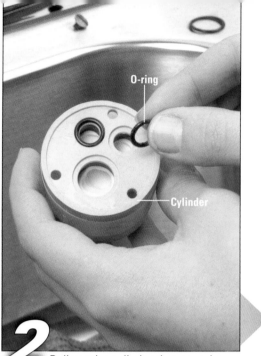

2 Pull out the cylinder that contains the disks and take it to a home center or hardware store to find replacement parts. The O-rings can be pried out of the cylinder using your fingers.

AMERICAN STANDARD TYPE

Carefully note the order and direction of the parts as you disassemble a disk faucet so you can put them back correctly. Rubber seals and O-rings are usually located in two places in the faucet; you may have to partially disassemble the cylinder to get at some of them.

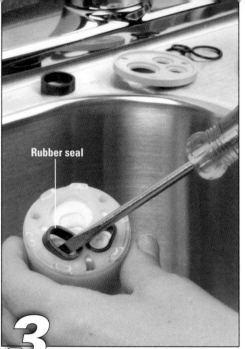

3 On some models removing the bottom plate reveals the rubber seals. Remove them with a small screwdriver, taking care not to nick the plastic housing. If the cylinder is cracked or scored, replace it. Otherwise buy a kit with the rubber seals and O-rings.

4 Before replacing the rubber parts, gently clean away scum and debris from the seats using a toothbrush or a nonmetallic abrasive pad. Rub a little silicone grease on the rubber parts.

5 Reassemble the cylinder. Install the cylinder so it faces the same direction as it did before.

DISK FAUCET WITH GASKETS

Instead of individual O-rings or rubber seals, some disk faucets use a rubber or nylon gasket. This way only one part is needed rather than two or three separate parts. To repair simply replace the worn gasket.

WHAT IF ...
The faucet leaks at the base?

Some single-handle disk faucets have large rubber rings at the base of the spout. These may wear out. Remove the worn rings with a standard screwdriver or knife. Take the old ring with you when shopping to find an exact replacement. Clean away any debris, coat the replacement parts with silicone grease, and reinstall. To repair the diverter and the kitchen sprayer, see page 83.

If water drips below the faucet and you find wet spots in the cabinet floor, feel with your hand and check with a flashlight to find the highest wet spot. You may need to tighten a supply tube where it hooks to the faucet.

BALL FAUCETS

On the outside a single-handle faucet looks a lot like a disk faucet, but it has a narrower cylinder under the handle. Inside is a metal or plastic ball with grooves and holes. When the handle turns, the grooves or holes line up with rubber-sealed inlets in the faucet body to allow water to flow.

This type of faucet can become clogged by small particles. If water flow is slow or erratic, disassemble and clean the inlets.

Getting the parts

If water seeps out below the handle or drips out the spout, tighten the cap or the cap-adjusting ring. If that does not solve the problem, buy a rebuild kit for your model. If water seeps out the base of the faucet, replace the O-rings. If water drips from the spout, replace the seats and springs. Less commonly a ball is damaged and needs to be replaced.

PRESTART CHECKLIST

☐ **TIME**
Less than an hour for most repairs

☐ **TOOLS**
Hex wrench, screwdriver

☐ **SKILLS**
Shutting off water, dismantling a faucet, installing small parts

☐ **PREP**
Shut off the water, close the sink stopper, and place a rag in the sink to catch any parts

☐ **MATERIALS**
Repair kit (including O-rings, seats, springs, and other plastic parts), perhaps a new ball

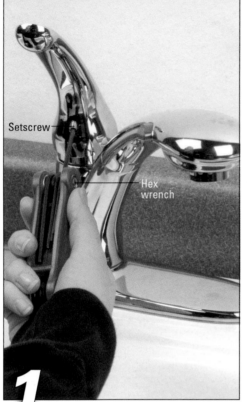

Setscrew

Hex wrench

1 **Shut off the water** and turn the faucet on until water stops running. Loosen the handle setscrew with a hex wrench, sometimes included in a repair kit. Lift off the handle and unscrew the cap.

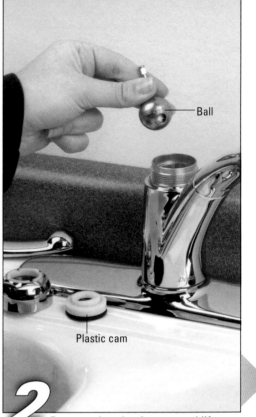

Ball

Plastic cam

2 Remove the plastic cam and lift out the ball. If the ball is worn, replace it along with the seats and springs.

DELTA AND PEERLESS

Handle

Adjusting ring

Setscrew

Cap

Spout

Aerator

Cam

Cam washer

Ball

Seats, springs

O-ring

O-ring

Escutcheon

"One-touch" spout option

Aerator

Hose

A spring presses each seat on a ball faucet against the ball. Replace weak springs or worn seats.

Spring

3 Carefully insert the tip of a screwdriver into a seat and pull it out. This may take a couple of tries for each seat.

4 Use the same technique to remove the springs. Clean or flush out debris in the faucet body. Purchase springs and seats for your faucet model.

5 Replace the springs and seats and press them into place with your finger. Insert the ball so it sits snugly. Add the washer and screw on the adjusting ring. You may need a special wrench to tighten the ring. If the faucet still leaks, tighten the ring further.

WHAT IF ...
You find debris?

If small particles partially clog the inlets, first wipe away as much as you can. Slowly turn the water back on to flush out more particles. If you have old galvanized pipes, you may need to do this regularly.

WHAT IF ...
The faucet leaks at the base?

To cure a leak at the base of the faucet below the handle, pull or twist off the spout. Pry or cut off the old O-rings, coat the faucet body lightly with silicone grease, and slip on the new O-rings. When you reattach the spout, make sure it slides all the way down.

STANLEY PRO TIP
Metal or plastic ball?

An inexpensive plastic ball is easily scratched, so it may wear out in less than a year, especially if your water contains debris. A metal ball is worth the extra cost because it lasts longer.

CARTRIDGE FAUCETS

Several manufacturers make single-handle cartridge faucets. Each model has a cartridge of a slightly different design. A cartridge may have a cylinder with grooves or it may be tapered so water can pass through when it is turned.

Getting the parts

If water leaks out the spout, you'll have to replace or repair the cartridge. If a leaky faucet's cartridge is plastic, replace it; if it is metal you may need to replace only the O-rings. If water wells up below the handle, replace the O-rings around the faucet body. Many repair kits contain both the cartridge and the O-rings.

PRESTART CHECKLIST

☐ **TIME**
Less than an hour for most repairs

☐ **TOOLS**
Screwdrivers, hex wrench, perhaps a stem puller

☐ **SKILLS**
Shutting off water, dismantling a faucet, installing small parts

☐ **PREP**
Shut off the water, close the sink stopper, and place a rag in the sink to catch any parts

☐ **MATERIALS**
Replacement cartridge or O-rings and seals, silicone grease

Hex wrench

1 **Shut off the water.** Turn on the faucet until the water stops running. To remove the handle pry off the decorative cap and remove the screw, using a hex wrench or screwdriver as needed. Lift off the handle.

Handle attachment mechanism

2 Unscrew the cap or retaining ring. If you find a handle-attachment mechanism like the one shown, note how it is attached so you can replace it correctly.

DELTA AND PEERLESS TYPES

Handle cap
Hot/cold indicator
Handle
Housing

Handle adapter
Pivot stop
Retainer nut
Washer
Diverter
Washer
Retaining clip
Cartridge

On some models the handle attaches directly to the cartridge. On others a mechanism between the handle and the cartridge makes for smooth operation.

3 Many cartridges can be removed simply by pulling up with pliers. If it is stuck you may need to buy a stem puller designed for your faucet.

Stem puller

4 Remove the spout. Pry off any damaged O-rings and replace them with duplicates. Apply a thin coat of silicone grease and replace the spout.

Spout

O-ring

5 Replace either the O-rings on the cartridge or the entire cartridge. If the cartridge is not greasy, apply a thin coat of grease and push it into position.

Cartridge

Silicone grease

Special pullers

Some faucets have cartridges that can be removed only with a manufacturer-specific pulling tool. Trying to remove the cartridge without the proper tool can damage the cartridge and faucet.

WHAT IF ...
Your cartridge is a different type?

A plastic cartridge that slips into a cartridge casing (left) should be well greased. If hot and cold are reversed after installing it, remove the cartridge and turn it 180 degrees. Some brass cartridges (center) require several O-rings of different sizes. Another type (right) uses O-rings as well as rubber seats.

TUB AND SHOWER STEM COMPRESSION FAUCETS

Tub and shower faucets work much like sink faucets, but they are oriented horizontally rather than vertically. In addition their parts are usually larger. A two-handle stem shower faucet has a stem with a washer that presses against a seat to seal off water, just like the faucet shown on pages 62–63. A three-handle unit adds a stemlike diverter to direct water up to the shower or down to the tub spout.

Getting the parts

Often leaks can be fixed simply by replacing the washers. Even if you need to replace the seats or stems, it usually makes sense to repair rather than replace an old shower faucet, because replacement requires opening the wall. If parts are hard to find, order them at a plumbing supply store.

PRESTART CHECKLIST

☐ **TIME**
An hour or two for most repairs

☐ **TOOLS**
Screwdrivers, perhaps a handle puller, adjustable wrench or groove-joint pliers, perhaps a stem wrench or seat wrench

☐ **SKILLS**
Shutting off water, dismantling a faucet, installing small parts

☐ **PREP**
Shut off the water, close the tub stopper, and place a rag in the tub to catch any loose parts

☐ **MATERIALS**
Washers, O-rings, seats, perhaps new stems

1 **Shut off the water.** Turn both handles on until water stops flowing. Pry off the handle cap, remove the screw, and pry off the handle. You may need to use a handle puller (page 63). Unscrew the stem sleeve and pull off the escutcheon.

2 If the stem protrudes far enough past the wall surface, loosen it with an adjustable wrench or groove-joint pliers. For a recessed stem, use a stem wrench.

THREE-HANDLE STEM SHOWER FAUCET

A two-handle stem shower unit works much like a stem sink faucet. A three-handle faucet adds a diverter to direct water.

3 If water seeps out around the handle, replace a worn packing washer or stuff thread packing around the stem and into the cavity behind the packing nut (page 63).

Packing washer

4 If water drips out the spout or the showerhead, replace a worn washer with an exact duplicate.

Washer

5 If replacing the washer does not stop the leak or if washers wear out quickly, remove the seat with a seat wrench and replace it. Or grind the seat smooth with a seat grinder (page 63).

Seat

Seat wrench

RECESSED STEM
Using a stem wrench

Stem nut

Stem wrench

If the stem nut is behind the wall, you won't be able to unscrew the stem with an adjustable wrench or pliers. Use a stem wrench, a deep socket wrench made to fit a bathtub stem.

WHAT IF ...
The diverter leaks?

The diverter on a three-handle tub faucet is essentially a stem. When its washer presses against the seat, water cannot rise up to the showerhead and is diverted to the tub spout.

You repair a diverter in much the same way as you do a hot or cold stem. Replace the washer at the bottom and replace any O-rings and other removable parts.

O-ring

Washer

TUB AND SHOWER CARTRIDGE FAUCETS

Once you shut off the water and remove the handle and escutcheon, you can quickly determine whether your single-handle tub and shower faucet is a cartridge, ball, or disk type (pages 68–73).

Getting the parts

Tub cartridge faucets work just like sink cartridge faucets (pages 72–73). Usually the faucet only turns water on and off; a diverter valve on the spout directs water to the showerhead or the spout. A number of manufacturers make cartridges of varying designs, so take the cartridge with you when you shop for parts. You may need to replace the entire cartridge. Follow the steps as shown to remove it.

PRESTART CHECKLIST

☐ **TIME**
An hour or two for most repairs

☐ **TOOLS**
Screwdriver, perhaps a hex wrench, groove-joint pliers, perhaps a cartridge puller

☐ **SKILLS**
Shutting off water, dismantling a faucet, installing small parts

☐ **PREP**
Shut off the water, close the tub stopper, and place a rag in the tub to catch any parts

☐ **MATERIALS**
Cartridge or repair kit for your faucet model, silicone grease

1 **Shut off the water** and turn the faucet on until water stops running. To remove the handle you may need a hex wrench, which is sometimes included in a repair kit. Remove the screws holding the escutcheon and slide out the escutcheon.

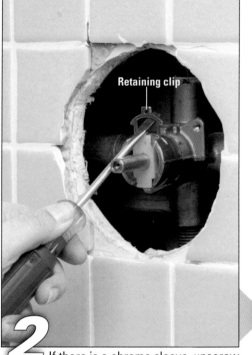

2 If there is a chrome sleeve, unscrew it or pull it out. Use a small screwdriver to pry out the retaining clip that holds the cartridge in place.

MOEN, KOHLER/BRADLEY TYPE

Tub and shower cartridge faucets are similar to their sink counterparts. Twisting the handle rotates the cartridge, which routes the water through the resulting passageways.

3 Some cartridges can be removed easily with pliers; others require a special cartridge-pulling wrench (usually available at hardware stores or home centers) made for a specific brand of faucet.

Cartridge-pulling wrench

4 If the cartridge is in good shape, replace the O-rings and any other replaceable parts. (Often, however, it doesn't cost much more to replace the cartridge.) Rub the O-rings with a thin coat of silicone grease.

O-ring

5 Insert the new or repaired cartridge into the faucet body, oriented as it was originally. Slide in the retaining clip and replace the handle and escutcheon.

Retaining clip

WHAT IF ...
You find this cartridge?

This cartridge works by virtue of its tapered shape, rather than a series of grooves. Note the cartridge's orientation when you remove it so you can put it back the same way. If hot and cold are reversed after you reinstall the cartridge, turn it 180 degrees.

Antiscald faucets

Even a short burst of scalding water can be painful and dangerous, especially for young children. So plumbing codes often require new tub and shower faucets that prevent the flow of very hot water. Some temperature-balancing or antiscald faucets prevent cold water from being turned off; others have a thermostatic device that reduces hot water flow when it senses the water is too hot.

An antiscald valve is usually marked. Sometimes by rocking the faucet you'll hear a click that indicates the unit has an antiscald valve. In some cases you can replace a standard cartridge in an older valve with an antiscald cartridge.

TUB AND SHOWER BALL FAUCETS

A ball faucet has a metal or plastic ball with grooves that control flow (page 70). Small springs press rubber seats against the ball. Replacing the seats and springs usually will stop a leak. The ball may also need to be replaced.

Tightening the adjusting ring with pliers or a special tool may stop a leak. If water flow is slow or erratic, remove the seats and springs and flush out any debris.

PRESTART CHECKLIST

☐ **TIME**
An hour or two for most repairs

☐ **TOOLS**
Screwdrivers, adjustable wrench, groove-joint pliers

☐ **SKILLS**
Shutting off water, dismantling a faucet, installing small parts

☐ **PREP**
Shut off the water, close the tub stopper, and place a rag in the tub to catch any parts

☐ **MATERIALS**
O-rings, seats, and other rubber parts, silicone grease, perhaps a new cylinder

1 **Shut off the water** and turn the faucet on until it drains. Remove the handle and escutcheon. Pry off any retaining clips, unscrew the retaining ring, and pull out the cylinder.

2 Take the cylinder with you to buy replacement parts. Most O-rings can be removed easily with your fingers. Replace all rubber parts. With a rag under the faucet body, slowly turn on the shutoff to flush out debris.

3 Apply silicone grease to the rubber parts. Reinsert the cylinder, reattach the retaining clip (if there is one), and screw on the adjusting ring. If the faucet leaks tighten the ring.

DELTA/PEERLESS TYPE

Housing assembly · Springs · Seats · Rotational limit stop · O-ring · Escutcheon · Faucet body · Push-button diverter · Cap assembly · Adjusting ring · Spacer

A ball faucet has an adjusting ring, which controls how tightly the cylinder (which contains the ball mechanism) presses against the seats. Sometimes inlets become clogged with tiny bits of debris.

TUB AND SHOWER DISK FAUCETS

This faucet works like a sink cartridge faucet (pages 72–73) and repairs are similar.

If water drips out the spout or seeps out around the handle, buy a kit and replace all the rubber parts. Inspect the cylinder and replace it if you see signs of wear. If your model has plastic rather than ceramic disks, replace the entire unit.

Depending on the model you may need to partially disassemble the cylinder to get to all the rubber parts.

PRESTART CHECKLIST

☐ **TIME**
An hour or two for most repairs

☐ **TOOLS**
Screwdrivers, adjustable wrench, groove-joint pliers, cleaning brush

☐ **SKILLS**
Shutting off water, dismantling a faucet, installing small parts

☐ **PREP**
Shut off the water, close the tub stopper, and place a rag in the tub to catch any parts

☐ **MATERIALS**
Repair kit for your model of faucet, silicone grease

1 **Shut off the water** and turn the faucet on until water stops running. Remove the handle and the escutcheon. Unscrew three screws to remove the cylinder.

Rubber seat

2 Remove rubber seats with your fingers. Clean the openings with a toothbrush or an abrasive pad. Replace the rubber seats with duplicates. Rub a bit of silicone grease over the seats.

O-ring

3 Do the same for all other rubber parts. If you need to pry out an O-ring, you may need to use a small screwdriver. Work carefully to prevent nicking the plastic housing.

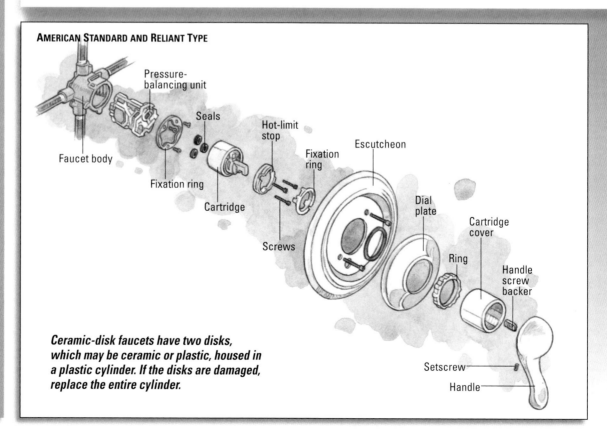

AMERICAN STANDARD AND RELIANT TYPE

Pressure-balancing unit

Seals

Hot-limit stop

Fixation ring

Escutcheon

Faucet body

Fixation ring

Cartridge

Screws

Dial plate

Cartridge cover

Ring

Handle screw backer

Setscrew

Handle

Ceramic-disk faucets have two disks, which may be ceramic or plastic, housed in a plastic cylinder. If the disks are damaged, replace the entire cylinder.

DIVERTERS

Most single-handle shower faucets simply turn water on and off; a pull-up diverter valve on the spout determines whether water goes up or down. Some models, however, have a diverter built into the handle.

Getting the parts
You may be able to find repair parts in a kit for a specific faucet. If not, standard O-rings and washers may fit. In some cases the seal is made with brass parts and no washers; simple cleaning and light sanding may solve the problem.

A corroded diverter stem or one with a weak spring should be replaced. A plumbing supply house should be able to order it. While you are waiting for the part to arrive, wrap duct tape around the handle of the diverter to keep it from pushing too far in. This will allow you to use the shower while waiting for the replacement part.

Push/pull type

Diverter

1 **Shut off the water** and turn the faucet on until the water stops running. Remove the handle and the escutcheon. Use groove-joint pliers or an adjustable wrench to remove the diverter unit.

O-ring

2 Remove and replace any worn rubber parts. If the diverter itself is worn, you may be able to buy a replacement.

BUILT-IN DIVERTER

Valve body

Diverter

O-ring

When pushed in, a washer at the end of the diverter seals the opening so water cannot rise up to the showerhead. A spring inside the diverter counteracts the effect of water pressure so the diverter can be easily pushed and pulled.

TUB SPOUTS

A tub spout may be screwed onto a threaded pipe or anchored to a nonthreaded pipe with a setscrew. Before you start to unscrew a spout, check underneath to see if there is a setscrew.

If water seeps from behind the spout, it may be attached to a threaded pipe that is loose. Remove the pipe, wrap its threads with pipe-thread tape, and use a pipe wrench to tighten it.

If given a choice spend a little more for a brass spout. It will last longer than a bargain-bin spout, which may be made of thin metal or even plastic that wears and stains quickly.

PRESTART CHECKLIST

☐ **TIME**
Less than an hour for most repairs

☐ **TOOLS**
Screwdrivers, hex wrench, groove-joint pliers, pipe wrench, caulk gun

☐ **SKILLS**
Unscrewing and reinstalling a spout

☐ **PREP**
There is no need to shut off the water; place a towel in the bottom of the tub to catch any debris or caulk

☐ **MATERIALS**
New spout, pipe-thread tape, tub-and-tile caulk

Pipe-thread tape

1 Use groove-joint pliers or a pipe wrench to remove an old spout that is threaded on. Clean the end of the pipe and scrape away any caulk on the wall. Wrap the pipe threads clockwise with two or three turns of pipe-thread tape.

Masking tape

2 Screw on the new spout by hand. Wrap masking tape or a cloth around the spout, or wrap electrician's tape around the jaws of groove-joint pliers, and tighten the spout firmly. If the pipe is copper, avoid overtightening, which can strip the threads.

SETSCREWS
Removing a spout held with a hex-head screw

Some spouts attach with a setscrew. Loosen the screw with a hex wrench and slide off the old spout.

Spout retrofit kit

Spout

Thread adapter

Washer

Hex wrench

Adapter pipe

Thread tape

Not all spouts are the same. Some are threaded where they meet the wall; others have threads deep in the body of the spout. You may be able to replace the pipe coming out of the wall or purchase a retrofit kit (shown) that helps make the transition.

INSTALLING A FLEX-LINE SHOWER

Installing a shower in a bathtub without one is a big job. An easier solution is a flex-line shower unit. It installs quickly, and its removable showerhead is a handy feature.

The surrounding walls should be covered with tile or other water-resistant material. If you have a claw-foot tub that does not abut the walls, purchase a circular shower curtain.

PRESTART CHECKLIST

☐ **TIME**
About an hour for most units

☐ **TOOLS**
Drill with masonry bit, screwdriver, hammer, groove-joint pliers or pipe wrench

☐ **SKILLS**
Drilling holes in tile, assembling parts

☐ **PREP**
No need to shut off the water; place a towel in the bottom of the tub to catch any parts

☐ **MATERIALS**
Flex-line shower unit, pipe tape, plastic anchors

1 Remove the old spout and screw on the one that comes with the shower unit. See page 81 for steps.

2 Hold the showerhead bracket or template in place and mark for mounting holes. Press the tip of a nail on a mark and tap with a hammer to make a small chip as a starter hole. Drill holes with a masonry bit.

3 Tap plastic anchors into the holes and attach the showerhead bracket with the provided screws. Snap on its decorative body. Screw the flex line to the tub spout and slip the showerhead into the bracket.

FLEX-LINE SHOWER UNIT

This unit has a diverter spout so water can run through the spout or up to the showerhead. Some showerheads provide a pulsating water flow.

Buy a high-quality shower Look for a brass (rather than plastic) showerhead and a heavy-duty flex line.

KITCHEN SPRAYERS

Kitchen sink sprayers are easy to repair. Instead of repairing one, though, you could install a one-touch faucet (page 87).

If pressure is low make sure the hose is not kinked. If that's not the problem, disassemble and clean the sprayer. If that fails turn off the water and check the diverter.

If water comes out of the sprayer even when its valve is not depressed, replace the sprayer body and valve.

(page 87)

PRESTART CHECKLIST

☐ **TIME**
An hour or two for most repairs

☐ **TOOLS**
Screwdriver, groove-joint pliers, long-nose pliers, toothbrush, knife

☐ **SKILLS**
Dismantling and reassembling a unit with small parts

☐ **PREP**
Shut the water off only to work on the diverter valve; lay down a small towel for organizing small parts

☐ **MATERIALS**
Replacement parts for the sprayer and diverter, perhaps a new sprayer, silicone grease

1 Pull the sprayer out and use pliers to dismantle the spout, keeping track of all its parts. Clean them with a toothbrush. If parts are caked with minerals, soak them overnight in vinegar.

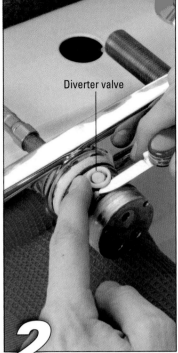

2 If cleaning or replacing the sprayer does not solve the problem, **shut off the water**. Remove the spout and find the diverter valve. On this model it is in the faucet body. Pry out the valve with a knife.

Diverter valve

3 Replace worn parts or the entire diverter valve. Clean away any debris and coat the rubber parts with silicone grease. Reinstall and test.

O-ring

SPRAYER AND DIVERTER

On a disk faucet and other single-handle models (left), the diverter valve is typically placed horizontally in the faucet body. On a two-handle faucet (right), the valve is likely situated vertically in the center of the spout.

Setscrew
Adjusting ring
Hub assembly
Cartridge
Diverter valve
Aerator
Sprayer body
Sprayer valve
Hose guide
Adjusting ring
Diverter valve
Aerator
O-ring
Mounting nut
Sprayer hose

INSTALLING A KITCHEN FAUCET

The three holes in a kitchen sink accommodate most new kitchen faucets. Some faucets require a fourth hole for a sprayer.

Installing a faucet requires working in cramped conditions. If you are also replacing the sink, install the faucet before installing the sink (pages 216–219). Otherwise do what you can to make the worksite comfortable (page 43).

Braided supply tubes make the job easier. Buy tubes long enough to reach from the faucet to the stop valves. If there are no stop valves under the sink, now is a good time to install them (pages 118–119).

Most people find single-handle faucets easier to use. Make sure the spout is the right length for your sink. A heavy, solid-brass unit will outlast a less expensive unit. The faucet should come with a warranty that includes the sprayer.

PRESTART CHECKLIST

☐ **TIME**
About 2 hours to install most faucets

☐ **TOOLS**
Screwdriver, adjustable wrench, groove-joint pliers, basin wrench, putty knife

☐ **SKILLS**
Shutting off water, working under a sink, attaching plumbing parts

☐ **PREP**
Shut off the water and remove the drain trap

☐ **MATERIALS**
New faucet, plumber's putty, pipe-thread tape, masking tape

Supply tube
Stop valve
Sprayer hose

1 **Shut off the water** and turn the faucet on until the water stops running. From underneath use a wrench or pliers to hold the stop valve still while you loosen the supply tube nut with another wrench or pliers. Disconnect the sprayer hose from the faucet or simply cut the hose.

Basin wrench

2 With a basin wrench loosen the nut on the one or two mounting shanks. If there is a sprayer hose guide, loosen it from underneath with a basin wrench as well. On other types of faucets, you may need to loosen a center mounting nut.

ONE-HANDLE INSTALLATION

Many newer faucets mount with a center ring and nut. Two more mounting nuts connect at the other two holes in the sink. Usually flexible supply tubes are needed to reach the stop valves.

Mounting nut
Center ring
Nut

Putty rope

Mounting nut

Base of sprayer support

Sprayer hose

Center faucet hole

3 Lift out the old faucet. If you feel resistance check underneath to make sure everything has been disconnected. In rare cases an old faucet will have supply tubes that are sweated on. See page 118 for how to cut away the old supply tubes.

4 If the faucet does not have a rubber gasket (see below), roll out a rope of plumber's putty and press it into place on the bottom of the new faucet. Make sure it is thick enough at all points to completely seal the faucet body.

5 If you have a sprayer, install the sprayer support, tightening the mounting nut first by hand, then with a basin wrench. Don't overtighten. Run the sprayer hose through the sprayer support and through the center faucet hole.

CENTER MOUNTING NUT

Bracket

Nut

A center-mount faucet attaches to the sink with a single bracket instead of two tailpieces doubling as hot and cold supplies. Typically a bracket is snugged up against the sink with a nut. With center mounts supply tubes can be installed before the faucet is set into the sink.

WHAT IF ...
The faucet has a gasket?

Some faucets have a rubber gasket, so they do not need a rope of putty. Make sure the gasket is centered and unwrinkled before tightening the mounting nuts.

STANLEY PRO TIP
Cleaning a gunky deck

Masking tape

Clean old putty off the sink deck before installing a new faucet. Mask around the faucet base with tape and scrape with a plastic putty knife. Clean the surface with an abrasive pad and mineral spirits or alcohol.

INSTALLING A KITCHEN FAUCET _continued_

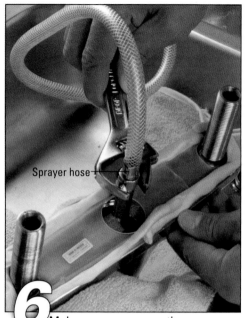

6 Make as many connections as possible before installing the faucet to minimize work under the sink. In this case the sprayer tube can be attached; mounting nuts must be attached from underneath before supply tubes can be installed.

Sprayer hose

7 Slip the new faucet into place. If the faucet has inlets and a mounting nut in the center, getting all those tubes through the center hole will be a tight fit. Take care not to scratch the threads. If you need to bend a copper tube, do so gently to avoid kinking it.

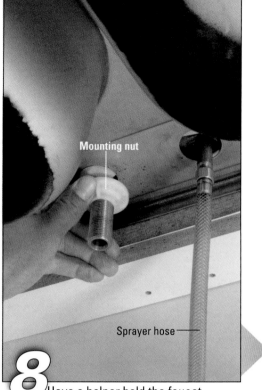

Mounting nut

Sprayer hose

8 Have a helper hold the faucet straight while you install the mounting nuts underneath. For this type first apply the mounting nuts and tighten them finger-tight. Check that the faucet is mounted straight before tightening with a basin wrench.

Supply tube options

Flexible plastic

Copper

Chrome-plated

Braided stainless steel

Braided plastic

Flexible plastic supply tubes are the least expensive but are not allowed by code in some areas. Plain copper and chrome-plated tubes are long-lasting but require careful measuring, cutting, and bending. Braided tubes are long-lasting and are the easiest to install.

WHAT IF ...
Copper runs to stop valves?

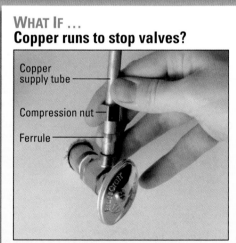

Copper supply tube

Compression nut

Ferrule

Many plumbers prefer to install copper or chrome-plated copper supply tubes rather than flexible lines. This saves a bit of money and makes for a slightly more solid installation. Cut the supply tubes with a tubing cutter (pages 110, 126) and bend them with a tubing bender (page 20). Attach the compression fitting (page 111).

9 Fasten each supply tube by hand to the faucet base. Then tighten the connection using a basin wrench.

Supply tube

Basin wrench

10 Screw on and tighten the supply tubes to the stop valves. Use two wrenches or pliers to prevent bending the pipes connected to the stop valves.

11 If you bumped the drain trap while working, you may have loosened its joints. To check, fill the sinks with water, remove the stoppers, and watch for any leaks. Tighten leaky joints.

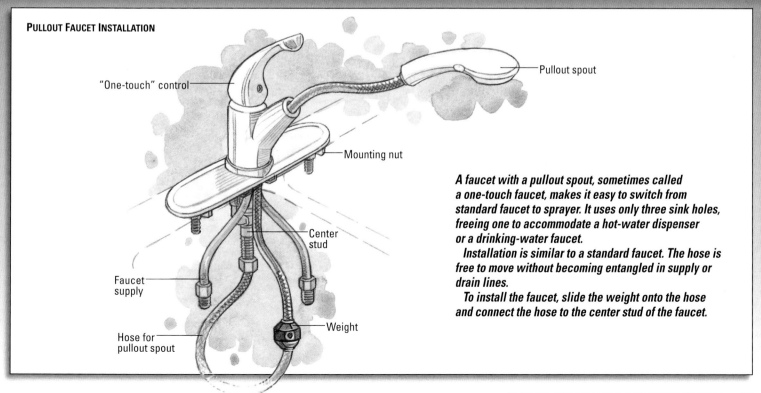

PULLOUT FAUCET INSTALLATION

"One-touch" control

Pullout spout

Mounting nut

Center stud

Faucet supply

Weight

Hose for pullout spout

A faucet with a pullout spout, sometimes called a one-touch faucet, makes it easy to switch from standard faucet to sprayer. It uses only three sink holes, freeing one to accommodate a hot-water dispenser or a drinking-water faucet.

Installation is similar to a standard faucet. The hose is free to move without becoming entangled in supply or drain lines.

To install the faucet, slide the weight onto the hose and connect the hose to the center stud of the faucet.

INSTALLING A WIDESPREAD FAUCET

Widespread faucets offer increased design latitude. Unlike centerset or fixed-base units, you can place the components 8 inches apart or more.

Consider countertop thickness before purchasing your faucet. Granite, marble, or other materials may be thicker than the thread length on many faucet bodies. You may be able to use a faucet extension kit for thick materials or countersink the mounting holes on the underside of the sink for short stems.

Sink styles matter too. A drop-in sink with precast or precut mounting holes saves time and work, but an undermount sink with the faucet installed in holes drilled in the countertop allows you more freedom in placing the faucets and accessories.

Installation of a widespread faucet follows the same general procedures required for a centerset model. If working with a new drop-in sink, you may be able to install all the faucet parts before installing the sink.

1 Unpack the parts and make sure nothing is missing. The spout is installed first for some models, the valves for others; follow the manufacturer's instructions. Apply plumber's putty or silicone to the bottom of the flange and insert the spout or valve.

2 With a helper holding the unit from above, tighten the retaining nut or T-fitting or whatever mechanical device secures the faucet element to the sink deck or countertop. Some units require only hand-tightening. Others call for a faucet wrench. In any case tighten then center the unit in the hole.

PRESTART CHECKLIST

☐ **TIME**
About 3 to 4 hours

☐ **TOOLS**
Screwdriver, putty knife, adjustable wrench, slip-joint pliers, basin wrench, hole saw

☐ **SKILLS**
Shutting off water, working under a sink, attaching plumbing parts

☐ **PREP**
Install sink, drill faucet mounting holes if necessary

☐ **MATERIALS**
New faucet and accessories, plumber's putty or sealant

Other techniques make installation easy

Some recent innovations have made installation of both centerset and widespread faucets quicker and almost error free. Some manufacturers offer snap-in fittings, which provide watertight installation without wrenches. Spout bodies and valves mount and are secured from the top with allen screws and wrenches, a feature that keeps you out from under the sink. Preinstalling the fixtures on a countertop can make this remodel job ready for use in an hour or so.

Spray hose housing

Flange

3 Apply plumber's putty or silicone sealer to the spray-hose housing flange and insert the spray-hose housing in the deck or countertop. With a helper holding the housing from above, tighten the nut from below. Assemble the head to the spray hose and install the hose in the center outlet of the T-fitting.

4 Following the manufacturer's instructions assemble the supply tubes and any other parts to the valve bodies. Seal the flanges with plumber's putty or silicone and insert the completed units in their respective holes. If the valve bodies feature a straight copper pipe, install the valve with this pipe facing the outside of the sink. Tighten the mounting nuts.

5 Seal the botttom of the mounting flange of the soap dispenser and insert the threads into the mounting hole. Tighten the mounting nut and assemble the dispenser unit as specified by the manufacturer.

Cutting holes for an undermount sink

Mounting techniques for undermount sinks can vary widely from manufacturer to manufacturer and model to model.

Some require only the installation of mounting clips. Others are held in place by a framed carriage built by the installer.

In almost all cases installing an undermount requires you to cut out the sink hole first, guided by a model-specific template provided by the manufacturer. Then, using the template or specification sheet supplied with the faucet parts, drill out the holes for the spout, valves, and accessories. For most materials use a carbide-tipped hole saw of the correct diameter.

INSTALLING A BATHROOM FAUCET

A bathroom sink typically has three holes. The faucet usually comes with a pop-up stopper assembly.

Except for a wall-hung sink with no cabinet or pedestal below, the workspace can be cramped. If you have a pedestal sink, check to see whether the bowl is securely attached to a wall bracket. If so you may be able to remove the pedestal while you work (pages 188–189). If you have a sink with a cabinet below, it may be easier to detach the trap, remove the sink, and set the sink on sawhorses to install the faucet.

If there are no stop valves under the sink, install them before putting in the new sink (pages 118–119).

Whether you reuse the old supply tubes or buy new ones, make sure they are long enough to reach the stop valves. Purchase fittings (either ⅜- or ½-inch) that will fit your stop valves.

PRESTART CHECKLIST

☐ **TIME**
About 2 hours to install a bathroom faucet with a pop-up drain assembly

☐ **TOOLS**
Screwdriver, adjustable wrench, putty knife, groove-joint pliers, basin wrench

☐ **SKILLS**
Shutting off water, working under a sink, attaching plumbing parts

☐ **PREP**
Shut off the water, remove the drain trap if needed

☐ **MATERIALS**
New faucet, new pop-up drain (usually comes with the faucet), plumber's putty, perhaps supply tubes

1 **Shut off the water** and turn the faucet on to drain it. Disconnect the supply tubes and the mounting nuts. Loosen the setscrew that holds the clevis strap to the lifter rod, pinch the spring clip, and slide the clevis strap off the pivot rod. Pull out the old faucet and clean the sink deck (page 85).

Disconnected supply tube
Spring clip
Clevis strap
Pivot rod

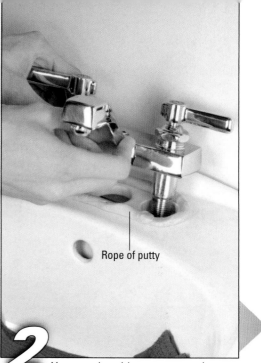

2 You may be able to connect the supply tubes to the new faucet using two wrenches. If no rubber gasket is provided, press a rope of putty to the sink deck or to the underside of the faucet body. Lower the faucet into place.

Rope of putty

TWO TYPES OF BATHROOM FAUCETS

A single-handle faucet (left) usually has copper supply tubes in the center and a mounting nut on each side. On a two-handle unit (right), the mounting nuts are below the handles.

Supply tube attaches here
Mounting nut
Supply tube attaches here
Mounting nut

Mounting nut

Basin wrench

Clevis strap

Pivot rod

Trap

Lift-rod setscrew

Clevis strap

3 Have a helper hold the faucet straight while you tighten mounting nuts from below. If the faucet is not solidly attached after hand-tightening, use a basin wrench to tighten the nuts further.

4 You can use the existing drain body or install a new one (see below). With the stopper closed all the way, slide the clevis strap onto the lift rod and the pivot rod, using the spring clip to hold it in place. Tighten the setscrew that holds the strap to the lift rod. Install the trap (pages 48–49).

5 Make sure the stopper seals water when the lift rod is pulled up and that it opens fully when the rod is pushed down. To adjust loosen the setscrew and move the clevis strap up or down.

Installing a drain body

Rope of putty

Flange

Pipe-thread tape

Tailpiece

1 Loosen the slip nut to disconnect the drain body from the trap. Remove the locknut under the sink and slide out the old drain body. Clean away caked-on putty. Place a new rope of putty around the hole, slip the new drain flange through the hole, and press it into place.

2 Twist the locknut onto the drain body and slip on the friction washer and the rubber gasket. Hold the flange with one hand while you hand-screw the drain body into it. Tighten the locknut with groove-joint pliers, making sure the drain body faces rear.

3 Install the pivot rod and install the clevis strap (Step 4 above). Apply pipe-thread tape to the threaded end of the tailpiece and screw it onto the drain body. Install the trap (pages 48–49).

TOILETS

Considering most are used thousands of times per year, toilets are remarkably durable. The bowl and tank are made of porcelain or vitreous china and will last a long time, as long as they don't get cracked. The mechanical inner workings, however, occasionally need repair. Most toilet repairs are easily within the scope of a do-it-yourselfer.

Sanitary conditions

Many people are understandably reluctant to touch the water in a toilet. With a few precautions, however, contact with unsanitary water can be avoided.

Water from the toilet bowl cannot back up into the tank; water in the tank is just as clean as water from a faucet. If you clean the bowl and flush several times, even the water in the bowl will be clean.

When a toilet is clogged, sewage may back up and flow onto the floor. Wear heavy-duty rubber gloves when cleaning.

You may need to insert a plunger into sewage to clear a clog. After doing so clean the plunger thoroughly—inside and out—with hot water and detergent.

How it works

A toilet bowl has a built-in trap. When water flows in from the tank through a series of openings under the bowl rim, the water level in the bowl rises until it is pushed through the trap and into the sewer line. Some bowls have a jet opening near the bottom to increase flushing power.

A wax ring seals the bowl to the toilet flange on the floor. Flushed water flows through a closet bend below the floor and directly to a large drain stack. This arrangement ensures that anything that makes it through the toilet will reach the stack and exit the house.

There are two mechanisms in the tank. The flush valve has a rubber flapper attached to a chain or, in older toilets, a rubber stopper attached to a lift rod. When the flapper or stopper rests on the flush valve seat, water is held inside the tank. When you push down on the flush handle, the flapper or stopper is raised, providing an opening for water to run out of the tank and into the bowl. When the tank is nearly empty, the flapper or stopper settles down onto the seat again, sealing the tank for filling.

The other tank mechanism is the fill valve assembly. Water flows through the valve into the tank until the water reaches a preset level, then automatically shuts off. Most older toilets have a brass ballcock fill valve attached to a float ball; when the ball floats high enough, the water automatically shuts off. A diaphragm fill valve is also attached to a float ball. A float-cup fill valve replaces the float ball with a plastic cup that slides up and down its shaft as the water rises and falls.

If the fill valve fails to shut off, the excess water flows down the overflow tube and into the bowl.

An emergency fix

If water starts welling up when you flush the toilet rather than swirling down into the bowl, you may be able to keep water from spilling onto the floor if you act quickly. Remove the tank lid, reach into the tank (remember, this water is clean), and push down on the flapper or stopper until it settles on the flush valve seat. Water will stop flowing. Take steps to clear the clog (page 95) before flushing the toilet again.

Nearly all toilet problems can be fixed quickly and inexpensively.

CHAPTER PREVIEW

Troubleshooting and repairs
page 94

Clearing a clog
page 95

Eliminating run-on
page 96

Installing a new float cup
page 97

Fill valve (float-cup type)

Float ball

Handle

Lift wire

Fill valve (ballcock type)

Tank

Fill tube

Overflow tube

Stopper flapper

Flapper

Bowl

Jet

Rim opening

Trap

Wax ring

Flange

Stack

Closet bend

No matter how old a toilet is, all its moving parts—the fill valve, the stopper, and the float—can be replaced, either with duplicate parts or with new mechanisms that perform the same duties reliably. If it's leaking it can be fixed by tightening a bolt or replacing a gasket. In the most extreme instance, you will have to pull up the toilet and replace the wax ring. A clog can almost always be cleared with a plunger or auger. The only time you need to replace a toilet is if the tank or the bowl is cracked.

Seeping and phantom flushes
page 98

Leaks from the tank
page 99

Maintaining a pressure-assisted toilet
page 101

Replacing a toilet seat
page 104

Replacing a toilet
page 105

TROUBLESHOOTING AND REPAIRS

No matter how old a toilet may be, replacement parts are readily available and usually not difficult to install. The only reasons to replace a toilet are if it is cracked or out of style.

To diagnose problems start by looking under the tank lid. If flushes are incomplete, check that the water level reaches the proper height—an inch or less from the top of the overflow tube. If the toilet constantly hisses or if water seeps into the bowl, the tank water level may be too high. The excess water is slowly overflowing into the overflow tube and into the bowl. Adjusting the water level is usually a simple matter. In some cases, however, the fill valve may need to be repaired or replaced.

If the toilet is clogged, use a plunger or an auger to clear the problem.

If water seeps out the bottom of the bowl when the toilet is flushed, the wax ring needs to be replaced (page 105–107).

PRESTART CHECKLIST

☐ **TIME**
Less than an hour for most repairs

☐ **TOOLS**
Screwdriver, groove-joint pliers, adjustable wrench, toilet plunger, pressure plunger, toilet auger, locking pliers, small mirror, toothbrush, bottle brush, nonmetallic scrubbing pad

☐ **SKILLS**
Making simple plumbing corrections

☐ **PREP**
Place a drop cloth on the floor; set the tank lid where it won't be damaged

☐ **MATERIALS**
Repair parts, perhaps a new float-cup assembly

Solutions to common toilet problems

Bowl overflows or will not flush freely: Clear a clog with a plunger, pressure plunger, or toilet auger (page 95).

Toilet does not flush: Check that the handle is connected to the flapper via a chain or to the stopper via a lift rod (page 96). Check that water is turned on and running into the tank.

Incomplete (short) flushes: Check the water level in the tank and adjust the float ball, chain, or lift rod (page 96). Flush the toilet and watch the flapper or the stopper; if it goes down too soon, replace it (page 98).

Handle is loose: Tighten the nut holding the handle to the tank. Check the handle's connection to the wire or the lift rod (page 96).

Water sprays out of the tank: Reattach the refill tube to the overflow tube (page 97).
Run-on: Adjust the float ball, stopper, or cup.

Replace a leaky float ball or stopper (page 96). If these measures do not bring the water level below the top of the overflow tube, repair or replace the fill valve (page 97).

Water seeps continuously into the bowl, making it necessary to jiggle the handle; you hear occasional "phantom flushes": Clean the flush valve seat and adjust the flapper or stopper. You may need to replace the flapper or stopper (page 98).

Leak from the tank: Check and tighten water supply connection. Tighten tank bolts. If the tank is cracked, replace it (pages 105–107).

Leak from the base of the bowl: Remove the toilet, replace the wax ring, and reinstall the toilet. If the bowl is cracked, replace it (pages 105–107).

THREE TYPES OF FILL VALVES

Float cup

Diaphragm

Ballcock valve

A float-cup assembly (left) and diaphragm valve (center) have plastic parts that look unsubstantial, but they are reliable. A ballcock valve (right) has brass parts that last for decades and rubber parts that can be replaced.

Clearing a clog

Plunger

1 You can usually clear a clog with a toilet plunger. Insert the plunger flange into the hole at the bottom of the bowl until it seals. Push and pull vigorously several times. Repeat the process as many as 10 times.

Pressure plunger

2 For tenacious clogs a pressure plunger exerts even greater force. Set it firmly in the bowl hole and pump it until you feel the pressure build. When the clog clears you will feel a sudden loss of pressure.

Toilet auger

3 If plunging does not clear a clog, use a toilet auger. Pull the auger's handle up, insert the auger, then crank while pushing down. The auger may push an obstruction through, or it may grab the obstruction so you can then pull it out (pages 58–59).

Water-saving toilets

Building codes require that new toilets use no more than 1.6 gallons of water per flush; older toilets use from 3 to 5 gallons.

Many early 1.6-gallon models, made in the mid-1990s, do not flush well. If yours is one of these, consider replacing it with a newer model that flushes more completely.

Newer gravity-flush models increase pressure by virtue of different hole designs that maximize water flow.

For even more flushing power, consider spending more for a pressure-assisted toilet, which uses pressurized air to make the water flow faster (page 187). However, this kind of toilet is noisy.

A pump-assisted toilet creates great pressure with less noise, but it is expensive and has an electric pump that must be connected to a power source.

WHAT IF ...
The clog is severe?

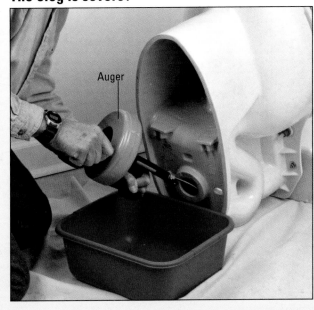

Auger

Occasionally a clog is too stubborn to be cleared by a plunger or auger. (Dumping construction materials, such as joint compound or tile-setting mortar, into a toilet can lead to this condition.) If you run into this problem, turn off the water, drain the tank, and remove the toilet (page 105). Turn the toilet upside down and chip away any caked-on debris. Then run an auger through it backward.

Eliminating run-on

1 If water runs continuously remove the tank lid and check the water level. If water is running over the top of the overflow tube, lower the level. If there is a float ball, bend its rod so the ball sits lower.

Float-ball rod

Overflow tube

2 A kinked or tangled chain may cause run-on. Detach it from the handle arm, undo the kink or tangle, and reattach it so there is about ½ inch of slack in the chain when the flapper is seated.

Flapper

Chain

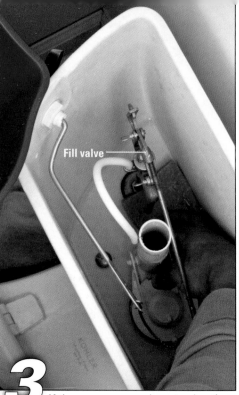

3 If these measures do not solve the problem, the fill valve needs to be repaired or replaced. The tank must be emptied for this and other repairs. **Shut off water to the toilet** and flush the toilet to remove most of the water. Use a sponge to remove the rest of the water.

Fill valve

WHAT IF …
The float cup needs adjusting?

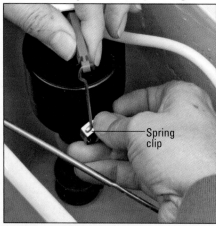

Spring clip

To adjust water level when there is a float-cup assembly, pinch the spring clip and slide the float cup up or down—up to raise the water level, down to lower it.

Adjusting the lift wire

Lift wire

The lift wire attached to a stopper must slide smoothly. If it doesn't, straighten it. You may need to bend the wire that connects the lift wire to the handle. Work carefully and test thoroughly until the lift wire slides without interruption every time.

Making handle adjustments

Handle-mounting nut

Arm

If a handle jiggles loosely, tighten the nut that connects it to the tank. Check the arm that connects to the flapper or stopper as well. Make sure it does not bump into any mechanisms in the tank.

Installing a new float cup

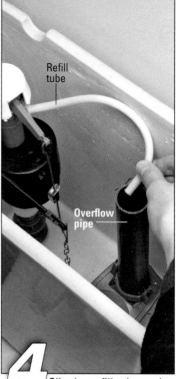

1 **Shut off water at the stop valve.** Flush the toilet to empty the tank. Disconnect the supply tube. Clamp locking pliers onto the nut at the base of the old assembly. Remove the nut under the tank with an adjustable wrench. Lift the assembly out.

2 Insert the new float-cup assembly through the hole in the tank. Hold it in place and tighten the mounting nut under the tank, following the instructions with the assembly. Make sure the cup is clear of obstructions.

3 Remove the flapper or stopper. Slide the new flapper down the overflow tube and adjust it so it flops down onto the center of the flush-valve seat. Attach the chain to it so there is about ½ inch of slack.

4 Clip the refill tube to the overflow tube. Reattach the supply tube and turn the stop valve back on. Let the tank fill and check for leaks.

Repairing a ballcock valve

1 If the rubber parts of a ballcock valve are damaged, you can replace them. Remove the float-rod linkage, which is attached with two screws. Pull out the plunger with pliers.

2 Clean away sediment in the valve, using a toothbrush or a soft wire brush. If the O-rings and the seat washer are worn, you may find it difficult to find replacements. In that case buy a new float-cup assembly and replace the entire assembly.

WHAT IF ...
There is a diaphragm valve?

Remove the clip or screws from the top of a diaphragm fill valve and lift out the bonnet. Pull out the plunger. Clean away any debris or slime. If the plunger or the diaphragm is worn, replace it or replace the entire unit.

Seeping and phantom flushes

Water runs into bowl: If water sometimes gurgles into the bowl until you jiggle the handle, the handle may be loose or in need of adjustment. Metal handle arms can be adjusted by gentle bending. The lift rod or chain may be stuck or snagged—adjust or replace if needed.

Phantom flushes: If water slowly seeps into the bowl, you may or may not hear it. A faint, "phantom" flush may occur every so often. In this case the flapper or stopper is not sealing tightly against the flush-valve seat. **Shut off the water** and flush, then clean the seat with a nonmetallic scrubbing pad.

Persistent problems: See whether the flapper or stopper is centered in the seat. Raising or twisting a flapper may solve the problem. If not, install a new one. Bring the old flapper to a home center so you can buy an exact replacement. If the new flapper does not seal tightly, try a different type.

WHAT IF…
The toilet has a weak flush?

1 If water flows weakly into the bowl, partially blocked rim openings or a blocked jet may be the culprit. **Shut off the water** and flush, then pour mineral cleaner into the bowl. Clean the siphon jet with a bottle brush.

2 Brush the rim openings with the cleaner and allow several minutes for it to soak in; repeat several times. A mirror will help you see if any openings are clogged. Auger a rim opening with a piece of insulated wire or a very small bottle brush.

A replacement flapper kit

Replacement flappers are available for virtually every toilet. This kit is ideal if you're having trouble getting a flapper to seal. It comes with its own seat, which seals tightly on top of an existing seat.

Leaks from the tank

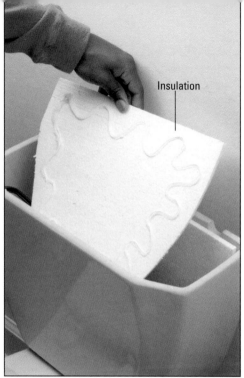

Leak at supply: If water leaks where the supply tube enters the tank, **shut off the water** and flush. Gently clamp locking pliers to the nut inside the tank and tighten the mounting nut under the toilet. If this doesn't solve the problem, you may need to replace the mounting-nut gasket inside the tank.

Leak between tank and bowl: **Shut off the water** and flush. With an adjustable wrench holding the nut under the tank, tighten the screw inside the tank. Don't overtighten; you may crack the tank. If this doesn't solve the problem, replace the rubber washers under the hold-down bolts.

Sweaty tank: If drops of condensation appear on the tank, buy a tank insulating kit. Drain and dry the tank. Cut each insulation piece to fit and attach it with the adhesive provided. For more infomation on fixing sweating tanks, see page 100.

Replacing a toilet seat

To remove an existing toilet seat, pry up any caps at the back of the seat to reveal the screw heads. Clamp locking pliers to the nut below and unscrew. Some plastic nuts have wings, so you do not need the pliers.

If old metal bolts are rusted tight, spray them with penetrating oil. If necessary cut through the bolts with a hacksaw.

Clean the top of the bowl. Hold the new seat centered over the bowl as you tighten the nuts (page 104).

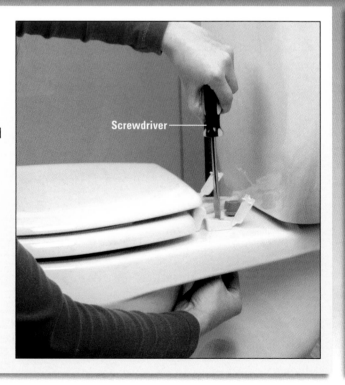

Water from the bowl means the toilet needs resetting

If water leaks from the bottom of the bowl when you flush, check the bowl for cracks. If there are none the wax ring needs to be replaced. Follow the steps on pages 105–107 to remove the toilet, install a new wax ring, and reinstall the toilet.

Fixing a sweating toilet

Turn supply valve off, flush, and dry tank with towel and hair dryer.

1 When a cold surface contacts warmer moist air, moisture will condense on the colder surface. Such condensation causes sweating toilet tanks, and over time this moisture can rot the floor. Insulation kits are available to prevent this. They require that the tank be flushed and dry.

2 After drying the tank thoroughly, follow the manufacturer's instructions to cut pieces from the insulation kit. You can make this job easier by making templates from stiff cardboard and using them to outline the insulation panels.

3 Test-fit the insulation and apply silicone caulk or the adhesive recommended by the manufacturer to the backside of the panels. Insert the panels in the tank and apply pressure as you're fitting them. Let the adhesive cure completely, turn the water on, and adjust the float valve if necessary.

Install an antisweat valve

Valve mixes hot and cold water

Warm water to toilet tank

Hot water line

Cold water line

1 An antisweat valve mixes a small amount of hot water with the cold water flowing into the tank, raising the tank temperature just enough to keep moisture from condensing on it. Some valves have a manual control to vary the mixture for different humidity levels.

2 **Shut off the water to the house.** Using the manufacturer's instructions as a guide, cut the water lines to the bathroom. Cut pipe to fit your installation. Dry-fit the pipe before soldering the joints, making sure everything fits perfectly. Keeping all the parts at the correct angles, presolder any joints that will lie too close to the joists when installed and might pose a fire hazard if soldered in place.

MAINTAINING A PRESSURE-ASSISTED TOILET

Pressure-assisted units differ from standard toilets mostly inside the tank. It's not mandatory (though it's helpful) to know exactly how they work (page 187). What's important is knowing what to do when a certain symptom exists.

These toilets are subject to the same problems as standard toilets—constant running, weak flushes, water leaks—and the repairs are easy.

The first cause of a faulty pressure-assisted unit is low water pressure. These toilets need water pressure between 20 and 80 pounds per square inch (some up to 125 psi) to function properly. If your pressure is too low, check for a clogged whole-house filter element that needs replacement, a faulty pressure-reducing valve in the main water line, mineral deposits in a primary or supply valve, or a clogged supply line or inlet screen. Pipes clogged by rust or minerals may require replacement.

Checking the pressure and flow

1 **Turn off the water** at the toilet supply valve. Disconnect the line from the toilet bowl with slip-joint pliers or an appropriate wrench. Catch the residual water from the line in a bucket. If available connect a pressure gauge to the line, turn the water on, and record the pressure.

2 You can reasonably estimate water pressure by checking the flow rate. Pour a gallon of water into a bucket and mark its volume on the side. Pour out the water and hold the toilet supply line in the bucket. Turn the water on for 30 seconds. If you have more than a gallon, your pressure is OK.

PRESTART CHECKLIST

☐ **TIME**
2 to 3 minutes to perform any given check; repair time varies with repair

☐ **TOOLS**
Slip-joint pliers, adjustable wrench, bucket, paper clip, toothbrush, screwdriver

☐ **SKILLS**
Dismantling and reinstalling various toilet parts

☐ **PREP**
Shut off water when necessary

☐ **MATERIALS**
Repair parts

STANLEY PRO TIP

Winterizing a pressure-assisted toilet

If your pressure-assisted toilet is in a cabin or other building that won't be heated during the winter, here's how to winterize it to protect it from freezing:
1. Turn off the main water supply valve to the dwelling.
2. Open all the water faucets and let them drain. Flush the toilet to relieve the pressure.
3. Set a bucket under the supply-line connection at the tank and disconnect the line. Let the water drain into the bucket.
4. Push down on the actuator and pull it up momentarily to allow air into the unit.
5. Follow the manufacturer's directions for winterizing the bowl.
6. Do not add any chemicals to the tank.

WHAT IF ...
There's water in the bottom of the tank?

A small amount of water in the bottom of the tank is normal. You can add a little vinegar to kill any odors.

A large amount of water, however, is not normal. It may mean there is a leak in the piping, a connection, or in the tank itself. Some high-chlorine water supplies may cause seals or other parts to fail. Do not use chlorinated water tablets in the toilet tank.

Cleaning the supply assembly screen:
Turn the water off and set a bucket under the supply assembly connection. Remove the supply line from the tank and pull up the assembly to gain access to the screen. Use a bent paper clip to remove the screen and clean off any deposits with an old toothbrush.

Checking the flush rod: With the water supply off, flush the toilet and gently lift up the flush rod. Measure the clearance from the top of the actuator to the bottom of the flush rod. To adjust loosen the actuator setscrew and raise or lower the actuator by rotating it clockwise or counterclockwise.

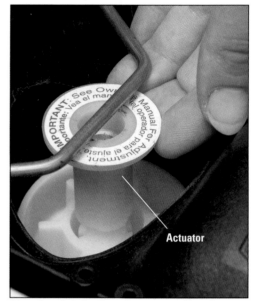

Clearing debris: Turn the water off to the toilet and flush it by pushing down on the actuator. When the unit begins to flush, carefully raise the actuator to allow debris to be flushed away through the lines.

Removing the supply screen on other models

On some models you don't need to remove the supply assembly to clean the screen. Try this before removing your assembly. Make a ⅛-inch right-angle bend in one end of a stiff paper clip. Insert the bent end in a hole near the edge of the screen. Turn the bend so it grabs the screen and pull down gently. The screen should pop out into your hand.

What parts are replaceable?

Replaceable parts vary from model to model. Parts are often available as repair kits or replacement assemblies, such as these for the unit shown in the steps: (A) lower supply assembly with hose, (B) upper supply assembly, (C) actuator with setscrew.

WHAT IF ...
I have to replace the actuator?

Proper vertical placement of the actuator is crucial to the operation of a pressure-assisted toilet. A built-in device allows you to position a replacement accurately. Screw the cartridge in until one black line shows. Turn the water supply back on and rotate the actuator clockwise in quarter turns until the water stops. Return the flush rod to its operating position.

Checking the actuator (flush-valve cartridge) for wear

1 Checking the actuator requires removing it, which means **shutting off the water,** moving the flush rod out of the way, and loosening the setscrew. To move the flush rod, disconnect it from the flush handle and lift it up and away from the actuator.

Flush rod · Actuator

2 Loosen the actuator setscrew and slide the rubber-coated handles of a pair of slip-joint pliers into the recesses at the top. Unscrew the actuator (counterclockwise) until you can pull it free.

Setscrew

3 Pull out the actuator and inspect the O-rings for any damage. If they are worn replace the actuator. Install the new cartridge (or replace the old one) by turning it clockwise. Turn the water back on and, if it still runs after it's full, tighten or loosen the actuator in quarter turns until it stops.

Checking the air regulator

Muffler cap hole · Muffler cap · Air regulator

1 To check the air regulator (air inducer), remove the muffler cap and flush the toilet. You should be able to hear the sound of air being drawn in. You can also place a couple of drops of water on the hole in the cap and flush the toilet. The water should be drawn into the cap. If it's not, go to Step 2.

Duck-bill valve

2 Inside the air regulator is a valve called the "duck-bill valve," and if it gets clogged with mineral deposits it prevents the air regulator from working properly. Remove the cap and the valve and clean the valve parts with a soft brush.

Checking for leaks

To check the flush-valve cartridge for leaks, pour a small amount of water into the cartridge housing area. If bubbles are coming from the center or the edge of the cartridge, replace it. If the vacuum breaker is leaking, it is likely that the water pressure is insufficient or the inlet-screen in the supply assembly is plugged.

REPLACING A TOILET SEAT

Replacing a toilet seat is one of the easiest repairs to make to a toilet.

If the current toilet seat is broken or its mounting hardware is worn and wobbly—and if you don't care much about style—you can probably find a replacement at your local hardware store. Most will carry an inexpensive basic seat and, perhaps, a better-grade one. If style matters, however, you can find a greater selection at your home center, design websites, or bath specialty outlets.

Almost all modern replacements mount in the fashion shown here. Some antique reproduction models, however, do not feature the plastic cap covering the plastic bolt. These reproductions have threaded studs integral to their design. Just push the studs through the holes in the bowl and tighten the nuts. In any case always make sure the replacement seat has the same contour as the bowl.

PRESTART CHECKLIST

☐ **TIME**
About half an hour

☐ **TOOLS**
Screwdriver, slip-joint pliers, possibly a hacksaw

☐ **SKILLS**
Removing and replacing plastic bolts

☐ **MATERIALS**
Replacement toilet seat, penetrating oil

1 Close the lid and look for two small plastic hinged covers at the back. These caps cover the mounting bolts. Slip the edge of a screwdriver or putty knife under the covers and snap them up. Don't worry if they break off at the hinges. The new seat will include replacements.

2 Hold the mounting bolt with a screwdriver and loosen the nut under the bowl flange with a slip-joint pliers. When loose enough unscrew it by hand. If the bolts are corroded or otherwise prove difficult to remove, spray the threads with penetrating oil. Cut stubborn bolts with a hacksaw.

3 Lift the old seat straight up out of the mounting holes and dispose of it. Set the new seat on the bowl, insert the mounting screws, and hand-tighten the nuts.

4 Align the seat so it's centered front to back and side to side and retighten the nuts by hand. Then hold the nuts with slip-joint pliers and tighten the bolts by turning them with a screwdriver. (If you hold the screwdriver and tighten the nuts with the pliers, you'll likely dislodge the seat.)

REPLACING A TOILET

Most new toilets come in two boxes: one for the bowl and one for the tank with all the moving parts installed.

The steps beginning at right show how to assemble the tank and bowl and how to install the toilet. You may install the bowl first and then attach the tank. If the existing toilet is heavy, you can detach the tank from the bowl before removing it. Keep your back straight and lift with the legs. Arrange for a helper if possible. Follow these same steps if your toilet is leaking from the base and you need to replace the wax ring.

You may install a standard, pressure-, or pump-assisted toilet. The rough-in distance—the measurement from the drain center and mounting holes to the back wall—is 12 inches for most toilets. Some are 10 inches. Measure the old toilet and buy a new one with the same dimensions.

PRESTART CHECKLIST

☐ **TIME**
About 2 hours

☐ **TOOLS**
Adjustable wrench, hacksaw, utility knife, putty knife

☐ **SKILLS**
Making simple plumbing connections, assembling a toilet

☐ **PREP**
Shut off water to the toilet; flush; use a sponge or rag to remove all the water you can from the tank and the bowl

☐ **MATERIALS**
Toilet, wax ring, flange bolts

1 **Shut off water** at the stop valve. Disconnect the supply tube at the tank and wall. Pry off any decorative caps and unscrew the nuts holding the bowl to the floor. If the nuts will not turn, cut through them with a hacksaw.

Cut down through nut.
Hacksaw

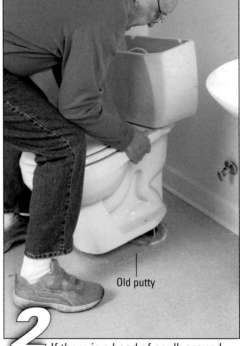

2 If there is a bead of caulk around the bowl at the floor, cut through it with a utility knife. If the toilet is old, check to see if the tank is bolted to the wall and remove the bolts. Grasp the toilet bowl on each side, pick it up, and set it on a drop cloth.

Old putty

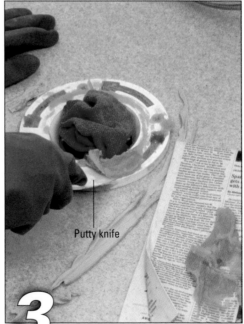

3 Place a large, damp rag in the hole to seal off sewer gas. Scrape away all putty and wax from the floor. Finish cleaning with a rag. If you are reinstalling the existing toilet, clean the bottom of its bowl in the same way.

Putty knife

4 Assemble the tank and the bowl of a new toilet following the manufacturer's instructions. A large spud gasket seals the opening below the flush-valve seat. Place a rubber washer under the head of each mounting bolt. Do not overtighten the nuts.

Mounting bolt
Spud gasket

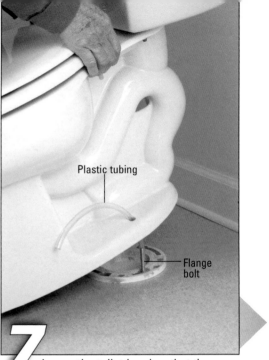

Wax ring

Flange

Flange bolt

Flange

Slip-on washer

Plastic tubing

Flange bolt

5 Press a new wax ring, flange pointed out (or down), on the underside of the toilet bowl. (Not all toilets or drainpipes accept a flanged ring; wax rings without the flange are also available.)

6 If the new toilet does not include them, buy new flange bolts. Use slip-on plastic washers to hold them temporarily in place, pointing straight up. Remove the rag from the hole.

7 Lower the toilet bowl so that the flange bolts poke through the holes. If it is difficult to line up the holes with the bolts, place a piece of plastic tubing over the bolt to guide it through the base as you lower the bowl.

STANLEY PRO TIP

Removing the wax ring

1 Place a plastic freezer bag over your hand for protection and grab the inside bottom edge of the wax ring. Grab as much of the bottom edge as you can and begin to lift the ring out slowly.

2 While continuing to pull the ring out of the flange, pull the bag over the ring with your other hand. Seal the bag and dispose of it. Scrape up the wax residue with a putty knife and stuff a large rag into the drain to keep out debris. Place duct tape over the rag to keep it from being dislodged if you have further demolition work to do.

8 Press down on the bowl with both hands to set the toilet firmly on the wax ring. Check the position of the toilet by looking at the toilet tank: It should be parallel to the wall and level.

Decorative cap

9 Tighten the nut on each side of the bowl, alternating sides. If the floor is uneven, use pennies as shims. Avoid overtightening. Stop tightening when the bowl feels solid when you sit on it. Carefully cut off the tip of each bolt and cover with a decorative cap.

Supply tube

Stop valve

10 Connect the supply tube, turn on the water, and test.

WHAT IF ...
The new floor is higher?

The combined thickness of flooring materials for a new tile floor may raise the level by as much as 1 inch. Raise the height of the toilet flange with an extender, available at most hardware stores and home centers.

An extender consists of rings that are stacked over the floor flange and sealed with silicone caulk. Add enough rings to bring the flange at least flush with and preferably about ¼ inch higher than the new floor.

Securing a toilet to an uneven floor

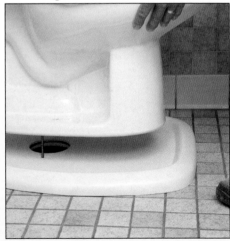

A toilet installed on an uneven floor can cause the wax ring to seal improperly and leak at the toilet base. Although you may be able to correct a slight unevenness by tightening the flange bolts, you run the risk of cracking the toilet base, a problem that may not show up until the toilet is used.

As an alternative install the toilet on a plastic base made specifically to remedy this problem. You also can insert coins as shown in step 9 above or plastic shims. Tap the shims in until they're snug. Then cut them at the base with a sharp utility knife.

PIPE REPAIRS

If a pipe suddenly springs a leak, you may be able to make a temporary repair by wrapping it tightly with electrician's tape. But a more permanent repair must be made as soon as possible.

If a pipe clamp (opposite page) does not solve the problem, you'll need to remove and replace sections of pipe, and possibly fittings as well. This chapter shows how to cut, assemble, and join copper, steel, and plastic pipe, as well as how to make repairs to cast-iron pipe. In addition it shows how to repair and replace valves, quiet noisy pipes, and thaw frozen pipes.

Pipe repair can be time-consuming, especially if the pipes are hard to reach. You may spend more time cutting into and patching walls than working on the plumbing.

Running new lines

You can use the techniques in this chapter to make a pipe repair or to install a new line for additional service. Usually simply installing a tee fitting allows you to run a new supply line. Armed with this knowledge you can tackle a simple project like a laundry room (pages 252–253) as long as the drain line does not have to travel more than about 5 feet.

Installing new service, on the other hand, is usually a complicated matter. Drain lines in particular must follow strict guidelines and must be properly vented (pages 14–15). Contact a professional plumber for any project more complicated than a simple laundry room hookup.

CHAPTER PREVIEW

Pipe repairs call for learning special skills. With a little practice, you can handle most jobs.

Repairs to copper pipe
page 110

Silencing pipe noises
page 112

Repairs to cast-iron pipe
page 113

Repairs to plastic pipe
page 114

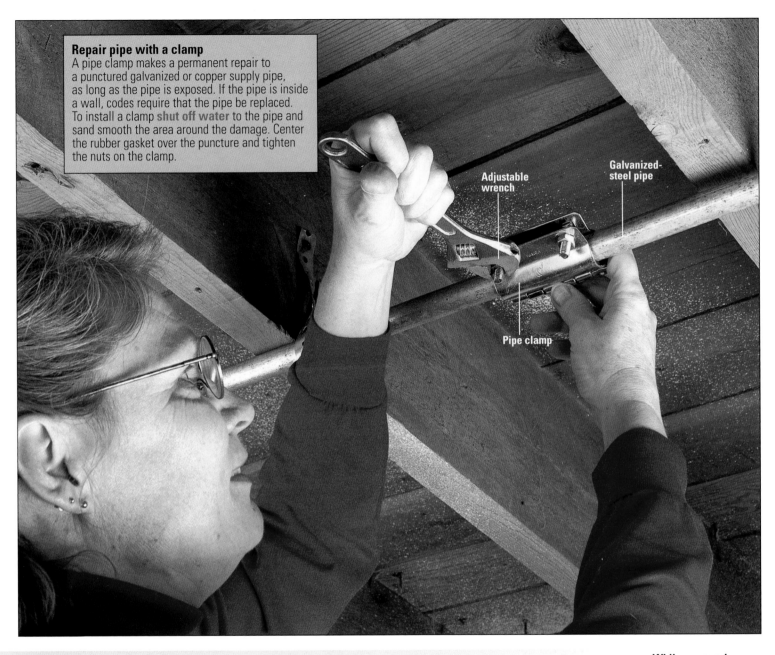

Repair pipe with a clamp
A pipe clamp makes a permanent repair to a punctured galvanized or copper supply pipe, as long as the pipe is exposed. If the pipe is inside a wall, codes require that the pipe be replaced. To install a clamp **shut off water** to the pipe and sand smooth the area around the damage. Center the rubber gasket over the puncture and tighten the nuts on the clamp.

Adjustable wrench

Galvanized-steel pipe

Pipe clamp

Leaks at stop valves and supply tubes
page 116

Installing a stop valve on copper pipe
page 118

Installing a stop valve on steel pipe
page 119

Replacing a valve
page 120

Thawing pipes and winterizing
page 122

While a properly applied clamp makes a permanent repair, you may prefer to replace a damaged section. To make repairs to copper pipe, see pages 110–111; plastic, pages 114–115; cast-iron, page 113; steel, pages 134–135.

REPAIRS TO COPPER PIPE

Because of its durability copper is the preferred material for most water supply lines. However copper pipe can leak when dented, punctured, or weakened from corrosion. Joints can degrade too.

Even if you have galvanized or plastic supply pipe in your house, you may want to use a transition fitting and switch to copper when making a repair or extending a line. When joining copper pipe to steel pipe, be sure to use a dielectric fitting (page 135) to avoid corrosion.

Type M copper pipe is fine for most residential work. Buy lead-free solder and flux paste.

For more detail on how to sweat copper pipe, see pages 126–127.

Sweating a large copper drain line calls for a large propane torch; you're probably better off hiring a pro for such work.

Compression fittings (opposite) require no special skills to install, but they are expensive. Use them only where they will be exposed; any joints hidden in a wall must be sweated.

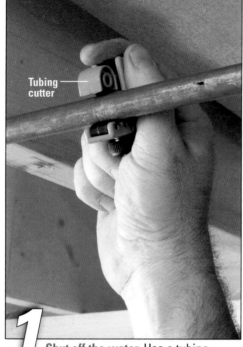

1 **Shut off the water.** Use a tubing cutter to cut each side of the damaged area. Screw the cutter tight, rotate it a full turn, tighten, and rotate again until the cut is complete. If there is not enough room, cut with a hacksaw. Exert gentle pressure to avoid flattening the pipe. File off burrs.

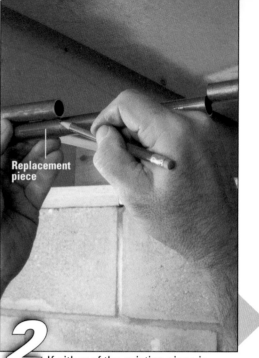

2 If either of the existing pipes is movable, you can use standard couplings (page 26). If not, use slip couplings (Step 3). Measure the replacement piece by holding it in place. It should be the same length. Cut the new piece with a tubing cutter.

PRESTART CHECKLIST

☐ **TIME**
An hour or two for most repairs

☐ **TOOLS**
Groove-joint pliers, tubing cutter, hacksaw, multiuse wire brush, flux brush, propane torch, fiber shield

☐ **SKILLS**
Using a pipe cutter, handling a propane torch

☐ **PREP**
Shut off the water; drain the line; position a cookie sheet or protective shield to protect flammable surfaces

☐ **MATERIALS**
Copper pipe and fittings, flux, solder

COPPER SUPPLY SYSTEM

Rigid copper joints are soldered together. The resulting joints, if made correctly, are at least as strong as the pipe itself. To add a supply line, install a tee fitting. Use a compression fitting (opposite) only if it will remain exposed for inspection.

3 Ream and polish the pipe and couplings using a multiuse brush (page 127). Brush on flux and slide a coupling on each side, position the replacement piece, and slide the couplings back halfway. (To install a standard coupling or elbow, give it a slight twist as you push it all the way into place.)

4 Protect framing and nearby walls with a cookie sheet or fiber shield (page 20). Aim the torch so the tip of the blue flame touches the middle of the fitting. When the flux sizzles after 5 seconds or so, move the flame to the opposite side and heat it briefly. Touch solder to the joints.

5 Once solder has been sucked into the joint all around, wipe the joint with a rag to smooth the solder and eliminate any drips. **Fold the rag several times and/or wear leather gloves.** Repeat for the other side of the fitting. **Check the work area an hour later to be sure nothing is smoldering.**

Patch a pipe with a tape kit

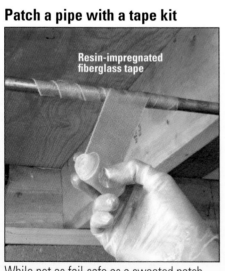

While not as fail-safe as a sweated patch, fiberglass patch tape can provide a quick, long-lasting cure for a leaky pipe. The kit includes tape impregnated with resin, gloves, and a lubricant that helps you squeeze out voids and bubbles.

STANLEY PRO TIP

Bread trick for wet pipe

If a pipe keeps dripping after you have shut off the water, jam a wad of soft white bread (not whole grain or crusts) into the pipe. Sweat the joint quickly, before the wad becomes saturated. Once the repair is made and the water turned on, open a nearby faucet. The bread will dissolve and flush out. (Or check your home center for gel beads that work the same way.)

COMPRESSION FITTINGS

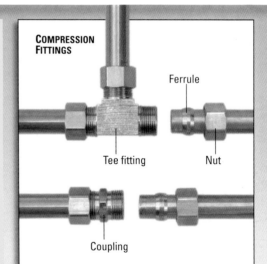

Compression fittings often make sense in tight places where it is difficult to solder. To install one, slide the nut, then the ferrule, onto the pipe. Slip the fitting onto the pipe, slide the ferrule into the fitting, and tighten the nut. No thread tape or pipe compound is necessary.

SILENCING PIPE NOISES

Pipes that rattle and hammer are not only annoying, they also may eventually come apart at the joints. Take steps to stop the noise and prevent possible leaks.

The most common noise is water hammer, a rattle that occurs when water is turned on or off by a faucet or an appliance, such as a dishwasher or washing machine. The solution is to install a shock absorber, also called an air chamber, which provides a cushion to dampen the water's movement.

The following instructions show how to install a shock absorber using threaded fittings. You can also fabricate one for plastic pipe using a piece of pipe and a cap fitting; see pages 128–129 for instructions on gluing.

After a few years the air chamber may fill with water and lose its ability to soften water hammer. Draining and refilling the line will replenish the chamber with a cushion of air.

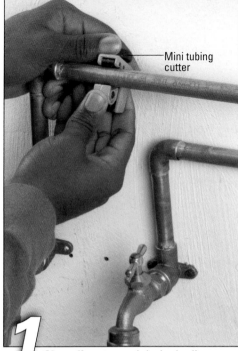

Mini tubing cutter

1 **Shut off water** and drain the line. Measure the shock absorber to determine how much pipe must be cut out; remember that pipe will be inserted into the absorber at each end. Cut the pipe with a tubing cutter if possible; otherwise saw carefully with a hacksaw.

Shock absorber

Compression fitting

Ferrule

2 On each side of the absorber location, slip a compression nut on the pipe, threaded side toward the absorber, then slip on a ferrule. On each side of the shock absorber, push the nut over the ferrule and finger-tighten the joint. Use an adjustable wrench to complete the installation.

PRESTART CHECKLIST

☐ **TIME**
An hour or so to install a pipe shock absorber

☐ **TOOLS**
Tools for working with copper (page 110), plastic (page 114), or steel pipe (page 119)

☐ **SKILLS**
Cutting and joining copper, plastic, or steel pipe

☐ **PREP**
Shut off the water and drain the line

☐ **MATERIALS**
Shock absorber for your type and size pipe, materials for joining the pipe, possibly insulation

Adding pipe insulation

Insulation

A pipe may vibrate when water runs through it, causing it to rattle against a nearby framing member. Cushion the pipe by slipping on foam insulation pieces. Firm loose pipes with pipe clamps or hanger brackets.

WHAT IF ...
There is no access to pipes?

This type of shock absorber is made for use in a laundry room. Simply detach each washer hose from its hose bib, screw on the shock absorber, and attach each hose.

REPAIRS TO CAST-IRON PIPE

Old cast-iron drainpipe can behave unpredictably. Sometimes a small section of a pipe starts to crumble or a joint begins to leak even though most of the pipe is sound.

If a cast-iron pipe is failing at several points, the most economical solution is to replace it with PVC pipe. This is a job for a professional.

Older cast-iron joints were sealed with molten lead, but this is not a danger to your health because only wastewater passes through the pipes.

SAFETY FIRST
Support cast-iron pipe

Cast-iron pipe is very heavy and must be held in place with special clamps attached to framing members. Never disturb these clamps; if one weakens, a long section of pipe could come crashing down.

PRESTART CHECKLIST

☐ **TIME**
An hour to clean and patch a joint; less time to patch a hole

☐ **TOOLS**
Wire brush, hammer, cold chisel, putty knife

☐ **SKILLS**
Cleaning metal, applying putty

☐ **PREP**
Make sure that the pipe is well supported

☐ **MATERIALS**
Repair paste or plumber's epoxy

Cold chisel

1 If water or a bad smell comes from an old leaded joint, use a cold chisel and hammer to gently tap the lead back into the joint. Use a wire brush and rag to clean away the corrosion.

2 Fill the resulting void with cast-iron pipe repair paste. Use a putty knife to apply the paste.

WHAT IF ...
A cast-iron pipe has a hole?

If a pipe rusts through or is punctured, clean the opening with a wire brush and fill the hole with two-part plumber's epoxy. Check the manufacturer's instructions for drying time. Don't use the pipe until the patch has completely set.

 STANLEY PRO TIP

Replacing a section of cast-iron pipe

If more than a small area is damaged, this is a job for a professional. Hire a plumber to cut out a section of the pipe and replace it with PVC pipe (pages 114–115).

First the pipe must be supported both below and above the area to be removed. At least one new pipe clamp must be installed. It may be necessary to build a wooden frame and attach the clamp to it.

Once the pipe is cut, attach a section of PVC pipe to the cast-iron pipe using neoprene sleeves at both ends. After the installation is complete, you may or may not be able to remove the new clamp, depending on the situation.

REPAIRS TO PLASTIC PIPE

White PVC pipe is the current material of choice for most drain lines. Existing black ABS pipe can be replaced with PVC. If you use a transition fitting, you can connect PVC to galvanized drainpipe. Special fittings also allow you to attach PVC to cast-iron pipe.

Using PVC for supply lines is not allowed by many building codes; check with your local building inspector before using it. CPVC is approved for many outdoor uses, such as lawn sprinkler systems.

Plastic pipe is easy to assemble, but take care to do it right. Joints must be primed and glued completely or they may leak. If you install a fitting that makes a turn, such as a tee or an elbow, use alignment marks to ensure the fitting faces the right way. Mistakes can't be corrected—if a glued joint points in the wrong direction, you must cut out the faulty section and start over. PVC pipe is inexpensive, so before you tackle the real thing, practice cutting and gluing pieces until you feel proficient.

1 Cut PVC pipe using a PVC saw, a hacksaw, or most any saw with fine teeth. A miter box helps hold the pipe to make perpendicular cuts.

PVC saw

2 Scrape the inside and outside of the sawed edge with a utility knife to remove burrs.

PRESTART CHECKLIST

☐ **TIME**
About an hour to make a simple repair

☐ **TOOLS**
PVC saw and miter box, utility knife, tape measure, felt-tip pen, PVC pipe cutter

☐ **SKILLS**
Measuring, cutting PVC

☐ **PREP**
Spread a drop cloth to catch any spilled primer and glue

☐ **MATERIALS**
PVC pipe and fittings, primer, cement

WHAT IF ...
Flexible plastic is used for a repair?

Compression/threaded coupling

Compression coupling

Flexible PEX supply pipe is approved in some areas. The pipe's flexibility makes it easy to turn corners. Fittings attach with compression joints, so no gluing is needed and mistakes can be easily corrected. However these fittings cannot be hidden behind a wall.

SAFETY FIRST
Beware of fumes

PVC primer and cement are flammable and have unpleasant and dangerous fumes. Keep flames and sparks away and open a window to provide ventilation. Cap the cans when they are not in use. Tighten the caps firmly when done.

Also be sure to use the correct primer and cement for your type of plastic pipe. PVC and CPVC require different products. The wrong primer and cement can ruin the installation.

Coupling

Replacement piece

Cement applicator

3 Assemble the pieces in a dry run to make sure everything fits. Disassemble the pieces, keeping track of the order in which they will be reassembled.

4 Apply primer to the pipe ends and to the insides of the fittings. The strip of primer on the pipe should be wide enough so that some can still be seen after the fitting is attached. Apply cement to the outside of the pipe, then to the inside of the coupling.

5 Immediately insert the pipe into the fitting and give it a slight twist. Some cement should ooze around the joint. Hold the joint for about 20 seconds, then wipe away any excess cement. Wait at least 30 minutes before running drain water through the pipes.

STANLEY PRO TIP: **REPAIR TO A SUPPLY PIPE**

Cut PVC or CPVC supply pipe with the scissorslike PVC pipe cutter. Deburr, make a dry run, apply primer, and glue pieces together just as you would for drainpipe (Steps 2 to 5 above).

Because water pressure is greater in a supply pipe than a drainpipe, wait several hours for the cement to fully cure before you run water through the pipes.

A similar tool can be used to cut flexible pipe and tubing.

PVC pipe cutter

Adding a tee fitting for a new line

To add a drain line, cut the pipe and install a tee fitting. Use alignment marks to make sure the tee is facing the right way. Once the tee is installed, assemble the lengths of pipe and fittings needed to reach the new location.

LEAKS AT STOP VALVES AND SUPPLY TUBES

If water is dripping onto the floor of a cabinet below a sink, leaky supply tubes may be the cause. More likely, however, a stop valve or supply-tube connection is the culprit.

To find the source of a leak, shine a bright flashlight into the cabinet and feel the pipes and tubes, stopping to dry your hand every so often. You can also dry the area, place dry newspaper under the suspect plumbing, and watch for spots of water.

A solid chrome-plated copper supply tube looks and feels more stable than a flexible braided tube. But the solid tube is actually more likely to develop a leak because it is inflexible. When bumped a braided tube is less likely to be damaged. Still many people prefer the appearance of a solid tube.

Tightening stop valve connections

Adjustable wrench

1 If water leaks at the stop-valve spout, use an adjustable wrench to tighten the nut that connects the supply tube to the valve. (If the valve moves brace it with another wrench.) If water leaks from where the supply tube enters the faucet, tighten the nut with a basin wrench.

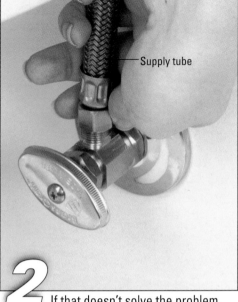

Supply tube

2 If that doesn't solve the problem, **shut off the water** at the stop valve. Unscrew the nuts at either end and remove the supply tube. Replace with a flexible braided tube or install a new solid supply tube (opposite).

PRESTART CHECKLIST

☐ **TIME**
Less than an hour to tighten nuts or install a new supply tube

☐ **TOOLS**
Adjustable wrench, basin wrench, tubing bender, tubing cutter

☐ **SKILLS**
Measuring and cutting a tube, connecting a compression fitting

☐ **PREP**
Place a bucket or towel below the leaking plumbing; make the area comfortable for working

☐ **MATERIALS**
Solid or braided supply tube

STOP-VALVE QUALITY

An inexpensive stop valve (below left) has plastic inner parts, making it more likely to break down. Its inner parts must be removed before sweating. The more substantial unit (below right) has all-metal inner parts that are long-lasting and don't need to be removed before sweating.

A stop valve has a stem much like that in a compression faucet. The packing washer and stem washer can be replaced, but it's easier to simply replace the entire valve.

Replacing a solid supply tube

1 Bend a chrome-plated copper or plain copper supply tube carefully by hand or use a tubing bender (page 20).

2 Insert one end of the tube into the faucet inlet, hold the other end near the stop valve, and mark it for a cut. Make the cut with a tubing cutter. (See page 126 for how to use a tubing cutter).

— Tubing cutter

3 At the upper end slip on the mounting nut and a ferrule. Poke the tube into the faucet inlet, slide the ferrule up to the inlet, and tighten the nut. Slip a nut and ferrule onto the lower end of the tube and attach to the stop valve in the same way.

Nut
Ferrule

Buy the right supply tube

³⁄₈" stop valve

¹⁄₂" stop valve

A toilet inlet usually is larger than a faucet inlet. When buying a braided tube, check whether it is made for a toilet or a faucet.

Stop valves have spouts that are either ¹⁄₂ inch or ³⁄₈ inch in diameter. Be sure to buy a tube made to fit your valve.

A common mistake is to buy a supply tube that is too short. Play it safe and buy a tube that's longer than you think you need.

WHAT IF ...
You use a plastic supply tube?

A plastic supply tube seals using a ball-shaped end held firmly by a nylon nut. Some have a rubber ferrule as well.

KINK-PROOF SOLID SUPPLY TUBES

These solid supply tubes bend without kinking. One is chrome-plated metal with a plastic liner to prevent kinks; the other is ribbed so it can be bent easily.

Installing A Stop Valve On Copper Pipe

Every faucet and toilet in a home should have its own stop valve so you can easily make repairs. Installing one is usually not difficult, though you may find yourself working in cramped quarters.

Take care to buy the correct valve. Its inlet must accommodate the size of pipe coming from the wall (usually ½-inch but sometimes ¾- or ⅜-inch). Its threaded spout must match the size of the supply tube—either ½- or ⅜-inch. You can install a compression or a sweatable valve.

If the pipes are plastic, simply cut with a close-work hacksaw and cement the valve in place (pages 128–129).

To shut off the water where there is no existing stop valve, see page 8. Some water will remain in the pipes and tubes after water has stopped flowing out of the faucet, so place a bucket and towel underneath.

Prestart Checklist

- ☐ **Time**
  One or two hours

- ☐ **Tools**
  Tubing cutter or close-work hacksaw, combination wire brush, two adjustable wrenches, flux brush, propane torch, fiber shield

- ☐ **Skills**
  Cutting and joining copper pipe

- ☐ **Prep**
  Shut off the water; drain the line; place a bucket or towel to catch debris

- ☐ **Materials**
  New compression or sweatable stop valve, flux, solder, possibly a new supply tube

Close-work hacksaw

1 **Shut off the water** to the line and drain the line by turning on a faucet at a lower location. If there is room cut the copper pipe using a tubing cutter. Otherwise cut slowly and gently with a close-work hacksaw, as shown.

Ferrule

Nut

2 Sand the outside of the cut pipe with a combination wire brush, emery cloth, or sandpaper until it is shiny. Slide a nut and ferrule onto the pipe.

STANLEY PRO TIP

Use two wrenches

Adjustable wrench

Slide the stop valve all the way onto the pipe. Hold the valve with one adjustable wrench while you tighten the nut with the other.

STANLEY PRO TIP

Remove stem before soldering

Valve stem

A shutoff valve may have rubber washers and O-rings or other parts that can be damaged by heat. Before sweating a valve remove all the inner parts.

It will take more time to heat a brass valve than it takes to heat a copper fitting, so have patience. Apply solder as you would for a copper fitting (page 127).

Allow the fitting to cool before replacing the inner parts.

INSTALLING A STOP VALVE ON STEEL PIPE

If an old galvanized pipe comes out from the wall, installing a shutoff valve is usually a straightforward job; simply screw a threaded stop valve onto the pipe.

If possible unscrew the supply tube at the bottom only, so it remains attached to the faucet or toilet above. If this is not possible, you may have to cut through the supply tube with a hacksaw and replace the tube after installing the valve.

Unscrew the parts up to the nipple that sticks out of the wall. Look into the pipe with a flashlight. If it is partially filled with mineral deposits, replacing it will increase the faucet's (or toilet's) water pressure.

To shut off the water where there is no existing stop valve, see page 8. Some water will remain in the pipes and tubes after water has stopped flowing out the faucet, so you might want to place a bucket or a thick towel underneath.

PRESTART CHECKLIST

☐ **TIME**
One or two hours

☐ **TOOLS**
Two pipe wrenches, adjustable wrench, possibly a hacksaw

☐ **SKILLS**
Cutting and joining steel pipe

☐ **PREP**
Shut off the water; drain the line; place a bucket or towel below the pipe to be cut to catch debris

☐ **MATERIALS**
New threaded stop valve for your size of pipe, pipe-thread tape, possibly a pipe nipple

1 **Shut off the water** and drain the line by turning on a faucet at a lower location. Hold the steel pipe still with one pipe wrench while you remove the elbow with another wrench. If you can't budge the elbow, slip a length of 1¼-inch steel pipe on the wrench handle for more leverage.

Pipe wrench

2 Clean the pipe threads and wrap pipe-thread tape clockwise around the threads several times. Screw the stop valve onto the pipe and tighten with an adjustable wrench. (Don't crank hard with a pipe wrench or the valve might crack.)

REFRESHER COURSE
Working with steel pipe

Measure to find the pipe lengths you need; be sure to take into account the distance the pipes will travel inside fittings and valves.

Wrap each pipe end with several windings of pipe-thread tape and use a pipe wrench to firmly tighten each pipe and fitting in order. Tighten with a tool no smaller than a 14-inch pipe wrench; a smaller tool may not have enough power.

Galvanized steel pipe

Pipe-thread tape

Black gas pipe

14" pipe wrench

Match supply tubes with stop valves
Stop valves have spouts that are ½-inch or ⅜-inch diameter. Buy supply tubes to fit the valves and faucet connection.

REPLACING A VALVE

A plumbing system should have a main shutoff valve that controls water to the whole house and intermediate shutoff valves that control water for various areas of the house. There also should be shutoff valves on the incoming cold supply line for a water heater and stop valves (also called fixture shutoffs) that control water leading to individual faucets and appliances.

If an old shutoff valve—usually a gate or globe type—leaks at the packing nut, make sure it's all the way open or closed. If it still leaks try tightening the packing nut with pliers or an adjustable wrench. (Don't crank down too hard, or you could crack the nut.) If it still leaks or if it fails to completely shut off water, follow the steps at right to repair or replace it.

Stop valves are often cheaply made and may fail to shut off water completely or may leak from the packing nut. Replace a faulty stop valve with a ball-type model, which costs a little more but is very reliable.

A globe valve inhibits water flow even if it is in good working order. Replacing it with a ball valve may increase water pressure.

Servicing an old valve

Gate valve

String packing

If water leaks from the packing nut of a gate valve, replace the packing washer or the string packing. If the valve does not shut off water completely, try removing the gate and cleaning out any debris in the valve body. If that does not solve the problem, replace the valve.

Stem washer

Globe valve

If water leaks out the packing nut of a globe valve, replace the packing washer or string packing. If the valve fails to shut off water completely, replace the stem washer with an exact replacement. If that does not solve the problem, replace the valve.

PRESTART CHECKLIST

☐ **TIME**
An hour or two to repair or replace a shutoff valve

☐ **TOOLS**
Groove-joint pliers, pipe wrenches, wire brush, flux brush, propane torch, fiber shield, adjustable wrench

☐ **SKILLS**
Working with supply pipe

☐ **PREP**
Shut off water upstream from the valve

☐ **MATERIALS**
Repair parts or a new valve, pipe-thread tape, flux, solder

GLOBE, GATE, AND BALL VALVES

Globe valve

Gate valve

Ball valve

A globe valve has a stem washer that presses against the chamber to shut off water. A gate valve has a wedge-shape gate (shown) that moves up and down, or a cylindrical gate that pivots, to control water flow. A ball valve has a spherical gate that opens or closes when the handle rotates a quarter-turn.

Installing a new valve

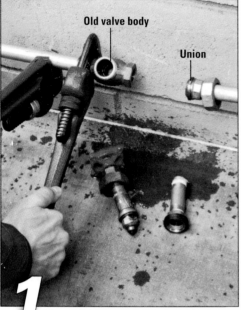

Old valve body

Union

1 If possible open a nearby union and disassemble a few pipes to get to the existing valve. If not, follow the steps on pages 134–135 for breaking into steel pipe. If the supply pipes are copper, see pages 126–127.

Pipe-thread tape

Nipples

2 The new valve will be about the same size as the old one, so you shouldn't have to change any pipe lengths. (Otherwise have on hand a selection of nipples.) Wrap all threaded pipe ends with several windings of pipe-thread tape and assemble the parts.

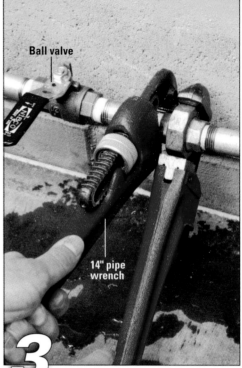

Ball valve

14" pipe wrench

3 Tighten the pipes and fittings as you go using two 14-inch pipe wrenches. Finish by assembling and tightening a union. Test for leaks.

Installing a gas shutoff valve

1 A house shutoff is usually on the gas meter. To shut off gas to the entire house, turn the valve slowly a quarter-turn with a pipe wrench. **To make sure no one turns the gas back on, padlock the valve.**

Gas-rated pipe-thread tape

2 **Open a window to vent any residual gas. Ignite no flames.** Using two pipe wrenches (Step 3, above) to avoid straining any of the pipe joints, remove the cap or old valve. Apply gas-rated pipe-thread tape clockwise.

Pipe wrench

Valve

Adjustable wrench

3 Screw the valve onto the pipe. Gripping the gas pipe with a pipe wrench, use an adjustable wrench to tighten the valve in place. Turn the gas on at the house shutoff. Test your work using liquid soap or test fluid (page 135).

THAWING PIPES AND WINTERIZING

Pipes that are not sufficiently insulated may freeze during cold weather. The result could be a minor inconvenience—the pipes may be undamaged and the water will flow again when they thaw out. Or it could be a burst pipe.

Exposed pipes are easily insulated or heated. If the pipes are inside a wall, the job may be difficult. If the exterior wall is the inside wall of an attached garage, consider attaching solid foam insulation on the garage side of the entire wall. Otherwise you'll have to remove the exterior or interior wall covering (whichever is easier), insulate the pipes, and then reinstall the wall covering.

If the weather forecast calls for extreme cold and you fear that a pipe may freeze, open a faucet or two on the line just a crack, so water comes out in little more than a drip. Moving water freezes more slowly than still water.

PRESTART CHECKLIST

☐ **TIME**
An hour or two to protect exposed pipes; much more time to protect pipes behind walls

☐ **TOOLS**
Portable heater, hair dryer, or heat gun; carpentry tools if you need to get at hidden pipes

☐ **SKILLS**
Identifying and locating the pipes that need to be protected

☐ **PREP**
Check the history of freezing pipes in your home; locate the vulnerable ones

☐ **MATERIALS**
Insulation (various types), electric pipe-heating tape

Insulate vulnerable pipes: Wrap exposed pipes with sections of foam insulation (page 112) or fill the surrounding area with fiberglass batts, loose-fill cellulose, or spray foam (shown). Leave part of the pipe exposed to warm, interior air.

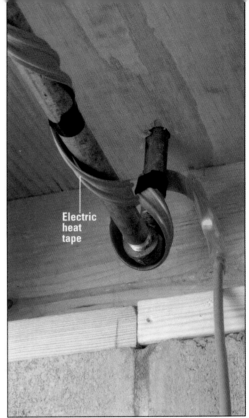

Install heat tape: Newer types of electric pipe-heating tape are easy to install and turn themselves on only when needed. Wrap the tape around the pipe and plug the unit into a reliable electrical receptacle. Follow the manufacturer's instructions. Never overlap electric heat tape.

WHAT IF ...
Your pipes freeze?

When water stops flowing during cold weather, you know that at least one pipe has frozen. (If only the hot water flows, you know the cold-water pipe has frozen.) A frozen pipe may or may not crack; you'll find out only after the water thaws. Just in case watch the pipes continually and **be prepared to shut off** **the water.** Have pipe repair materials on hand. If a pipe is exposed, thaw it by pointing a hair dryer or heat gun at it (left). (Don't get too close with the heat gun, and watch carefully for any drip or spray of water.) If the pipe is hidden in a wall, aim a portable heater at the area (above).

WINTERIZING A CABIN

If a cabin will be left unheated during the winter, take steps to prevent pipe damage due to freezing water. In addition to the steps shown, turn off the main shutoff valve and open a pipe nearby to let water drain out. Drain all water-using appliances, such as the dishwasher and clothes washer. If the cabin has hot-water heat, drain the heating system. Some cabins have small drain valves on the pipes; open them.

At the electrical service panel, shut off power to an electric water heater.

If the water heater is gas, shut off the gas that runs to it.

Even after draining the system, water will remain in traps. Pour about 3 cups of full-strength antifreeze into every toilet bowl.

Pour about a cup of antifreeze into each sink.

After shutting off power or gas, drain the water heater.

Drain hose bib

Pour about 2 cups of antifreeze into every shower and floor drain trap.

Drain each accessible trap before adding antifreeze.

Drain each stop valve.

Drain well pump.

Protect your outdoor hose bib with an indoor shutoff valve

PVC saw

1 Using a PVC saw or scissors-type PVC cutters (page 115), cut out a section of pipe. Take into account the fact that the pipes will slide into the valves at each side. Remove burrs from the pipes (page 128).

2 Make sure the valve fits. Apply primer outside the pipe and inside the valve. Cement one pipe and one side of the valve. Immediately slip the valve onto the pipe. Give it a slight twist and hold it for 30 seconds. Glue the other side.

Hose bib insulator

When cold weather approaches disconnect and drain all outdoor hoses. To protect the outdoor faucet (called a hose bib or sill cock), shut off the line that runs to it and open it to drain the water.

To protect it further, strap on a foam insulator like this one. A long-term solution is to install a freezeproof sill cock that has the valve body indoors, protected from freezing temperatures.

WORKING WITH PIPE

utting and joining the various types of pipe—copper, plastic, and steel—call for special techniques. These methods can be learned in an hour or two. This chapter teaches you how to work with the materials you choose.

Practice, practice

Though you may never learn to install plumbing as quickly as a professional plumber, with practice you can make joints that are every bit as strong and durable as those made by the pros.

But these techniques take practice, so buy extra pipe and fittings and practice until you can make straight cuts. Experiment to find out how far a pipe pokes into a fitting so you can measure accurately. Clamp a pipe to a vise on a workbench and join it to a fitting. Keep practicing until you are confident that your joints are tight and secure.

Preparing the worksite

Working in tight spots is usually what makes plumbing difficult. Evaluate the working conditions and take time to make things as comfortable as possible. Remove all obstructions. Place a bucket under any pipe that might leak as it is disassembled. In confined spaces have plenty of large towels on hand to soak up spilled water and to cushion your back, head, and knees. Protect floors with a drop cloth.

You may need to pull an existing pipe away from a wall or framing member in order to cut and join a new line to it. Remove a clamp or strap or two and pull gently. Copper pipe can kink if you pull it too hard. Unscrewing a steel pipe fitting can stress corroded threads enough to cause a leak.

Before working on any project, practice the golden rule of plumbing: **Shut off the water** and turn on a faucet to make sure the water is off. When working on drain-waste-vent pipes, **shut off the water,** flush all the toilets, and tell household members not to use the drainage system.

Make the jobsite safe. When sweating copper pipe protect all flammable surfaces and have a fire extinguisher ready. When working on a drain line, keep the room ventilated in case noxious fumes escape. **Shut off a gas line before working on it.**

Cutting and joining pipe requires skills that can be learned in just an hour or two.

CHAPTER PREVIEW

Working with copper pipe
page 126

Installing plastic drainpipe
page 128

Working with CPVC and plastic supplies
page 130

Working with PEX tubing
page 132

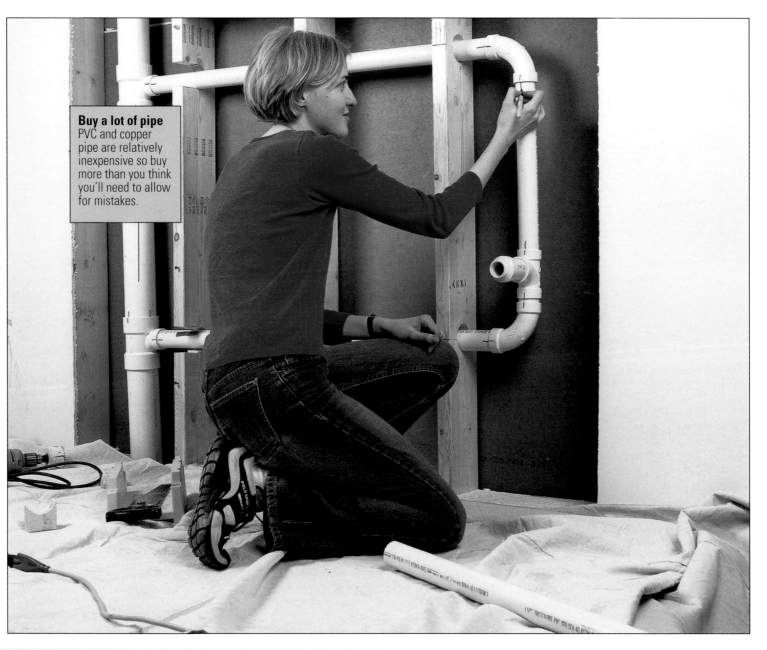

Buy a lot of pipe
PVC and copper pipe are relatively inexpensive so buy more than you think you'll need to allow for mistakes.

Advanced plumbing projects call for special preparations. Clear away furniture and lay down a thick, absorbent drop cloth. A drop cloth will protect the floor from dropped tools and fittings. In addition it will soak up any residual water and catch any spilled primer, putty, and debris.

Installing steel pipe
page 134

Working with cast-iron drainpipe
page 136

Running pipes through walls and floors
page 138

Connecting new to old
page 140

Working With Copper Pipe

A properly soldered (or "sweated") joint on copper pipe is as strong as the pipe itself. A poorly soldered joint will leak.

Work systematically because each step depends on the previous one: The pipe must be cut straight and all burrs removed. The inside of the fitting and the outside of the pipe must be clean. Flux must be applied for the solder to adhere. The solder must be fully drawn into the joint.

Pipe ends and fittings must be perfectly round. If either is dented or even slightly flattened, it is all but impossible to restore the original roundness. Cut the pipe again or buy a new fitting.

Cutting with a tubing cutter ensures roundness. If space is tight and you must cut with a hacksaw, do it slowly and gently. If you must bend a pipe to move it away from a wall, work carefully.

Prestart Checklist

☐ **Time**
About 15 minutes to cut a pipe and join a fitting

☐ **Tools**
Felt-tip marker, tubing cutter or hacksaw, multiuse wire brush, flux brush, propane torch (preferably with a trigger igniter), fiber shield

☐ **Skills**
Cutting pipe, soldering

☐ **Prep**
Protect any flammable surfaces with a fiber shield or cookie sheet

☐ **Materials**
Copper pipe and fittings, flux, solder (95 percent tin for drinking water supply), damp rag

1 Hold a pipe in place to measure for a cut or use a tape measure. Take into account the distance the pipe will fit into the fitting. Mark with a felt-tip marker or a pencil.

Felt-tip marker

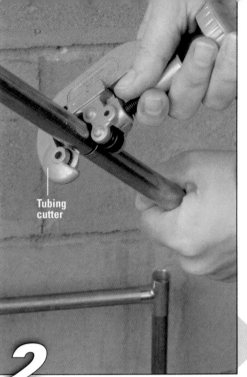

Tubing cutter

2 Use a large tubing cutter or a small one if space is tight. Align the cutting wheel with the cut mark. Twist the knob until the wheel starts to bite into the pipe. Rotate the cutter once, tighten a half turn or so, and repeat until the pipe is cut. Assemble all the parts of a joint in a dry run.

Refresher Course
Sweating a brass valve

Meltable parts

If a valve has any plastic parts—as is the case with most stop valves—disassemble the valve and remove all the meltable parts. Heat the brass valve body as you would a fitting. It may take a bit longer to heat than a fitting. After sweating wait for the valve to cool before replacing the plastic parts.

Protect walls and framing from the torch flame

While caught up in the sweating process you may not notice that the flame is charring a joist or wall surface. Protect flammable surfaces with a fiber shield (page 20) or use an old cookie sheet or two. **Keep a home fire extinguisher handy.**

If you can't pull a pipe more than a half inch away from a wall or framing member, don't worry about heating all around the fitting. As long as you heat two opposite sides, the solder will draw evenly around the joint.

Avoid MAPP gas, an alternative to propane fuel. It produces an extremely hot flame and is not recommended for most residential work.

After the job is complete, **check the area an hour later to be sure no flammable surfaces are smoldering.**

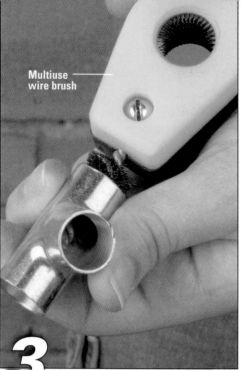

3 Using a wire brush made for the size of the fitting, ream out every inside opening until it is shiny. Oil from your hand may weaken the joint. If you accidentally touch a brushed opening, ream it again.

4 Brush or sand the outside of the pipe to be joined until it shines by inserting the pipe end in the multiuse brush and spinning the brush a few times. Rebrush or resand if you touch the shiny area.

5 Using the flux brush (it often comes with the can of flux), apply flux to all the inside openings of the fitting and to the outside of the pipe. Take care to keep the flux brush away from any debris; clean it if any particles stick to it.

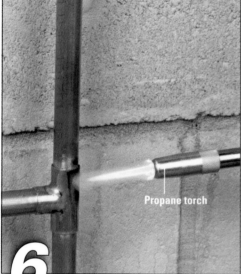

6 Ignite a propane torch and point the flame at the fitting near the joint—not at the pipe and not at the joint. The tip of the blue portion of the flame should just touch the fitting. Move the flame back and forth so you heat two opposite sides of the fitting.

7 When the fitting starts to smoke, remove the flame and touch the tip of the solder to the joint. If it does not melt, heat again. Once the fitting is hot enough, the solder will be drawn into the joint. Move the solder around so the entire joint is soldered.

8 Immediately repeat the process for any other joints in the fitting. This will go quickly because the fitting is already hot. Once all the joints are soldered, quickly wipe all the joints with a damp rag. Avoid bumping the fitting for 10 to 15 minutes.

INSTALLING PLASTIC DRAINPIPE

Plastic PVC pipe and fittings are inexpensive and easy to install. However do not take this work lightly. Once glued together a joint is rock-hard and cannot be adjusted. If you make a mistake, you'll have to cut out the section and start all over again.

Making a dry run

To prevent a mistake cut and assemble the pipes in a dry run: Cut and temporarily join five or six pipes and fittings and make sure that the last pipe in the run is facing the right direction. Use a felt-tip pen to make alignment marks on all the joints where the fitting must face correctly. Disassemble, keeping careful track of the order of installation. Apply primer to each pipe end and each fitting. Apply cement and join each pipe in order.

PRESTART CHECKLIST

☐ **TIME**
About an hour to cut and assemble five or six pipes and fittings

☐ **TOOLS**
Felt-tip marker, PVC saw or backsaw and miter box or power miter saw, deburring tool

☐ **SKILLS**
Sawing, measuring, working methodically

☐ **PREP**
Make a drawing of the drain/vent assembly; clear a path for the pipes

☐ **MATERIALS**
Primer and cement for your type and size of pipe (opposite)

1 When measuring allow for the distance the pipe will travel inside the fitting. Use a felt-tip marker to mark the pipe. You can use a hacksaw or backsaw to cut PVC, but a plastic-pipe saw is easier to use. A power miter saw with a fine-cutting blade is easiest of all. Cut it square.

Plastic-pipe saw | Miter box

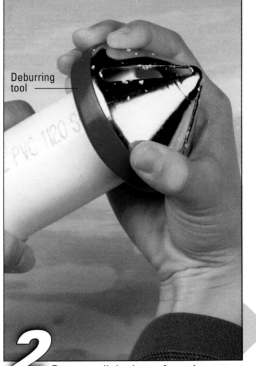

Deburring tool

2 Remove all the burrs from the cut pipe end. You can do this by scraping with a knife, but a deburring tool does a better job and is easier to use. Assemble cut pipes and fittings in a dry run (below).

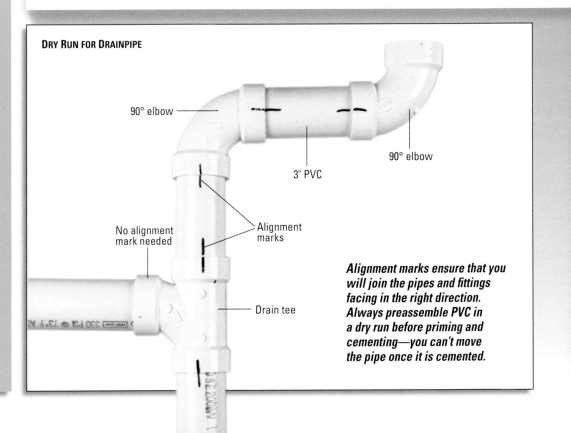

DRY RUN FOR DRAINPIPE

90° elbow

90° elbow

3" PVC

No alignment mark needed

Alignment marks

Drain tee

Alignment marks ensure that you will join the pipes and fittings facing in the right direction. Always preassemble PVC in a dry run before priming and cementing—you can't move the pipe once it is cemented.

PVC cement

3 Apply primer to the inside of the fitting openings and to the pipe ends. The applicator should be wet enough to produce a fairly dark line but not so wet that the primer drips. Place the pieces where they will not get dirty. If debris sticks to the primer, it will be difficult to join the pipes.

Primer applicator

4 Apply cement to the inside of one fitting opening and to the end of one pipe. Work quickly—the cement starts to set up in a few seconds.

5 Push the pipe into the fitting and twist so the alignment marks line up. Hold for a few seconds, then wipe with a damp cloth. In a minute the joint will be strong enough so you can assemble the next piece. After 15 minutes you can run unpressurized wastewater through the pipes.

WHAT IF …
You are connecting ABS pipe?

Most codes require PVC for drain lines, but if you already have black ABS pipe in your home, local codes may allow you to add to your system using the same material instead of making a transition to PVC.

Cut and assemble the black ABS pipe in much the same way as you would PVC pipe. Use a plastic-cutting saw or backsaw with a miter box, remove the burrs, and put pipe and fittings together in a dry run. Use a sharpened, light-colored crayon to make alignment marks.

Instead of primer apply ABS cleaner to pipe ends and fitting openings. Use special ABS cement to glue together the pieces. Push the pieces together and twist.

To connect PVC pipe to existing ABS pipe, use a no-hub fitting (page 137).

ABS cleaner applicator

Use the right products

Check the label on a can of primer or cement to make sure it's made for your type of pipe. Local inspectors may or may not approve of "all-purpose" cement. The larger the pipe's diameter, the bigger the applicator should be so you won't have to dip it twice. As a general rule an applicator should be about half the diameter of the pipe to be joined.

WORKING WITH CPVC AND PLASTIC SUPPLIES

Check local codes before installing plastic supply piping; many building codes do not permit it for interior use.

CPVC and other types of plastic pipe are often used for irrigation systems and other outdoor work. Because plastic pipe can be broken when hit, some codes allow it only for underground installations and require metal pipe above ground.

Often rigid plastic supply pipe is used with flexible tubing such as PEX, both for outdoor and interior installations. In a typical irrigation system, rigid pipe is used for long runs and flexible tubing is used for shorter runs leading to sprinkler heads.

PRESTART CHECKLIST

☐ **TIME**
About an hour to cut and join five or six pieces of pipe and fittings

☐ **TOOLS**
Felt-tip marker, PVC pipe cutter or plastic-pipe saw and miter box, deburring tool, groove-joint pliers

☐ **SKILLS**
Cutting, measuring, cementing

☐ **PREP**
Cut holes behind walls or under floors to clear a path for the supply pipes

☐ **MATERIALS**
Plastic supply pipe approved by local codes, appropriate primer and cement, damp rag, flexible pipe, compression fittings

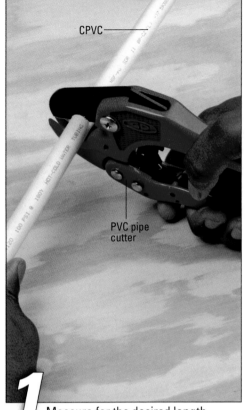

CPVC

PVC pipe cutter

1 Measure for the desired length and mark the pipe with a felt-tip marker. Cut small-diameter plastic pipe with a PVC pipe cutter (shown) or a saw and miter box.

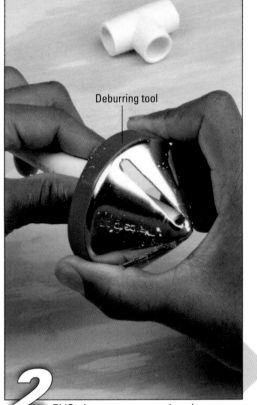

Deburring tool

2 PVC pipe cutters cut cleanly, but if you use a saw or there are any burrs, use a deburring tool to smooth the inside and outside of the cut end. Dry-fit the pipes and make alignment marks.

PLASTIC PIPE SYSTEM

Assemble the parts in a dry run and draw alignment marks so when you put the pieces together again they will face the right directions.

Galvanized steel pipe

Steel to CPVC transition fitting

CPVC to PEX transition fitting

PEX tubing

Alignment mark

Elbow

Tee

3 Using a small can with a small applicator brush, apply purple primer to the inside of the fitting and the pipe end. Place the pieces on a surface where they will not get dirty.

Cement applicator

4 One pipe and fitting at a time, apply cement to the inside of the fitting and to the pipe end.

5 Quickly insert the pipe into the joint and twist. Where there are alignment marks, make sure they meet. Hold for a few seconds and then wipe the joint with a damp rag.

Breaking into plastic pipe with a compression tee

Cut line   Cut line

Threaded adapter

1 Plastic compression tees are ideal for breaking into an existing line where it is difficult to glue a standard tee. Note the distance that the pipe should be inserted into each end of the compression tee—usually ¼ inch. Mark the length of the tee and the insertion points (your cut lines).

Rubber gasket   Nut

2 **Turn off the water and drain the system.** Use a plastic-pipe saw or other fine-tooth saw to cut the pipe. Deburr the pipe (see Step 2, opposite). Slip the nut and rubber gasket onto each end of the pipe. Bend the pipe out slightly to slip the tee into place.

3 Tighten the nuts with groove-joint pliers. **Do not overtighten.** Add the extension to the line, following the steps above for cementing plastic pipe. Turn on the water to test the extension.

WORKING WITH PEX TUBING

Cross-linked polyethylene (PEX) is strong, durable, and can handle hot as well as cold water. It is approved for interior plumbing in many areas of the country—especially the South—and is gaining acceptance elsewhere.

PEX is an installer's dream. It is easily cut and flexible enough to make gentle bends around corners. To join compression fittings no special tools or materials are required—just a pair of pliers or an adjustable wrench. More permanent fittings require a special crimping tool (see Steps 2 and 3). Where approved by local codes, PEX is an ideal material if you want to replace old galvanized pipes because it can be snaked through walls.

PEX systems can use a manifold fitting (Step 2), which allows you to install one water supply line to a location and then add branch lines to various fixtures.

PRESTART CHECKLIST

☐ **TIME**
About an hour to run and install about 50 feet of pipe with five fittings

☐ **TOOLS**
Drill, plastic tubing cutter or plastic-pipe cutter, crimping tool, reaming tool, adjustable wrench

☐ **SKILLS**
Understanding of supply pipes

☐ **PREP**
Bore holes for running pipe through joists or studs

☐ **MATERIALS**
PEX tubing, compression fittings, crimp rings

1 Holes for PEX tubing need not be carefully laid out in a straight line. PEX can be bent around corners, but don't make too sharp a bend or the tubing may kink. In most cases you can run the pipe through the holes and then cut it in place. Drill 1-inch holes for ½-inch tubing.

Flexible tubing cutter

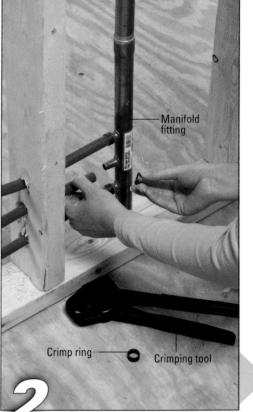

Manifold fitting

Crimp ring — Crimping tool

2 Make sure the tube end is cut straight and that the cut end is free of burrs. To make a crimped connection, slide the crimp ring onto the tube and slip the tube onto the fitting.

PEX FITTINGS

Transition fittings allow you to join PEX to other pipe materials. Be sure to use fittings approved for the types of pipe you are connecting.

- PEX pipe
- Compression elbow
- Crimp tee
- Composite-to-PEX union
- Compression tee
- Copper pipe
- Composite pipe
- Composite compression stop valve
- Copper-to-composite tee

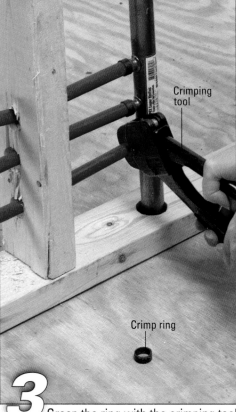

3 Grasp the ring with the crimping tool and squeeze until you feel the ring compress. Tug on the connection to make sure it is solid.

Crimping tool

Crimp ring

4 To install a stub out, temporarily screw the drop-ear elbows, mark the tubing for cutting, and cut with a tubing cutter.

Drop-ear elbow

5 Remove the elbow, attach it to the tubing using the crimping tool, and reattach the elbow. To ensure against rattling noises when water is turned on and off, clamp the pipe firmly every couple of feet. Where pipe runs through a hole, tap in a wooden shim.

Installing composite pipe

Tubing cutter

In addition to straight polyethylene pipe, composite pipe, with an aluminum core sheathed in plastic, is approved in some areas for water supply and gas lines. Cut it with a tubing cutter.

Reaming

Use a reaming tool to true the tubing into round and clean out the inside of the cut end. Insert the tool and give it a couple of twists. Make sure no scrapings are left inside the tube.

Ferrule

Adjustable wrench

Slip a nut and a ferrule onto the tube end, then slip the tube onto the fitting. Finger-tighten, taking care not to cross-thread. Then tighten the nut with one full turn (no more), using an adjustable wrench or pliers.

INSTALLING STEEL PIPE

New water supply lines are usually copper or plastic, but if you need to repair or extend a galvanized pipe system, it makes sense to use the same material.

Almost all gas lines are black threaded pipe, which is installed the same way as galvanized pipe (opposite).

Measure carefully, keeping in mind that ½- and ¾-inch pipe goes about ½ inch into each fitting. Then have a home center or hardware store employee cut and thread pieces to these exact measurements.

A more flexible strategy is to estimate your pipe and fitting needs. Then you can buy long pipes as well as a variety of nipples—short lengths of threaded pipe ranging from 1 to 12 inches. Also buy extra couplings. When you come close to the end of a run, you probably can create the correct length simply by combining nipples and couplings.

PRESTART CHECKLIST

☐ **TIME**
About an hour to cut into a line and install several fittings and pipes

☐ **TOOLS**
Hacksaw or reciprocating saw, two pipe wrenches (14-inch wrenches are a good choice), groove-joint pliers

☐ **SKILLS**
Careful measuring and planning, firm tightening using a pipe wrench

☐ **PREP**
Shut off water. If there is a nearby union fitting, you may be able to avoid cutting a pipe.

☐ **MATERIALS**
Threaded pipe lengths and nipples, pipe-thread tape or pipe joint compound

1 **Shut off water to the line.** To tap into the middle of a line when there is no nearby union fitting, cut through a pipe with a reciprocating saw equipped with a metal-cutting blade or with a hacksaw. Unscrew the pipe on both sides of the cut.

Reciprocating saw

Metal-cutting blade

2 Before threading a pipe into a fitting, wrap the threads with several windings of pipe-thread tape. With the pipe end facing you, wrap clockwise. Or brush pipe joint compound onto the threads of the pipe end and the inside of the fitting.

Pipe-thread tape

GALVANIZED PIPE SYSTEM

Nut

Washer

Sweated brass female end

Screw-on dielectric transition fitting

Elbow

Nipple

Braided supply tube

Pipe-thread tape

Stop valve

Tee-fitting

Union female end

Union male end

Union nut

Threaded pipe must be installed consecutively, meaning you cannot break into a line unless you use a special fitting called a union.

14-inch pipe wrench

Tee-fitting

Union component

Union component

Union nut

Tape measure

3 Twist on a pipe or fitting by hand. If it does not turn easily, the joint is not straight and the threads are crossed. Back up and try again. Then firmly tighten each pipe or fitting using a 14-inch pipe wrench. You may need a second wrench to hold the adjacent piece steady.

4 Once the tee-fitting for the new line is installed, add a nipple and slip on the nut for the union, checking that the threads are toward the joint. Apply tape and install half of the union. Set the second half of the union in place and measure for the final section of pipe.

5 Attach the second half of the union to the final piece and install. The union halves should line up so they can set against each other. Slip the union nut up and hand-tighten. Then fully tighten the nut with a pipe wrench to complete the union.

Dielectric fitting for transition to copper

Galvanized steel pipe

Nut

Sweated brass female end

Screw-on transition fitting

Plastic washer

Copper pipe

To install a dielectric union, screw the threaded part onto the steel pipe. Before sweating the brass fitting of the copper pipe, slip on the nut and sleeve and push them well away from the heat of the torch. Once the fitting is sweated and cools, join the two parts. Use only groove-joint pliers to tighten the nut.

STANLEY PRO TIP: **Safely joining black gas pipe**

1 Before working with black threaded gas pipe, **shut off the gas** and ventilate the room. Follow the steps shown above but use black pipe and fittings instead of galvanized. Wrap threaded ends with special yellow pipe-thread tape, made for use with gas pipe.

2 After installation turn the gas back on and test for leaks. Spray gas-joint testing fluid or brush liquid soap (shown) or soapy water on a joint. If you see bubbles there is a leak. Tightening the nipple or valve will likely stop the leak. Retest.

Working With Cast-Iron Drainpipe

To extend or repair cast-iron drainpipe, make the transition to PVC drainpipe. Several types of no-hub fittings are available to join iron and plastic; check local codes to see which are accepted. A no-hub fitting has a neoprene sleeve and clamps that are tightened around the cast-iron pipe and the plastic piece to hold them in place and make a watertight joint. Such fittings are considered a permanent joint.

Cast-iron pipe is heavy, so work carefully and use a helper. Support pipe with clamps and framing before cutting it. Add clamps above and below the new joint or leave the frame permanently in place.

Prestart Checklist

☐ **Time**
A full day to support, cut, and install a replacement piece with two banded couplings; an hour or two to install a saddle-tee fitting (opposite)

☐ **Tools**
Carpentry tools, cast-iron snap cutter or circular saw with metal-cutting blade, tools for installing plastic drainpipe (pages 128–129), hex screwdriver or torque wrench

☐ **Skills**
Good carpentry skills, measuring, attaching with bolts

☐ **Prep**
Examine how the existing pipe is clamped; determine how best to hold it firmly as you work

☐ **Materials**
Riser clamps, plastic pipe or fitting matching cast-iron pipe, banded couplings

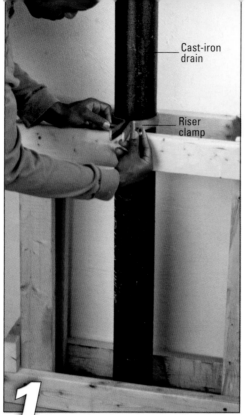

Cast-iron drain

Riser clamp

1 **Secure the pipe above and below the point that will be cut** so that neither end can fall or move sideways while you work. To be safe build a frame like the one shown here and attach the pipe to it with riser clamps.

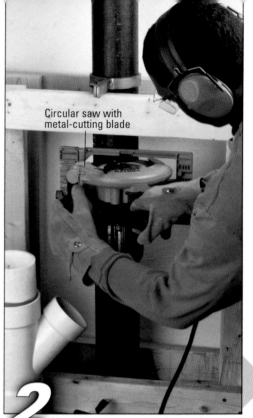

Circular saw with metal-cutting blade

2 Next to a snap cutter (below), the quickest way to cut cast iron is with a circular saw equipped with a metal-cutting blade. **Wear eye and ear protection.** If a circular saw will not reach all the way around, cut all or part with a reciprocating saw equipped with a metal-cutting blade.

STANLEY Pro Tip: **Make a quick, clean break with a snap cutter**

Another way to cut cast-iron pipe is with a snap cutter, which can be rented. After supporting the pipe above and below, wrap the cutter's chains around the pipe. Each chain link has a little wheel cutter. Follow manufacturer's instructions. Typically a handle sets the ratchet for loosening or tightening. Set it for tightening; pump the lever slowly until the chain is tight. Continue ratcheting until the cutting wheels crack through the pipe. Cut both sides and, wearing gloves, remove the scrap piece of pipe.

Cast-iron pipe

Lever

Ratchet-setting handle

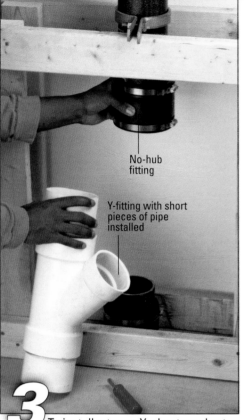

No-hub fitting

Y-fitting with short pieces of pipe installed

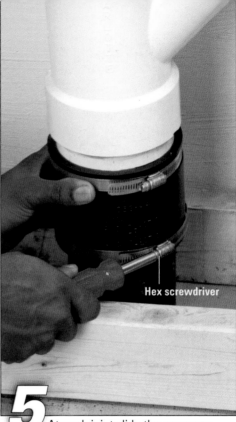

Hex screwdriver

3 To install a tee or Y, glue two short pieces of pipe to each end of the fitting (pages 114–115), making sure the resulting component will fit snugly between the pipes. Slip the no-hub fitting onto each of the cast-iron pipe ends.

4 Position the fitting or replacement piece between the two cut cast-iron ends and pull the neoprene sleeve over the plastic.

5 At each joint slide the neoprene sleeve of the no-hub fitting so it's centered on the joint. Tighten the band nuts using a hex screwdriver. Some codes may require the use of a torque wrench, which will stop tightening when you reach the proper band tightness.

Installing a saddle-tee drain fitting

Grinder with metal-cutting blade

Silicone sealant

Neoprene sheet

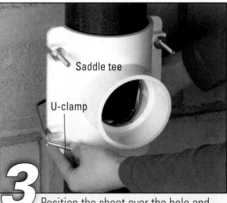

Saddle tee

U-clamp

1 If it's approved by your local inspector, a saddle fitting is easier and quicker to install. Cut a roughly circular hole in the cast-iron pipe using a grinder equipped with a metal-cutting blade (shown). The hole should be slightly larger than the opening in the fitting.

2 Hold a neoprene sheet for the fitting against the hole and trace the outline of the hole. Cut a hole in the sheet that's slightly larger than the hole in the pipe. Squeeze silicone sealant around the hole.

3 Position the sheet over the hole and press the plastic fitting over it. Slip a U-clamp around the back of the pipe and slide its threaded ends through the plastic fitting. Screw on the two nuts finger-tight. Attach the other clamp the same way, then tighten all four nuts.

RUNNING PIPES THROUGH WALLS AND FLOORS

Once you've drawn a plan for new plumbing service, develop a strategy for running the pipes. In a new building or addition where the framing is exposed, this is easy. If you are remodeling be prepared to make changes in the plan once you've removed the wallcovering and flooring.

Replacing finished surfaces after plumbing (especially patching walls) usually takes several days. A large wall patch—even replacing an entire wall—takes only a little more time than a small patch, so open plenty of space for working.

Once you've opened the vent and drain lines, running the supplies—which usually run alongside drain-waste-vent (DWV) lines—will be relatively easy.

PRESTART CHECKLIST

☐ **TIME**
For a modest bathroom two or three days to cut into walls and flooring and run pipes through framing

☐ **TOOLS**
Demolition tools, drill with various bits and hole saws, reciprocating saw, level, tools for installing pipe

☐ **SKILLS**
Carpentry, knowledge of your home's structure, installing pipe

☐ **PREP**
Have your plan approved by the local building department

☐ **MATERIALS**
Pipes, fittings, clamps, and assembly materials listed on your plan

Cutout for new stack

1 If you need to run a new stack (pages 14–15), assess your framing. An installation with a toilet must have a 3-inch drain, which can be installed only if the stud wall is made of 2×6s or larger (2-inch pipe can be run through a 2×4 wall). Remove the wall surface up to the ceiling.

2×6 stud

Reciprocating saw

2 Cut a hole with some wiggle room for the new pipe. For a 3-inch pipe, use a drill and reciprocating saw to cut a hole about 4¼ inches × 10 inches through both the bottom plate of the room you are working in and the top plate of the room below. Cut away a 10-inch × 2-foot section of flooring.

Stabilizing and protecting pipes

Shim

Whenever possible run pipes through holes in the center of framing members.

To keep pipes from rattling, line the holes with felt or use wood shims. Slip a shim under the pipe and tap in until it is firmly in place, but not tight, to allow for expansion.

Metal plate

If notches are needed make them as small as possible; they weaken the framing member. Metal plates protect pipes from nails.

2½" hole

1½" vent pipe

3 Assemble the approved fittings onto the top of the drainpipe. Take special care that they face the right direction. The drainpipe should be longer than needed—you can cut it to size from below later. Slip the pipe down through the hole.

4 You may need to cut a hole in the wall of the room above or below to guide the vent pipe up or the drainpipe down. In the attic you may be able to run the vent over to tie into an existing vent. If not, drill a hole in the attic ceiling and have a roofer install a roof jack for the vent pipe.

Right-angle drill

Hole-cutting saw

5 Anchor the drainpipe with straps. Cut a smaller opening in the ceiling for the vent pipe. For a 1½-inch vent pipe, a 2½-inch hole is sufficient. Guide the vent pipe up through the hole and into the attic or room above and slip its lower end into the fitting at the floor.

Running pipe through a floor

This hole is ⅜ inch lower than hole in previous joist

Running drainpipe through joists calls for meticulous work. The holes must follow a straight line across the floor and must ascend or descend so the pipe will be sloped ¼ inch per foot. (If joists are 16 inches on center and pipes run across them at a right angle, holes should differ in height by about ⅜ inch.)

Running pipe through a wall

Code may require slope toward main drain

Drain

Main drain

Trap adapter

Slope toward main drain

Drain

Vent pipes may run level, though some codes may call for a slight slope toward the main drain. All drain lines must be sloped. For a precise slope strike a level line on the studs and measure down ¼ inch per running foot. Codes may call for fireproof caulking in walls.

CONNECTING NEW TO OLD

The most common way to connect a new drain, vent, or supply line to an existing line is to install a tee fitting.

Shut off water to existing supply pipes and drain the lines. Flush all toilets and caution others not to use drains. After opening a drain line, make sure no one uses a sink or faucet that drains into it. Seal any open drain lines with a rag to block fumes.

If joining pipes of different materials, make sure the transition fitting conforms to local code.

Typically it doesn't matter exactly where you join to an existing pipe, but the new service must be precisely located. So it's usually easier to start pipe runs at the new location and travel toward the existing pipes rather than vice versa.

PRESTART CHECKLIST

☐ **TIME**
Usually less than two hours to connect new to old once pipes are run

☐ **TOOLS**
Cutting and fitting tools for any type of pipe you will be working with, carpentry tools, reciprocating saw, hex-head driver

☐ **SKILLS**
Cutting and joining the type of pipe used in the project

☐ **PREP**
Run new pipes from the new service location to the existing pipe; install the last pipe a little longer than it needs to be so you can cut it to length when you make the connection to the old pipe

☐ **MATERIALS**
Joining materials for the type of pipe you are using, transition fittings

Pipe slopes down ¼" per foot

5" piece

Tee

5" piece

1 To join a new plastic drainpipe to an old steel pipe, run new pipe into the room. Prime and glue two 5-inch pieces of pipe to a tee fitting. Temporarily run pipe—longer than it needs to be—so it comes near the old pipe. (When running pipe across a stud wall, you may need to notch-cut some of the holes, using a reciprocating saw.) Dry-fit the tee assembly onto the new pipe and hold it next to the existing pipe. Mark the existing pipe for cutting. You may need to cut the opening larger than the tee assembly to accommodate the neoprene sleeves on the banded couplings.

WHAT IF ...
You need to connect new PVC to old ABS?

Neoprene sleeve rolled back to slip over PVC

No-hub fitting

Even though there are specialty primers and cements intended for joining PVC pipe to an old ABS line, local codes may not permit connecting in this manner. Instead use a no-hub fitting, which has a neoprene sleeve and metal clamps, to hold it firm. Some municipalities may require that the fitting be accessible for future repairs.

2 Support the pipe above and below with riser clamps so it cannot drop or sway as you work, and so the PVC fitting will not have to bear the weight of the drain. You probably will need to install a new stud or two as well as blocking for the upper clamp.

3 Slide a no-hub fitting onto each end of the old pipe, slide back the banded coupling, and fold up the neoprene sleeves. Position the tee assembly. Fold the neoprene sleeves over the assembly and slide the metal bands over the sleeves. Tighten the nuts with a hex-head driver.

4 Cut the new pipe to exact length and test that it fits into the tee fitting; you may need to loosen the nuts and rotate the fitting slightly. Prime and glue the pipe to the fitting (page 115).

Tapping into supply lines

To tap into existing copper lines, **shut off the water.** With a tubing cutter cut an opening in each pipe that is about an inch shorter than a tee fitting. Dry-fit the tees. If the pipes are rigidly installed, remove a clamp or two so you can pull the pieces apart slightly.

Dry-fit the pipes that will be inserted into the tees and draw alignment marks. Disassemble, wire-brush the fittings and pipe ends, brush on flux, and sweat the joints (pages 126–127).

Joining copper to existing galvanized pipe

To tie a new copper line into an old galvanized line, follow the steps on pages 134–135 for installing a new galvanized tee fitting. Screw a galvanized nipple into the tee and connect the copper line to the nipple using a dielectric union (page 135).

SYSTEM REPAIRS & UPGRADES

Home plumbing systems periodically need maintenance and appliance upgrades. These chores are moderately difficult—more involved than "easy installs" but not as complicated as a bathroom or kitchen renovation. Some projects may call for running short lengths of new supply pipe or gas pipe but no elaborate drain-waste-vent installations.

Some building inspectors will want you to obtain a permit for any installation, no matter how small. Others don't want to conduct inspections unless an installation requires running new pipes. To be safe consult with your local building department before tackling any of the projects described in this chapter.

An inspector may provide valuable advice for some of the more complicated connections, such as connecting water, gas, or electric lines to a water heater (pages 148–151) or solving water pressure problems (pages 152–153).

Other sources of advice and help

If you have a gas water heater, call the gas company to check for gas leaks and carbon monoxide (which can build up dangerously if the flue is not installed correctly). They may perform these checks for free.

If your main drain line is clogged, have the city inspect its portion of the drain line; again this should be free.

If you have an old home or if your plumbing is too complicated for you to understand, do not hesitate to call a plumber. A plumber's hourly rate may be high, but a pro has experience with a variety of plumbing problems and can perform some tasks so quickly that it may be well worth the money.

These maintenance and upgrade projects are straightforward and can be done in a weekend.

CHAPTER PREVIEW

Repairing a gas water heater
page 144

Repairing an electric water heater
page 146

Replacing a water heater
page 148

Increasing water pressure
page 152

Shut off water before draining.

Pressure-relief valve

SAFETY FIRST
Shut down water heater before draining

Always turn off the water heater before draining. With an electric water heater (shown), shut off electric power at the service panel (page 146). With a gas unit shut off gas at the burner control unit (page 144).

If water in your area is mineral-laden, draining the water heater once a year will prolong its life. Shut off the water and the gas or electricity before draining. Once the water has drained, close the drain valve, turn on the water, and wait for the unit to fill before restoring gas or electric power.

Drain valve

Use a hose to run water to a floor drain or use a bucket, shutting off the drain valve with each filling.

Installing a water filter
page 154

Installing an on-demand water heater
page 156

Maintaining a water pump
page 158

Maintaining a water softener
page 159

REPAIRING A GAS WATER HEATER

Most repairs to a gas water heater are made at the burner control. If your heater leaks the tank is rusted through and the entire unit must be replaced (pages 148–150). Here's a quick troubleshooting guide to gas water heater problems:

■ If the unit suddenly stops heating water, try relighting the pilot. If it does not stay lit, the thermocouple probably needs to be replaced (right). If that does not solve the problem, you may need to clean the burner.

■ If the flame is mostly yellow rather than mostly blue, clean the burner.

■ If water isn't heating sufficiently even though the thermostat is turned up and the flames are blue, drain the tank and refill it (page 143).

■ If you have hard water, unscrew and remove the anode rod once a year. Look for a 1-inch nut in the top of the heater. Loosen the nut; the anode rod will be attached. If it's encrusted with minerals, replace it to get more efficient operation.

Replacing a thermocouple

Control

Thermocouple

Pilot bracket

1 If a pilot light won't stay lit after you've followed the lighting directions, **turn the gas control knob to OFF.** It's often easiest to detach the thermocouple and pilot supply tube at the control and, using a stubby screwdriver, disconnect them from the burner. Pull out the thermocouple.

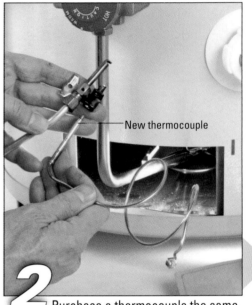

New thermocouple

2 Purchase a thermocouple the same length as the old one. Unroll it carefully to avoid kinking. Insert the tip into the pilot bracket so the pilot flame will heat it. Reinstall the thermocouple and the supply tube and attach them at the control. Turn the gas back on and light the pilot.

PRESTART CHECKLIST

☐ **TIME**
About an hour to replace a thermocouple; two to three hours to service a burner

☐ **TOOLS**
Long matches or a barbecue lighter, screwdriver, adjustable wrench, thin wire, soft metal brush, vacuum cleaner

☐ **SKILLS**
No special skills are needed

☐ **PREP**
Clear the area; you may need to shut off the gas

☐ **MATERIALS**
New thermocouple of the correct length, new pressure-relief valve

GAS WATER HEATER

Anode rod

Burner control

Drain valve

Burner

Pilot bracket

Instructions printed on the unit will explain how to relight a pilot light. The thermocouple signals the control unit to keep gas flowing to the pilot light; if the thermocouple fails the light will not stay lit.

Servicing a burner

1 If flames are yellow or erratic, remove and clean the burner. **Turn the gas control knob to OFF.** Unscrew and pull the gas tube, burner tube, and thermocouple from the control. Reach inside the chamber and pull the burner unit out or down until it unclips. Carefully pull the unit out.

2 Unscrew the burner unit from the gas tube. Clean the pilot gas tube with a soft wire brush or poke a thin wire down into its hole.

3 Turn the burner upside down and shake out any debris. Vacuum the jets to remove all dust. Use a thin wire to make sure the opening in the gas tube is clear and vacuum out any debris. Reassemble, reinstall, and relight. If the burner still malfunctions, call for service.

SAFETY FIRST
Check the flue

The flue on a gas water heater should pull all fumes up and send them out of the house. To check that a flue is working, light a match, blow it out, and hold it near the flue. Smoke should be sucked up into the flue. If it isn't, check that all the connections are tight. Have the gas company inspect to be sure.

Maintaining a gas water heater

Keep your heater alive longer by following these tips:

■ In areas with hard water, a gas water heater will last no more than 10 years. If you drain the unit once a year (see page 143), you will lengthen the unit's life and increase its efficiency.

■ The higher a thermostat is set, the shorter the life of the water heater. Set the temperature to just as hot as you want and no higher.

■ A damaged or incorrectly installed flue will lead to elevated levels of carbon monoxide. Install a carbon monoxide detector near (or directly above) the water heater to warn of this dangerous gas.

■ New water heaters are well insulated, but an older unit will benefit from a slip-over insulation blanket made specifically for water heaters.

Pressure-relief valve

A temperature- and pressure-relief (TPR) valve is a safety device that provides an outlet for water in case the unit overheats. To test that it's working, pull up on the little lever; water should flow out. If not, or if water drips from the valve, install a replacement.

REPAIRING AN ELECTRIC WATER HEATER

Most repairs to an electric water heater involve the two elements and their thermostats. If water leaks onto the floor, the tank is rusted through, and the unit must be replaced (pages 148–151).

■ If water is not hot enough, try turning up the thermostat settings for both elements.

■ If the unit suddenly stops heating water, press the reset button, usually on the high-limit cutoff. If you hear a click, the unit is reset and the problem may be solved. Also check that power is reaching the unit; call in an electrician if you are not sure.

■ If water gets warm but not hot, replace the upper element and/or thermostat.

■ If the hot water runs out quickly, replace the lower element and/or thermostat.

■ If the unit is noisy, drain the tank and refill it. If that does not solve the problem, remove and clean the elements.

■ If water is too hot even with the thermostats turned down, replace either the thermostat or the high-limit cutoff.

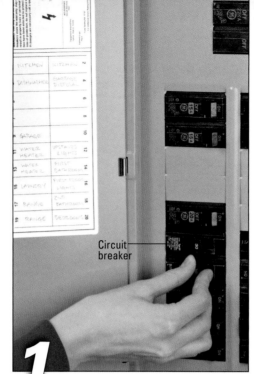

1 The amount of power an electric water heater uses is dangerous. Check with an electrician if you are unsure about shutting off power. At the service panel **shut off the breaker or unscrew the fuse controlling the water heater. Be sure no one will turn power on while you work.**

Circuit breaker

Voltage tester

DANGER

Access panel

Protective cover

2 Close the water shutoff valve above the tank. Drain the tank (page 143). Remove the access panel and the protective cover. Press the two prongs of a voltage tester against the terminal screws that the wires are connected to; test all possible combinations. Be certain the power is off.

PRESTART CHECKLIST

☐ **TIME**
An hour or two for most repairs

☐ **TOOLS**
Screwdriver, voltage tester, groove-joint pliers

☐ **SKILLS**
Testing for electrical power, unscrewing and replacing devices

☐ **PREP**
Prepare the household for doing without hot water for a few hours; arrange for a work light while the power is off

☐ **MATERIALS**
New element, thermostat, or high-limit cutoff for your make and model of water heater

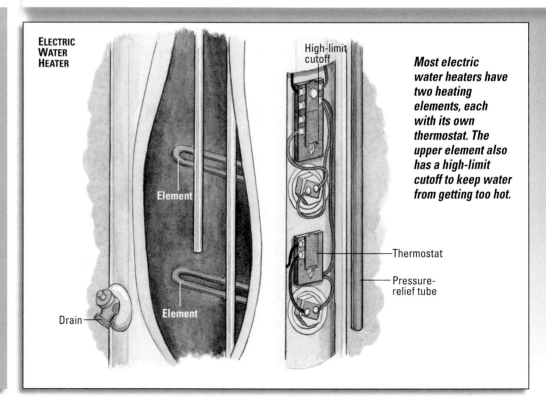

ELECTRIC WATER HEATER

Element

Element

Drain

High-limit cutoff

Thermostat

Pressure-relief tube

Most electric water heaters have two heating elements, each with its own thermostat. The upper element also has a high-limit cutoff to keep water from getting too hot.

3 Loosen the element's terminal screws and pull the wires away. You don't need to mark the wires—they can be attached to either terminal.

Element

4 Use groove-joint pliers to loosen and unscrew the element. Pull out the element. Have an appliance parts dealer test the element and buy a duplicate if it's defective. If the element is working, try replacing the thermostat.

Thermostat

5 Scrape away any debris from around the opening and clean it with a rag. Screw in the new element, replace the wires, replace the cover, and refill the tank. Set the thermostat (below), restore power, and test.

WHAT IF ...
A high-limit cutoff is defective?

High-limit cutoff

If water overheats or if the unit does not heat water and other solutions do not solve the problem, remove the high-limit cutoff from the upper element and take it in for testing. Replace it if necessary.

REPLACING THE THERMOSTAT

Thermostat

To remove a thermostat **shut off power** and test that power is off. Disconnect and tag the wires. Remove any mounting nuts or screws. Pry out the thermostat. Have the thermostat tested; replace it if necessary.

Resetting and adjusting a thermostat

Thermostat setting

150°F   90°F
125°F

A water heater is commonly set to 120 degrees. If water seems too hot or too cold, adjust the temperature up or down by about 10 degrees. After a day of use, you may want to adjust it another 10 degrees.

REPLACING A WATER HEATER

If the new water heater is the same size as the old one and has connections in the same places, hooking up the water, gas, and flue will be simple. If you need to move any lines, the job will take longer.

The system should include a shutoff valve for the cold water line to the water heater (but not for the hot water line) and the gas line. If not, install them when you install the new water heater.

In an area that experiences earthquakes, local codes may require that you chain or strap the water heater firmly to a wall.

Arrange for disposal of the old water heater. Your local waste hauler may have special requirements.

PRESTART CHECKLIST

☐ **TIME**
About a day for most installations

☐ **TOOLS**
Groove-joint pliers, screwdriver, pipe wrenches, adjustable wrench, tools for cutting and joining pipe, two-wheel cart, torpedo level, hammer

☐ **SKILLS**
Assembling supply pipe and gas pipe, maneuvering and leveling a large appliance, working with a flue

☐ **PREP**
Clear a path for removing the old unit; prepare the household to be without hot water for a day; check local codes

☐ **MATERIALS**
New water heater, shims, gas pipe or flexible connector, water pipe and/or flexible connector, heat trap nipples, pipe-thread tape, flue extension (optional), pressure-relief valve

Installing a gas water heater

1 **Turn off the gas shutoff valve** (so the handle is perpendicular to the pipe). **Shut off water** and allow the tank to cool. Drain the tank (page 143). If there is a gas pipe union, use two pipe wrenches to disconnect it. If there is a flexible connector (page 150), disconnect it.

2 Disconnect the water lines. If there is no flexible connector or union to disconnect, you may have to cut through a solid copper pipe. Use a tubing cutter to make a clean cut so you can connect the new line to it.

Flexible water connectors

If flexible water lines attach to the old water heater, simply unscrew the nuts with an adjustable wrench to disconnect. Check that the old fittings will work with the new; you may need to buy new lines or a male or female adapter. Check local codes.

Choosing a water heater

Different water heaters serve different needs. When shopping for a new unit:
■ Check the energy guide sticker on a water heater and choose one that's well insulated. Though it may cost a bit more, it will save money in the long run.
■ Consider buying a unit with an additional 10 gallons of capacity if family members complain that water runs out during showers. It may take more time to install and will use a little more energy.
■ Check the "rate of recovery"—how quickly the unit heats water. A water heater with a quick rate of recovery may solve the problem of running out of hot water.
■ Consider a unit with two anode rods, which attract sediment, if you have hard water. Regularly cleaning the rods can add years to the life of a water heater (page 144).

3 Once the flue has cooled, detach it from the water heater. Tie the flue up to keep it out of the way. With a two-wheeled cart, remove the old unit. Mineral deposits make it heavier than a new unit.

Torpedo level

Shim

4 Carry or wheel in the new water heater. Position it so the water, gas, and flue connections are as easy to reach as possible. Use a level to check the unit for plumb and shim the legs if necessary.

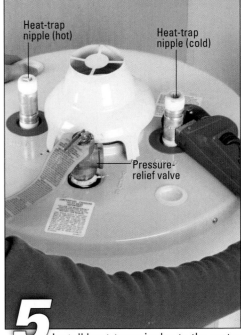

Heat-trap nipple (hot)

Heat-trap nipple (cold)

Pressure-relief valve

5 Install heat-trap nipples to the water heater inlets. Install the blue nipple, its arrow pointing down, to the cold water inlet. Install the red nipple, its arrow pointing up, to the hot-water inlet. Tighten both with a pipe wrench. Run PVC from the pressure-relief valve to a floor drain (page 151).

Choosing connectors

Local codes may have specific requirements for the type of pipe or connectors to be used when hooking up a water heater.

Unlike a range a water heater usually is not moved during its life. However it may vibrate while in use. Some building departments prefer flexible connectors, while others prefer hard piping—both for the water supplies and for the gas line. Always follow local codes.

If there is no floor drain nearby, you may want to place a drain pan under the water heater to catch water in case of a small leak.

Propane torch

Adapter

Solder

6 Before hooking up the supply lines, you may need to install an adapter. For a copper pipe that has been cut, sweat a male adapter to each pipe.

Corrugated supply tube

Heat-trap nipple

7 Connect the water supply tubes to the heat-trap nipples. Buy connectors approved by local codes, checking that they fit at both ends. If necessary use reducer fittings to make the transition.

INSTALLING A GAS WATER HEATER continued

8 <u>Connect the gas line.</u> A hard-piped gas line should have a drip leg to collect condensation and dirt that can hinder the burner's efficiency. Wrap the pipe threads with yellow pipe-thread tape (made for gas lines). Tighten connections securely using two pipe wrenches (page 119).

9 **Do not light the pilot until you are sure there are no leaks.** Turn on the gas. Test for leaks by spraying with gas-joint testing fluid (shown) or by pouring a strong soap-and-water mixture on each joint. Bubbles indicate a leak. Tighten leaky fittings. Recheck if necessary.

10 Follow the manufacturer's instructions for lighting the pilot. Usually this involves lighting the pilot while holding down the reset button and continuing to hold it for a full minute before releasing and turning on the burner.

CONNECT THE GAS LINE
Use a flexible connector

A flexible gas connector usually has a "FIP" fitting at each end. For the best burner performance, install a drip leg as shown.

Attaching a flue

1 If the new heater is the same height as the old water heater, you can simply hook up the flue in the same way. If you need to add piping, measure and cut pieces to fit with a pair of tin snips.

2 Connect the pieces by driving three or four sheet metal screws into each joint. Test to make sure the flue draws (page 145) and install a carbon monoxide detector in the room. If you have any doubts about the flue, have the gas company or a plumbing and heating contractor inspect it.

Installing an electric water heater

1 To replace an electric water heater, **shut off power** (page 146). Test to make sure power is off. Remove the electrical cover plate and carefully pull out the wires; remove the wire nuts and touch the bare wires with the probes of a voltage tester to make sure there is no power.

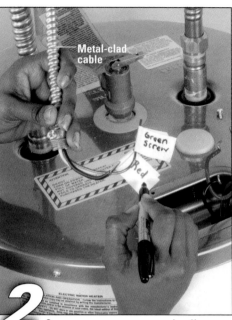

2 Once you are sure power is off, loosen the cable clamp screw and pull out the cable, which might be metal-clad (shown), nonmetallic cable, or wires running through conduit. Mark the wires for reattaching. Follow steps to disconnect the water lines and remove the old unit (pages 148–149).

3 Position the new unit, level it, and shim if needed. Run the electrical cable through the clamp and tighten it. Connect the ground wire to the ground screw. Splice the other wires and screw on wire nuts. Push the wires carefully into the cavity and replace the cover plate.

4 Install the water lines (page 149). Open the water shutoff valves and allow the tank to fill. Do not restore power yet.

5 Open both access panels and set the thermostats to the desired settings. Press the reset buttons until they click. Restore power.

Running a line from a relief valve to a drain

Install a drain tube to vent the water should the pressure-relief valve have to do its job (page 145). Run a 1-inch PVC line from the valve to a floor drain. Use a PVC adapter to make the transition.

INCREASING WATER PRESSURE

Check the water pressure entering your home; it should be 40 to100 pounds per square inch (psi). If the incoming pressure is OK, corrosion, sediment, or mineral buildup in galvanized pipes may be the problem. Horizontal lines and hot-water pipes are most prone to clogs. However any galvanized pipe can clog.

The ultimate solution is to replace old plumbing with copper pipes—a time-consuming and expensive job. Here are several simple solutions. The method shown will clear pipes but can also clean corroded joints where sediment alone was preventing leaks. **Use compressed air gently.** Clear pipes between a faucet and the water heater, then use the same method to clear pipes from the water heater to the main shutoff. Don't blast compressed air through a water heater—you could damage its lining.

PRESTART CHECKLIST

☐ **TIME**
Several hours to assemble the parts and to force out sediment with an air compressor

☐ **TOOLS**
Pipe wrenches, groove-joint pliers, air compressor, hand-crank auger, wire cutters, toothbrush

☐ **SKILLS**
Dismantling and assembling galvanized steel pipe

☐ **PREP**
Determine which pipes are clogged; map where the pipes run (pages 32–33)

☐ **MATERIALS**
Parts to connect an air compressor to a pipe, pan or bucket, perhaps new aerators

Forcing out sediment with an air compressor

1 **Shut off the clogged supply line** at a convenient spot on the street side of a union. At the other end of the pipe run to be cleared, disconnect pipes or remove a stop valve.

2 Attach the hose of an air compressor (a model that has a holding tank) to the pipe end. Making this connection requires several fittings; consult with a home center salesperson to assemble them properly.

Clearing aerators and screens

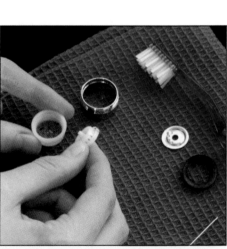

If water flows slowly at one faucet or appliance only, chances are that an aerator or a screen is clogged. At a washing machine shut off the hose valve and disconnect the hoses from the back of the machine. Pry out the screens in the machine's inlets or hose ends and clean them.

Use pliers to unscrew an aerator from the end of a faucet spout and clean all the little parts. Replace the aerator if it is damaged.

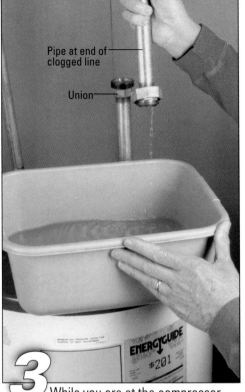

Pipe at end of clogged line

Union

3 While you are at the compressor, have a helper disconnect the union on the house side of the shutoff valve, such as a union near a water heater (shown). Place a pan or bucket under the union. Water contained in the pipes will flow out.

Compressor hose

COMPRESSOR

4 As soon as the union is disconnected, turn on the compressor. Water—along with a good deal of gunk—will gush out the pipe at the other end. Repeat this process once or twice to force out lingering sediment from the pipe.

Aerator

5 Reattach the union and the pipe or stop valve to the other end and turn on the water. Remove the aerators from all affected faucets and run water for a minute or two to flush out more sediment.

Augering supply pipes

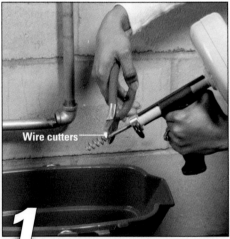

Wire cutters

1 To ream out a pipe, buy an inexpensive hand-crank auger and cut off its tip with a pair of wire cutters so it can fit into a clogged pipe. The resulting tool will run through straight sections of pipe only. **Shut off the water** and drain the line.

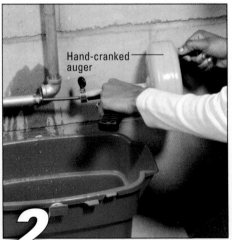

Hand-cranked auger

2 Disassemble the pipe at both ends. Push the auger through, turning the crank if necessary. Pull the auger out and flush the pipe with running water.

STANLEY PRO TIP

Replacing pipes

If water runs slowly throughout the house, replacing a few of the first pipes that enter the house may help substantially. If these pipes are exposed in a basement or crawlspace, replacing them will not be difficult.

Start as near to the street as possible and remove all the pipes—both horizontals and verticals—that you can easily reach. Before installing the new pipes, use a hose to run water backward through the pipes that you did not remove. If you will install copper pipe, connect it to a galvanized pipe with a dielectric union (page 135).

If a single faucet is sluggish, you may be able to remove and replace the short pipe (usually horizontal) to which the stop valve is attached. Often this pipe is clogged, and you'll see significant improvement when you replace it.

INSTALLING A WATER FILTER

Water from a public utility must meet strict health requirements. If you think that your water is unsafe) have it tested by a local health department, the utility company, or an extension service office of a state university.

Even safe water may have a bad taste or odor, and it may produce stains. A filter could be the solution.

If chlorine causes water to taste bad, a temporary solution is to run water into a pitcher and let it sit in the refrigerator overnight. By morning much of the chlorine odor and flavor will be gone, making the water more palatable.

Softening water
Hard water—water laden with minerals—can hinder the lathering action of detergent, making it difficult to clean clothes. Hard water may also stain fixtures and ceramic tiles and clog pipes. A water softener uses ionization to solve these problems. It also can remove rust from water.

PRESTART CHECKLIST

☐ **TIME**
An hour or two

☐ **TOOLS**
Tools for working with copper or galvanized pipe, groove-joint pliers, canister wrench

☐ **SKILLS**
Working with copper or galvanized supply pipe

☐ **PREP**
Find a convenient location to install the filter so that you can change cartridges easily

☐ **MATERIALS**
Water filter, pipe adapters, shutoff valve, perhaps a jumper wire with clamps

1 **Turn off the main water shutoff valve.** On the house side of the main shutoff, break into the supply line. If the pipes are galvanized, find a union or cut with a hacksaw and install a union (pages 134–135). Cut into a copper line using a tubing cutter.

2 Install a ball or gate shutoff valve on the house side of the water filter. Remove the insides of the valve before sweating the valve body in place. (Some plumbers like to install a bypass loop with additional stop valves so water can be rerouted should the entire filter unit need replacing.)

Problem-solving filters

A plumbing inspector or local contractor should know which type of filter works best for the water in your area. Here are some qualities of the most popular filter types.

PROBLEM	SOLUTION
Soap does not lather well; soap scum residue on clothes and fixtures	Water softener
Rust stains	Water softener or charcoal filter
Rotten-egg smell due to high sulfur content	Oxidizing filter or a chlorination feeder system
Chlorine odor and taste	Carbon filter
Water appears cloudy or dirty	Particle filter
Harmful bacteria or chemicals suspected	Reverse-osmosis filter

3 Purchase the adapters you need to connect the filter to your size and type of pipe. (These parts may come in a kit, but be sure they fit your pipes.) Install the adapters on either side of the filter. Hold the filter in place and measure for cutting the pipe that emerges from the new shutoff valve.

4 Slide nuts and ferrules onto the pipes on either side. Slip the filter onto the pipes, slide the ferrules and nuts over to the filter, and tighten the nuts.

5 Place a filter cartridge in the canister and twist the canister onto the filter unit. Tighten with a special canister wrench.

Undersink filters

If your main concern is the quality of your drinking water, there's no need to filter all the water entering the house. Install a small filter under the kitchen sink and hook it to the cold water. A unit like this can be installed simply by connecting tubes to the stop valve and faucet.

INSTALLING AN ON-DEMAND WATER HEATER

Long popular in Europe on-demand (or tankless) water heaters provide hot water seconds after turning on the faucet.

A compact on-demand unit can be tucked into a cabinet or closet. It costs more than a standard water heater but uses less energy, so it may pay for itself in a few years.

It heats 3 to 5 gallons per minute, plenty for a dishwasher or a shower, but probably not enough for both at the same time.

Installing one calls for running gas lines and supply lines and installing a vent. These pages show general installation steps; the manufacturer's literature provides more specific directions. A gas unit is shown; electric units are also

PRESTART CHECKLIST

☐ **TIME**
At least a day to run a gas line, install a vent, and connect plumbing for an on-demand water heater

☐ **TOOLS**
Drill, screwdriver, groove-joint pliers, tools for running water supply and gas lines, tin snips

☐ **SKILLS**
Working with supply and gas pipe

☐ **PREP**
Go over your plans with an inspector to make sure the installation will be safe

☐ **MATERIALS**
On-demand water heater, gas pipe and fittings, supply pipe and fittings, vent pipe and fittings

HOW AN ON-DEMAND WATER HEATER WORKS

Flue pipe · Flue · Hot water · Cold water · Heat exchanger · Main burner · Pressure-relief valve · Temperature adjustment · Pressure-relief tube · Hot water · Gas · Cold water

Water passes through the heat exchanger, where it is instantly heated by the main burner. Valves automatically turn on and off as needed.

1 Install the water heater in a code-approved location. The manufacturer's specifications determine acceptable distances between the unit and vent pipes and combustible surfaces. Make sure the room is well ventilated. Mount it using the hardware provided.

Mounting hook

2 Attach the pressure regulator, which ensures safe flow of gas to the unit. Run an approved gas line (page 25). Use ¾-inch pipe for any runs more than 10 feet; ½-inch pipe can be used for shorter runs. Connect the line to the regulator, turn on the gas, and test for leaks.

Pressure regulator

Gas-rated pipe-thread tape

Union

Drip leg

3 Copper is recommended for the water supply pipe, at least for 3 feet before and after the water heater. Install a pressure-relief valve (some manufacturers provide it) before the ball valve on the outgoing hot water line.

Pressure-relief valve

Hot water line

Cold water line

Ball valve

Setting water temperature

When you first use the unit, turn the gas valve switch off and wait for five minutes to clear out any gas (check the manufacturer's specific instructions). If you smell gas test for leaks. Once you are sure there are no leaks, turn the switch on and turn on the hot water of a nearby faucet. An automatic spark will light the pilot light, which will fire the burner. After 10 to 30 seconds, the pilot will go off while the burner remains on.

Turn on the faucet's hot water to maximum flow; wait a minute for the water to reach maximum heat. Turn the temperature dial counterclockwise to lower the heat and clockwise to increase the heat. If incoming water becomes colder in the winter, you may need to turn up the dial to achieve the desired temperature.

Installing vent piping

The water heater must be vented to the outside of the house in a code-approved manner, using flue pipes at least 5 inches in diameter (follow manufacturer's instructions). For the flue to draw efficiently, maximize the vertical rise—it should be at least 6 feet—and use as few elbows as possible. Test the flue before using to make sure it draws (page 145).

Flue pipe

Maintaining A Water Pump

Water pressure for water-well installations is maintained by a pressure tank installed in the line between the well pump and the residence.

Pressure to the tank is regulated by an electric switch that turns the pump on when pressure is low and off when the proper tank pressure is reached. The pressure switch may require periodic maintenance.

Before performing any maintenance steps on a pressure switch, **turn off the power to the switch.** The current required to run a well pump is potentially deadly. Open your breaker box and look for the breaker marked "well" or "pump." It may be a single large amperage (30 amp or more) breaker or two lower amperage breakers in tandem. If you're not sure which breaker is the right one, turn the main breaker to the house. (Do not leave the main power to the house off for periods long enough to defrost frozen foods or reduce the heat long enough to freeze pipes.)

If maintenance steps do not return the pump to service, replace the switch.

Prestart Checklist

☐ **Time**
An hour or so to perform routine maintenance and reset pump pressure switch

☐ **Tools**
Screwdrivers, emery cloth, pliers, small open-end wrenches

☐ **Skills**
Cleaning electrical contacts

☐ **Prep**
Shut off power to the pump

1 **Turn off the power to the well** and locate the pressure switch. It is likely to have some kind of plastic or metal cover secured with screws. Unscrew them and lift off the cover. Set it aside so it won't get damaged. (The easiest thing to do in a cramped well house is to step on a switch cover.)

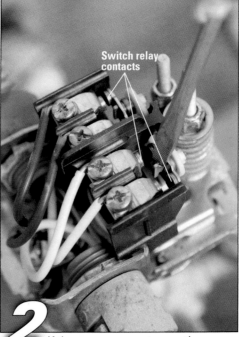

Switch relay contacts

2 If the pump was not operating, pry back the switch relay contacts and inspect them for pitting or burning. Clean the contacts (below) and perform any necessary pressure adjustments.

Cleaning the contacts

Emery cloth

To clean the pressure switch contacts, slide a length of emery cloth between them and pull the cloth across them several times. Reverse the cloth and repeat the process on the other side until all the contacts (usually eight or more) are shiny. Use pliers to unscrew an aerator from the end of a faucet spout and clean all the little parts. Replace the aerator if it is damaged.

Adjusting the switch

Pressure adjustment nut

Pressure switches are installed in conjunction with pressure gauges, and the switches are set to turn on at low pressure and off at a higher pressure (typically 20 and 40 psi, respectively). Adjustment instructions usually can be found on the inside of the switch cover. Use wrenches to turn the adjustment screws, following the manufacturer's instructions.

MAINTAINING A WATER SOFTENER

High concentrations of magnesium and calcium in water make it "hard." Soap and cleaning products do not work well in hard water, and the minerals stick to the sides of pipes in the form of scale, reducing the pipe's ability to conduct water or heat.

A water softener replaces the calcium and magnesium with sodium or potassium, which don't cause the same adverse effects. Replacement of the harmful minerals takes place in the softener, in which the hard water runs over a bed of beads coated with sodium ions. Periodically the softener needs to be recharged with sodium ions and will flush the accumulated calcium/magnesium water out a drain line.

Although a water softener is a simple device, brine lines and the injector filter in the system can become clogged. Inspect the brine tank and remove any crust with a vacuum cleaner. If you see iron deposits, use an iron-removing agent to clean the softener. If the timer or control unit is faulty, you can remove and replace it, but repair is best left to a trained technician.

PRESTART CHECKLIST

☐ **TIME**
About 2 hours to remove, clean, and reassemble the brine line and injector screen

☐ **TOOLS**
Needle-nose pliers, screwdriver, kitchen baster

☐ **SKILLS**
Making simple plumbing connections and disconnections

☐ **PREP**
Divert water with bypass valve

Checking the brine line and injector screen

1 Open the bypass valve so the line won't run water while you're working on it. Loosen the compression nut and disconnect the line. Inspect it for deposits, which you can often clean easily with a small screwdriver or miniature plastic bottle brush. Flush the line using a kitchen baster.

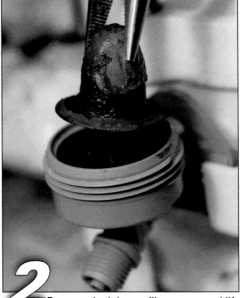

2 Remove the injector filter cover and lift out the screen. Check the nozzle (see the unit owner's manual). Clean the screen in soapy water and reinstall. Replace the filter screen if it is damaged or cannot be cleaned adequately.

WATER SOFTENER PLUMBING

Soft hot water — Water heater — Softener — Salt storage — Soft water — Bypass valve — Hard water — Hard water (to fixtures)

REMOVING & REPLACING A BATHTUB

Bathtubs and showers sustain heavy use and are frequently scoured, so it's not surprising they eventually need to be replaced. This chapter shows how to remove an old tub and install a new one, as well as how to install a tub or shower enclosure. If you need to install a new tub or shower with new plumbing, see the chapter "Installing a New Bathroom" (pages 170–203).

Some inspectors don't require an inspection for fixture replacements. As long as no new drain or supply pipes are to be installed, no permit will be required.

But check with your building department; this is a major job. It's to your benefit to have an inspector sign off on it. If you are running new lines for a shower (pages 190–191), be sure to schedule inspections.

Plan the whole job

Replacing a tub or installing a shower is a remodeling project, involving not only plumbing but also carpentry, wall repair, and perhaps tiling. Count the cost and prepare for all aspects of the job. Allow yourself plenty of time. Just patching and painting a wall can take several days.

Leaks below a bathroom

If water drips from the ceiling below a bathroom, incompletely sealed walls and floors or cracked tiles are usually the cause—not necessarily the plumbing. Even a small gap in caulking or grout can provide a pathway for stray water. By the time you notice a leak, there may be serious damage to walls, ceilings, and framing members. Every few months inspect the grout and caulk. Encourage family members to dry off in the tub or to use an absorbent rug so that water does not puddle on the floor.

Replacing a tub or installing a shower is a major project that can take more than a week.

CHAPTER PREVIEW

Removing a tub
page 162

Replacing a tub
page 165

Installing a prefab tub surround
page 168

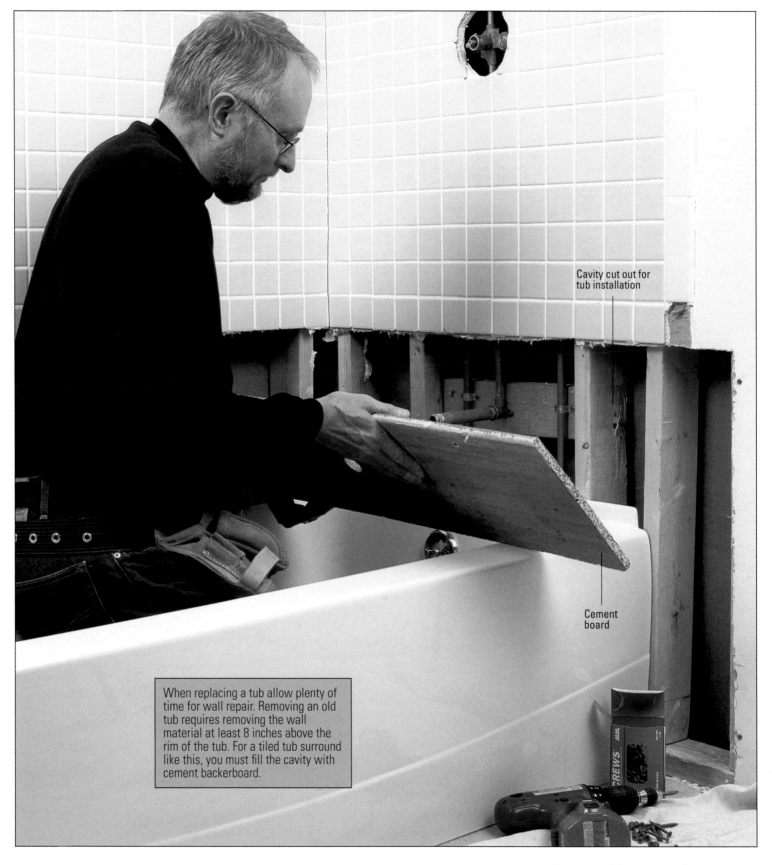

Cavity cut out for tub installation

Cement board

When replacing a tub allow plenty of time for wall repair. Removing an old tub requires removing the wall material at least 8 inches above the rim of the tub. For a tiled tub surround like this, you must fill the cavity with cement backerboard.

REMOVING A TUB

If your tub is chipped, difficult to keep clean, or just plain ugly, consider refinishing rather than replacing. You'll probably find several companies in the phone book that use various methods. Check samples of their work and read their guarantees carefully. Note that no refinishing method can produce a finish that is as hard and durable as a new tub.

Plan and prepare

If you decide to remove and preserve your old tub, measure it and make sure you will be able to get it past other fixtures and out the door. Remove the sink or the toilet if they will be in the way.

A drop cloth is probably not enough protection for the floor. Cut and tape pieces of plywood to the floor and cover with a drop cloth.

Sometimes old tiles can be removed and reused. However at least some will probably break. Either find tiles to match or plan to retile the walls. Or install a solid-surface tub surround (pages 168–169).

PRESTART CHECKLIST

☐ **TIME**
A full day

☐ **TOOLS**
Screwdriver, strainer wrench, flat pry bar, crowbar, hammer, drill, utility knife, sledgehammer

☐ **SKILL**
Basic carpentry skills, dismantling a trap

☐ **PREP**
Locate access to the tub plumbing in the basement or in an adjacent room; if necessary install an access panel (opposite)

☐ **MATERIALS**
Plywood and drop cloth to protect the floor

1 From inside the tub unscrew and remove the overflow cover plate. If a drain assembly is attached to it, pull it out. (A drain assembly with a plunger is shown.) Unscrew and remove the mounting bracket if there is one.

- Drain assembly
- Plunger
- Overflow cover plate

2 To disconnect the drain you may need to remove a screw or two and remove the strainer. Or you may need to lift out a stopper and a rocker assembly (page 166). Use a strainer wrench to remove the drain flange.

- Strainer wrench
- Drain flange
- Strainer

WASTE-AND-OVERFLOW INSTALLATIONS

- Overflow pipe
- Overflow pipe
- No-hub coupling
- Shoe
- Shoe
- P-trap
- Drum trap

The waste-and-overflow (WO) unit may connect directly to a drain trap or, in older systems, to a drainpipe that leads to a drum trap. It may connect with a slip nut or a no-hub coupling.

Access opening

Waste-and-
overflow unit

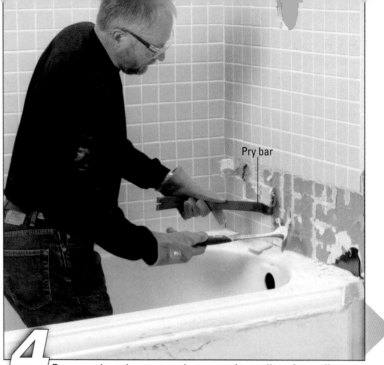

Pry bar

3 From an access panel behind the tub or from below, disconnect the waste-and-overflow (WO) unit from the drain line. Depending on the installation you may need to unscrew a slip nut or loosen the screws on a no-hub coupling (see page 165 for alternatives). If the parts are cemented plastic, you'll have to cut through a pipe. Remove the WO unit from the tub. (You may not need to remove the old WO unit if it will fit exactly on the new tub. Measure carefully.)

4 Remove the tub spout and remove the wall surface all around the tub to a height of about 8 inches. (If there are tub faucet handles, leave them in place if they are at least 8 inches above the tub.) Use a flat pry bar or putty knife to pry off tiles. Cut through drywall with a drywall saw. If the wall is plaster, use a reciprocating saw, taking care not to cut into the studs. Pry off or unscrew nails and screws.

WHAT IF ...
You need to install an access panel?

Drywall saw

¼" plywood
or hardboard

1 If there is no easy access to the plumbing behind the tub, install an access panel in the adjacent room. Use a drywall saw to cut a hole in the wall surface, spanning from stud to stud.

2 Screw 2×2 cleats to either side of the opening. Cut a piece of plywood 2 or 3 inches larger than the opening. Paint it to match the wall and attach it with screws.

REFRESHER COURSE
Add a ready-made panel

Purchase a ready-made plumbing-access panel for a quicker installation and a neater appearance. Follow manufacturer's instructions for cutting the hole and installation.

REMOVING A TUB continued

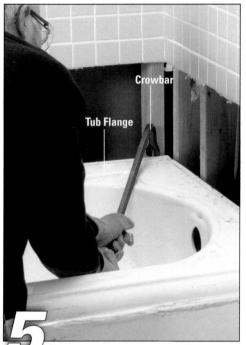

5 Pry out or unscrew any nails or screws anchoring the tub flange to studs. Where the tub rests on the floor, use a utility knife to cut through a bead of caulk, if there is one. Use a crowbar to pry the tub an inch or so away from the back wall.

6 Unless the tub is an old-fashioned claw-foot or other type of stand-alone, it will fit fairly tightly between studs on either side. That means you probably can't slide it out unless you cut away the wall surface on both sides. The best way is usually to lift the tub on one end. Pry up one end of the tub first with a crowbar, then with 2×4s. Working with a helper stand the tub upright.

STANLEY PRO TIP
Removing a cast-iron tub

A cast-iron tub weighs 300 to 400 pounds—a bear to remove. If you plan to discard it anyway, break it into manageable pieces. Wear eye protection and gloves. Cover it with an old drop cloth (to prevent pieces from flying) and hit it repeatedly with a sledgehammer.

Choosing a tub

Acrylic or fiberglass tubs are inexpensive, light, and easy to install. Some have finishes that are fairly durable, but they may become dull in time. An enameled steel tub has a sturdier finish but lacks insulating properties; bathwater will cool quickly. Enameled cast iron is the most expensive and heaviest material but may be worth the cost because it retains a gleaming finish for decades, fills quietly, and keeps water warm the longest.

Enameled steel

Acrylic

Enameled cast iron

REPLACING A TUB

An inexpensive replacement tub may be narrower than the old tub. Many people find a narrow tub uncomfortable, so buy one that's comfortable. Most tubs fit into a 60-inch opening, but some older ones may be longer. Measure to make sure your replacement tub will fit.

Some spa or whirlpool tubs fit a standard tub opening. Installing one is not much more work than installing a standard tub. A spa or whirlpool needs to plug into a GFCI (Ground Fault Circuit Interrupter) electrical receptacle. For a more elaborate whirlpool installation, see pages 192–195.

Preparing the floor and the walls
If the bead of caulk at the base of a tub has even a small gap, water that puddles on the bathroom floor will seep underneath the tub, quickly damaging any bare wood. To be safe install protective flooring on the entire floor, including the area the tub will cover.

PRESTART CHECKLIST

☐ **TIME**
   About a day to install a replacement tub where there is an existing drain

☐ **TOOLS**
   Drill, torpedo level, screwdriver, strainer wrench, putty knife, pry bar, hammer

☐ **SKILLS**
   Making drain connections in a tight spot, basic carpentry skills

☐ **PREP**
   Clear the area; cover the floor with plywood and a drop cloth

☐ **MATERIALS**
   Tub, waste-and-overflow unit, plumber's putty, pipe-thread tape, cement backerboard and tiles or other wall-finishing material, caulk

1 Check the drain and replace any damaged parts. Consult the manufacturer's literature and measure to make sure the drain is in the correct location. Purchase a waste-and-overflow unit (page 166) and determine how you will connect it to the drain line (below). Screw ledger boards to the studs at the height recommended by the manufacturer. Ideally the finish flooring material should run under the tub.

DRAIN CONNECTIONS

Waste-and-overflow (WO) units have been attached to drain lines in various ways over the years. Here are some of the most common methods. A rubber no-hub coupling (sometimes called a mission coupling) may be used to connect to a cast-iron or a plastic drain line. Usually the WO tailpiece connects to the drain via a slip nut. Whichever method you use plan so that you won't have a nasty surprise after the tub has been wrestled into position.

2 Working with the tub turned on its side, dry-fit the overflow tube and the shoe. Make any necessary cuts, then make permanent connections. Place the gasket on the overflow flange, position it behind the overflow hole, and insert the linkage.

Overflow tube
Gasket
Linkage

3 Inside the tub slip the screws into the overflow trim. Hold the overflow flange in place and hand-tighten one of the screws. Start the second screw and tighten both with a screwdriver.

Overflow cover plate

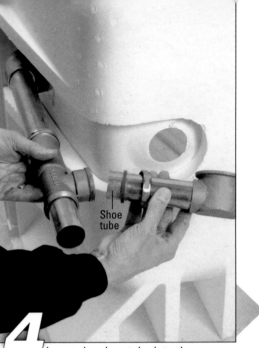

4 Insert the shoe tube into the opening in the overflow tube and slip the other end up into the drain hole.

Shoe tube

WHAT IF ...
You have an extra-deep tub?

Extension tube

If the tub is deeper than usual, the opening in the overflow tube may be too high for the shoe.

If so cut and install an extension for the overflow tube.

In some cases an extension is included with the waste-and-overflow unit.

BATHTUB WASTE-AND-OVERFLOW ASSEMBLIES

Lever
Overflow tube
Body
Linkage
Plunger

Lever
Overflow tube
Body
Linkage
Rocker arm

A plunger design has a brass cylinder (or plunger) that slides up and down through the overflow pipe to open or close the drain. A brass pop-up drain has a rocker arm that pivots to raise or lower the stopper. Many plastic units have no interior mechanism; instead the stopper itself is raised and lowered by the bather. This type drains more slowly than the other two.

Strainer
wrench

Plumber's
putty

5 Inside the tub place a rope of plumber's putty under the strainer or drain flange. Hold the shoe with one hand while you screw in the flange. Finish tightening with a strainer wrench. Clean away the squeezed-out putty with a plastic putty knife.

6 Before tilting and moving the tub, plan the move so you avoid damaging the waste-and-overflow unit, which protrudes below the tub. It may work best to rest the tub on 2×4s part of the time. Move the tub into position with a helper. You may have to tilt the tub as shown. Slide it into the opening and gently lower the tub in place. You might want a helper to guide the overflow tube into the drain line (see Step 8) while you do this. Slide the drop cloth or any other protective material out from under the tub. Protect the tub interior.

Torpedo level

7 Check the tub for level; an out-of-level tub may not drain completely. Attach the tub to the studs according to manufacturer's directions. You probably will nail or screw through an acrylic tub flange (shown). For a metal tub drive nails just above the flange.

Waste-and-overflow
tailpiece

8 Working from behind or below, connect the waste-and-overflow tailpiece to the drain line, using one of the methods shown on page 165. To test for leaks close the stopper and fill the tub. Open the stopper; watch and feel for any sign of wetness.

Backerboard

9 To fill the gap above the tub, cut and install strips of cement backerboard, which is more moisture-resistant than green drywall. Install tiles to fit, allow the adhesive to set for a day, and apply grout. Apply silicone or tub-and-tile caulk where the tiles meet the tub.

INSTALLING A PREFAB TUB SURROUND

A prefab surround quickly gives a tub and shower area a fresh look. High-quality units have durable finishes along with convenient niches and towel bars.

Make sure the unit you buy has panels with flanges that overlap so you don't have to cut the panels to fit precisely. With a standard 60-inch-wide opening, you probably won't have to cut at all, other than making holes for the spout and the faucet control or handles.

Preparing the wall surface

The walls should be smooth and even. Scrape away any peeling paint and patch any cracks or weak spots. Apply primer paint to the walls to ensure a strong bond with the adhesive. It's possible to install over tile, but the panels will have gaps at the front edges, which must be covered with tile or acrylic.

PRESTART CHECKLIST

☐ **TIME**
Several hours to install a solid-surface tub surround

☐ **TOOLS**
Level, drill, caulk gun (or tube), notched trowel, tape measure, utility knife

☐ **SKILLS**
Measuring and drilling holes

☐ **PREP**
Clean and prime the walls, close the drain, place a drop cloth in the tub; remove the spout and the faucet control or handles

☐ **MATERIALS**
Tub surround kit, manufacturer's recommended adhesive, tub-and-tile caulk, masking tape, cardboard for a template

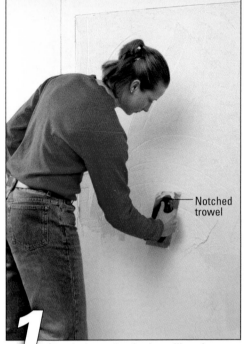

1 Check the order for installing the panels in the instructions. Position and mark the first panel to be installed, the center one in this case. Using a notched trowel or caulk gun (as specified by the manufacturer), apply adhesive to the area. Apply evenly so the panel will not be wavy.

Notched trowel

2 Press the center panel into place and smooth it with your palm. Install other pieces in the same way, following the manufacturer's installation procedures.

Center panel

PREFAB TUB SURROUND

Showerhead

Faucet control

Spout

Available acrylic or polystyrene tub surrounds may have a modern, decorative, or retro look and come in various colors. While these units are less permanent than tile, they install quickly, are relatively inexpensive, and will last for many years.

3 Place the piece that will cover the plumbing wall on a scrap piece of plywood. Make a template and cut holes using a utility knife or drill bits and hole saws of the correct size. Install the endpieces in the same way as the backpieces.

Utility knife

Overlapping flange

Masking tape

4 The panels can be adjusted before the adhesive hardens, which usually occurs about a half hour after application. Apply pieces of masking tape to ensure that their top edges form a straight line. (The bottom edges will be caulked, so they can be slightly uneven.)

Tub-and-tile caulk

5 Apply caulk to the space between the strips and a bead where the panels meet the tub. Practice applying even pressure to the tube while drawing smoothly along the joint. After applying the caulk smooth it with your finger. Clean any mistakes with a damp sponge.

MAKE A TEMPLATE

Cardboard

Spout stub out

To prevent mistakes in cutting holes, cut a piece of cardboard the same width as the panel to be installed. For each hole measure up from the tub and over from the corner panel and mark the center of each hole. (If the panel will overlap the corner panel, take that into account.) Cut holes with a utility knife.

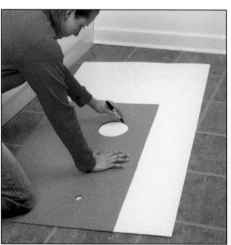

Hold the template against the wall as a trial run. Once you are certain the holes are correct, place the template over the panel and mark it for drilling the holes.

WHAT IF ...
You're installing a shower faucet?

If you need to replace the shower faucet, remove the wall surface. Follow the plumbing instructions on pages 190–191. Cover the wall with cement backerboard or water-resistant drywall (greenboard) .

INSTALLING A NEW BATHROOM

Installing a new bathroom with a toilet, sink, and tub is a challenging do-it-yourself project. You'll need a thorough understanding of plumbing systems and techniques. Developing a sound plan and working with a good helper will help ensure you get everything right.

Getting a handle on the plumbing

The following pages show how to install the three major bathroom plumbing fixtures in a common configuration. You'll find quite a few variations on this basic arrangement. Your situation may call for pipe runs that differ from those shown, so you may need to develop a unique plan that suits your home.

You'll need a good understanding of the basic skills and techniques of plumbing. Study the first chapter of this book, then determine how you will connect the new plumbing to the old. Pay special attention to the drain vents and make sure you use pipe types and sizes that conform to code. If possible hire a professional plumber to spend an hour or two giving you advice. This modest investment could save time and money later.

The entire project

Whether you are remodeling an existing bathroom or installing one in a new addition, you will need carpentry skills. Modifying the framing sometimes can make the plumbing work easier. Plan and install the plumbing so it damages joists and studs as little as possible; reinforce any framing members that have been compromised. It's usually best to run any electrical lines after the plumbing has been installed.

CHAPTER PREVIEW

A complete bath installation calls for thorough planning, sound plumbing skills, and patience.

Bathroom specs
page 172

The overall plan
page 173

Preparing the site
page 174

Running drain and vent lines
page 176

Running copper supply lines
page 182

Capping off supply lines allows you to test your work before installing final fittings; cap the lines, turn on the water, and check for leaks. Caps also keep out debris that could later clog faucets and spouts.

Tape off all drain openings or buy ready-made caps or fittings with knockouts.

Roughing in supply, drain, and vent lines is the most demanding part of a plumbing project. Once an inspector has approved the essentials of your project, you can finish the walls and install fixtures, hardware, and trim. In the meantime seal all drain openings to keep debris from falling into drain lines and sewer gas from entering the house.

Installing a bathroom vanity sink
page 184

Connecting a toilet
page 186

Installing a pedestal sink
page 188

Hooking up a shower or tub faucet
page 190

Installing a whirlpool tub
page 192

Building a shower enclosure
page 196

Installing a luxury shower
page 200

Building a wet wall
page 202

BATHROOM SPECS

Specifications for the placement of plumbing fixtures and the dimensions of pipes are intended to make the bathroom a comfortable space with plenty of capacity for incoming water and outgoing drains and vents. The specs shown here will meet the requirements of most building departments, but check local codes to be sure.

Bathroom layout

Where you place the toilet, sink, and tub may depend partly on the existing plumbing. Most homes have a wet wall, which is an interior wall that is thicker than most walls because it contains the main stack. Minimize long horizontal runs of drain and vent pipes by installing fixtures close to the wet wall.

Plan for a layout that is comfortable and convenient. The following pages show how to install a basic 5×8-foot bathroom— just enough room for the three major fixtures with adequate space between them.

Most codes require that no fixture be closer than 15 inches from a toilet's centerline. There must be at least 24 inches of space in front of the toilet (it's OK for a door to swing into this space).

Sinks and vanity sink tops range from 20 to 30 inches in width. A standard bathtub is 60 inches by 32 inches. If your plans call for a larger tub, alter the layout to fit it. The tub shown on pages 192–195 will be 36 inches wide once framing and tiles are installed.

The framing—not the finished wall— must be 60 inches wide to accommodate a standard tub length. If the opening is any smaller, the tub will not fit; if the opening is more than ¼ inch too long, making a tight seal along the wall will be difficult. Framing must be almost perfectly square.

Choosing materials

These plans call for 3-inch PVC pipe for the main drain and the short length leading from the toilet to the drain, and 2-inch PVC for the other drain lines and the vents. Local codes may call for a 4-inch main drain, and some plumbers prefer to run larger vent pipes.

Cast-iron drainpipe is making a comeback in some areas because it's quieter than plastic pipe. However cast-iron pipe should be installed by a pro. (You can reduce the noise of water draining through PVC by wrapping the pipe with insulation.)

Rigid copper pipe is the most common material for supply lines. However PEX or other plastic materials may be permitted in your area. Bathrooms are usually supplied with ½-inch pipe. For maximum water pressure, however, run ¾-inch pipe to the bathroom and use ½-inch for short runs only.

MINIMUM CLEARANCES

At least 15"

At least 15"

At least 4"

Width varies

At least 2"

Typically 32"

60"

Door should swing freely

At least 36" to nearest wall

24"

24"

At least 15"

A bathroom with a 5×8-foot interior space allows the minimum clearances that most municipal codes require for fixtures.

While exploring layout options maintain these clearances in your plan to assure ease of use and installation.

Standard dimensions

Make sure your plans follow these standard specs:

Drain and vent pipes

Toilet: 3–4 inches; 2-inch vent
Sink: 2-inch drain, connecting to 3-inch horizontal run; 2-inch vent
Tub/shower: 2-inch drain, connecting to 3-inch horizontal run; 2-inch vent
Main stack: 3–4 inches
Sink drain: 19 inches above floor
Toilet drain: 12 inches from wall

Supply pipes

Tub/shower: ¾-inch pipe
Sink, toilet: ½-inch pipe
Sink stub out: 19 inches above floor, 8–10 inches apart
Toilet stub out: 8 inches above floor

Tub/shower fittings

Tub control(s): 28 inches above floor
Spout: 6 inches above top edge
Showerhead arm: About 76 inches above floor
Shower control: 48 inches above floor

THE OVERALL PLAN

Once you have decided on the basic layout and have a general idea of how the drain and vents will run, make specific plans. Measure the existing room plan for new framing right down to the inch; take into account the thickness of the wall finishing material—usually ½ inch for drywall and perhaps another ⅜ inch for wall tiles. (See pages 40–41 for tips on producing drawings.)

Vents

Start by figuring the vents (pages 14–15). As a general rule the drain line for each fixture should connect to a vent within a few feet of the fixture. A true vent never has water running through it, although wet venting—routing drain water through a vent— is permitted in some situations.

This plan calls for running a new vent up through the ceiling and either tying into an existing vent in the attic or running out through the roof. Or you may be able to tie into an existing vent on the same floor.

Consider how new lines will affect existing vents. For instance if you install an upper-story bathroom and tie into an existing stack, you may end up draining water through a pipe that is now used as a vent.

Drains

In this plan a new main drain line for the bathroom runs down to the floor below. If the new bathroom is on the first floor, you can probably simply tie into the house's main drain line in the basement or crawlspace below. If the new bathroom is on the second floor, the bathroom's main drain will have to travel through the wall on the first floor and down to the basement or crawlspace. (See page 175 for how to trace the location of a drainpipe through an intervening story.)

If a drain line is nearby, you may choose to run a new drainpipe so it will join to it, rather than running a new line. However, it may be difficult to run a toilet's 3-inch (or 4-inch) drain to an existing line, especially if you have to go through joists.

In the room below the installation, the drain lines turn outward at 45-degree angles to avoid running 3- or 4-inch pipe through studs. If the room below is finished, you will need to build a soffit around these pipes (page 174) or run the pipes through the studs. This plan calls for a 3-inch horizontal drain; codes may permit 2-inch pipe.

Seal openings where pipes enter attics or crawlspaces to prevent drafts and to act as fire stops.

BATHROOM SUPPLY, DRAIN-WASTE-VENT OVERVIEW

The pipes supplying hot and cold water can run in any convenient configuration. However by running separate ¾-inch lines from near the water heater to the shower, water pressure (and temperature) will not be affected when someone uses another fixture in the house.

Waste/overflow

2" vent

2" vent

2" vent

Tee

2" trap

Tee

Cleanout

45° elbow

45° elbow

3×2 Y

4×3 reducing closet bend

Low-heel vent fitting

3×2 Y

Street elbow

Preparing The Site

A new bathroom often requires an extra-wide "wet wall" built of 2×6s or two side-by-side 2×4 walls. Because only 2-inch pipe runs through the walls, codes may permit a standard 2×4 wall. Except in an area with a warm climate, avoid running pipes in an exterior wall.

To convert existing space to a bathroom, you may need to move a wall. Before removing a wall make sure it's not load-bearing; check with a carpenter or structural engineer if you are not sure.

Whether you are framing a new space or remodeling an existing space, make sure the framing accommodates the tub.

Remove drywall or plaster from the areas where you will run plumbing. Clear out all cabinets, fixtures, and other obstructions.

If wiring is in the path of plumbing, **shut off power** to the circuit and test to make sure. You may want to remove cables and reinstall them after the plumbing is in place.

Prestart Checklist

☐ **Time**
A day or more to remove wallcoverings; about half a day to mark for positions of fixtures

☐ **Tools**
Framing square, tape measure, hammer, pry bar, level, drill, hole saw or jigsaw, circular saw, reciprocating saw

☐ **Skills**
Basic carpentry skills, planning for plumbing runs, careful measuring

☐ **Prep**
Have your plumbing plans approved by your building department.

☐ **Materials**
Lumber for any framing that's needed

1 Determine the exact center of the toilet drain. For most toilets this is 12 inches from the finished wall surface. If you will install ½-inch drywall, measure 12½ inches out from the framing. (Toilets with drains set 10 or 14 inches from the wall are available, though usually in white only.)

Framing square

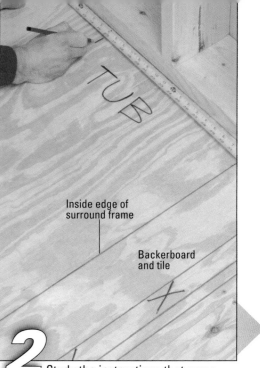

Inside edge of surround frame

Backerboard and tile

2 Study the instructions that come with the tub and the waste-and-overflow assembly to determine exactly where the tub drain needs to be (pages 165–167). Mark the tub outline on the floor. In this case the framing, backerboard, and tiling for a whirlpool tub must be added.

PLANNING FOR FINISHING THE ROOM BELOW

2×2

Attach with screws or nails.

Drywall

If the room below is finished, plan to frame around the plumbing to create a soffit. Simple 2×2 framing can be covered with drywall. To minimize noise wrap the pipes with insulation.

Tub supply location

Sink drain, marked for cutting with hole saw

Notch marked for drain/vent fitting

3 Mark the bottom plate for the location of the vent and drainpipes. Position the tub/shower vent so it will not interfere with the installation of the faucet (pages 190–191). You may need to move a stud or two to make room for the tub/shower faucet. Also mark where the supply lines will enter the room. Check all your measurements twice.

Circular saw

Hole for toilet flange

Reciprocating saw

4 Use a hole saw or saber saw to cut a hole in the floor for the toilet drain. Use a circular saw and a reciprocating saw to cut a section of flooring large enough to allow you to run the plumbing. Wherever you need to run pipes through joists, give yourself plenty of room to work.

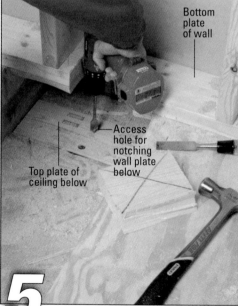

Bottom plate of wall

Access hole for notching wall plate below

Top plate of ceiling below

5 Drill holes or cut notches as needed. To make room for the toilet drain (pages 176– 178), a large notch must be cut in the bottom plate of the wall and the top plate of the ceiling below.

Holesaw

6 Using a hole saw cut 2¼-inch holes for the tub and sink drains. Remove a 12×14-inch section of flooring for the tub/shower drain—cut a larger opening if you don't have access from behind or below.

STANLEY PRO TIP

Running pipe through an intervening story

Light shining down wall cavity

If the new bathroom is on the second story, you will need to run a drainpipe down the wall of a first-story room. Don't tear into the wall to confirm the drain location. Instead cut the bathroom drain hole and position a bright light over it. Take measurements and drill a test hole in the basement. If the location is right, you'll see the light.

RUNNING DRAIN AND VENT LINES

Drain and vent lines must be positioned precisely, so you should install them before the supply pipes. It may be possible to simplify supply runs by moving a vent pipe over a few inches.

If you must run drainpipes across a floor, carefully calculate the amount of vertical space available; you must slope the drainpipe at ⅛ to ¼ inch drop per foot.

Sometimes it's difficult to visualize how drainpipes will travel through walls and floors. Once you start assembling the pieces and testing them for fit, you may need to modify your plans.

Some inspectors prefer horizontal vent pipes to be sloped so condensation can run back to the drainpipes; others don't consider this important. To be on the safe side, slope the vents.

PRESTART CHECKLIST

☐ **TIME**
Working with a helper, about two days

☐ **TOOLS**
PVC saw or power saw, level, carpentry tools

☐ **SKILLS**
Cutting and joining PVC pipe, running pipes through walls, connecting new pipe to old

☐ **PREP**
Have your plans approved by an inspector; prepare the room (pages 174–175)

☐ **MATERIALS**
PVC pipe and fittings to meet codes, PVC primer and cement, pipe strap, fitting to join to existing drainpipe

A. Running the main drain line

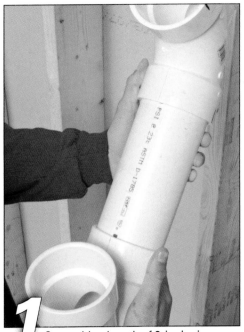

1 Start with a length of 3-inch pipe long enough to reach the basement or crawlspace. You may be able to cut it to exact length after it has been installed. Dry-fit a Y-fitting, a length of pipe, and a low-heel vent fitting as shown, aligning them precisely.

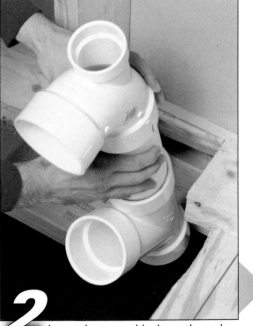

2 Insert the assembly down through the wall plates and temporarily anchor it. Make sure the Y-fitting is low enough to allow for installation of the other drain lines (Step 2, page 179). Once you are sure of the configuration, pull up the assembly and prime and glue the pieces.

FRAMING FOR A TOILET BEND

Wall plate

Cleat

Blocking

Cut joist

A joist may be in the way of a toilet bend; if so remove as much flooring as necessary to get at the framing. Cut the joist, install a blocking piece, and attach 2×4 cleats around the opening.

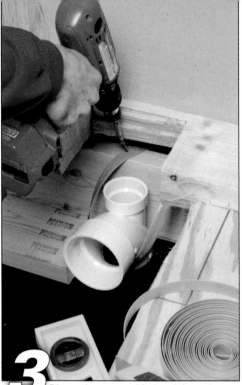

3 Place the assembly back into the hole. Secure the low-heel vent fitting to the framing with pipe strap. Secure the pipe from below as well.

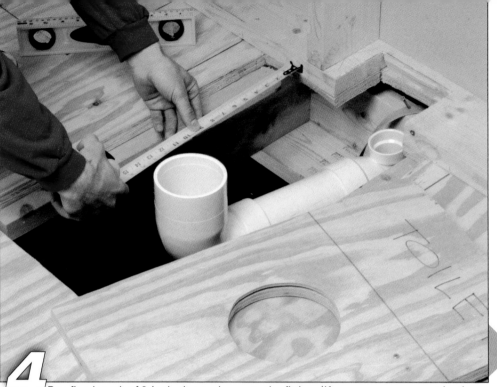

4 Dry-fit a length of 3-inch pipe and a 4×3 reducing closet bend to the low-heel fitting. Check that the center of the closet bend hole is the correct distance from the wall—in most cases 12½ inches from the framing to allow for ½-inch drywall. Check that the pipe slopes ⅛ to ¼ inch down to the fitting. (If necessary you can trim the top of the closet bend after the flooring has been replaced.)

Once you are sure the toilet drain setup is correct, mark the alignment of the fittings and disassemble. Prime and glue the pieces. Support the closet bend with a strap.

TOILET VENT OPTIONS

Elbow — Closet bend — 45° street elbow — 3×2 reducing Y

Elbow — 45° street elbow — 3×2 reducing Y — Closet bend

4×3 closet flange — Elbow — Reducer — 45° street elbow — 3×2 reducing Y

If the toilet drain does not connect directly to a vent, you must find another way to vent it. If the drain line runs away from the wall where you want the vent, use a reducing Y and a 45-degree street elbow to point the vent line toward the wall. The horizontal vent pipe runs right next to the closet bend.

If the vent wall is parallel to the drain pipe, install a 45-degree reducing Y and a street elbow to point toward the wall. You may need another elbow (of any degree) to position the vertical vent where you want it.

If the vent wall is opposite the drain line, use a reducing Y and a street elbow. The fittings can be pointed straight at the wall or at an angle, as needed.

5 Run a horizontal pipe to the existing pipe and assemble the parts needed for tying into it. All fittings should be Ys or drain elbows so wastewater can flow easily. Hold the horizontal pipe so it's sloped at ⅛ to ¼ inch per foot and mark the existing pipe for cutting (pages 140–141).

6 If the existing pipe is cast-iron, take care to support it securely before cutting. In the setup shown a 4×3 Y connects to the house drain using no-hub fittings (which should be used to connect to either cast iron or ABS). Once you are sure the

fittings are correct and the horizontal pipe slopes correctly, make alignment marks. Disassemble the parts, apply primer and glue, and reassemble the pieces in order, starting at the existing drain.

OTHER DRAIN CONFIGURATIONS

Your situation may call for another drain configuration. This example shows a single-floor home in which all the fixtures tie into horizontal pipes, which in turn run to the stack.

In this example for a two-story home, first-floor vent pipes run up to join the second-floor vents at the top of their runs, so that all the vents tie in at a point well above the second-floor fixtures.

B. Running individual drain lines

Vent hole

Safety glasses

Reciprocating saw

Tub/shower vent

Sink drain

Toilet vent

Street elbow

45° elbow

3×2 sanitary tee

Carpenter's level

Y-fitting

1 Slip lengths of 2-inch pipe down through the holes drilled in the floor plate for the tub and sink vents. Have a helper hold the pipes plumb as you mark the plate below for notching. Cut notches about an inch wider than the pipe to accommodate a fitting.

2 Cut and dry-fit the horizontal drainpipe and the fittings for connecting the tub and the sink drains. (A 3-inch horizontal pipe is shown, but your inspector may permit a 2-inch pipe.) Insert a street elbow into the Y and hold the other pieces in place to mark for cutting. Make sure the horizontal pipe slopes at a rate of ⅛ to ¼ inch per running foot. Install a reducing tee and a 45-degree elbow (or street elbow if you need to save room) for both joints. If the pipe will be accessible, install a cleanout on the fitting for the tub; otherwise install a drain elbow instead of a tee.

WHAT IF ...
You need to run a drain for a shower only?

Shower base

Tailpiece

Cemented 2" trap

Vent

Sanitary tee

A 1½-inch drain trap is often permitted for a shower, but a 2-inch trap will ensure quick flow of water and will be less likely to clog. A shower has no waste-and-overflow assembly, so the rough plumbing consists of a cemented trap that rises to the correct height for the shower base (page 196).

Tub/shower P-trap

2" pipe

3 To plumb the drain for the tub, dry-fit a 2-inch trap onto a length of 2-inch pipe that is longer than it needs to be. Study the directions for the tub to determine precisely where the trap should be located. Hold the trap-and-pipe assembly in place and mark it for a cut. Dry-fit and check that the horizontal pipe slopes correctly. Once all the parts are accurately assembled, draw alignment marks and prime and glue the pieces together.

C. Installing the vents

2" sanitary tee
2" sanitary tee
90°
2" elbow
2" pipe
Carpenter's level

Pipe strap
1×6 brace
Trap adapter
Sanitary tee
18"

1 Your codes may require the horizontal revent lines be as high as 54 inches above the finished floor, or at least 6 inches above the fixture flood level (the point where water will start to spill out). Use a carpenter's level to mark the studs for drilling holes. Run the horizontal vent lines sloped downward toward the fixtures at a rate of ⅛ to ¼ inch per running foot. Drill holes, cut pipes, and connect them in a dry run using drain fittings.

2 Install a sanitary tee facing into the room for the sink trap. The ideal height is usually 18 inches above the finished floor, but check your sink instructions to be sure. Cement a 1¼-inch trap adapter into the tee. Install a piece of 1×6 blocking and anchor the pipe with a strap.

RUNNING A VENT AROUND AN OBSTRUCTION

If a medicine cabinet, window, or other obstruction prevents you from running a vent straight up, you'll have to turn a corner for a short distance, then turn again to head upward. Horizontal runs should be at least 6 inches above the fixture flood level—the rim of a sink for example.

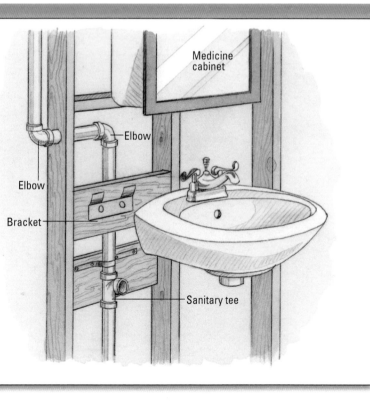

Medicine cabinet
Elbow
Elbow
Bracket
Sanitary tee

Running up through the ceiling

Hole saw

To run a vent pipe through the ceiling, first drill a test hole to make sure you won't bump into any joists in the attic. You may need to move the hole over a few inches. The top plate may be doubled, meaning you have to drill through 3 inches. You may need to drill with a hole saw first from below (shown), then from above.

Sanitary tee for testing

Reducer tee fitting

No-hub fitting

90° elbow

Main stack

3 In the attic tap into a conveniently located vent pipe. Following the steps shown on pages 140–141, cut the pipe and connect a reducer tee fitting. Use no-hub fittings to connect a PVC fitting to cast-iron or ABS pipe.

4 Run the new vent line over to the tee fitting. The pipes should slope gently away from the existing vent pipe so water can travel downward.

Your inspector may want you to include a tee fitting to be used for testing: Once the

drain system is assembled and cemented, plug the drainpipe at the lower end. Pour water into it until all the drain and vent pipes are filled with water. Allow the water to sit for a day to make sure there are no leaks.

INSTALLING A ROOF JACK

Check local codes for the correct way to install a roof jack. In most areas you will need to install a 4-inch pipe. Some areas allow for a plastic pipe to extend out the roof (shown); in other areas a metal pipe is required. Purchase a roof jack with a rubber flange that will seal a 4-inch pipe.

Cut the 4-inch pipe to roughly the same angle as the roof slope and hold it plumb, its top touching the attic ceiling. Mark for the hole, which will be oval. Cut the hole using a drill and a reciprocating saw.

You may need to cut some roofing shingles back. Slip the jack under the roof shingles at its upper half; the lower half of the jack rests on top of shingles. Poke the vent pipe up through the rubber flange. To anchor the jack lift up some shingles and drive roofing nails. If any nails are not covered by shingles, cover the heads with roofing cement.

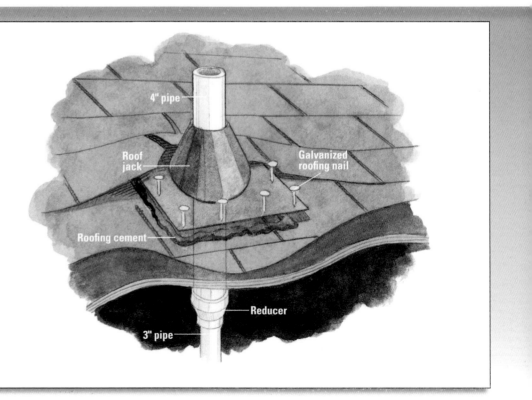

4" pipe

Roof jack

Galvanized roofing nail

Roofing cement

Reducer

3" pipe

RUNNING COPPER SUPPLY LINES

Copper is preferred for supply lines in most locales, although flexible or rigid plastic is permitted in some areas. Practice cutting copper pipe and sweating joints (pages 126–127) before you start.

Supply lines are usually routed so they do not cross drainpipes or vents. In most cases it's easier to make the horizontal runs in the crawlspace or basement. If you need to run pipes horizontally in the room, see the box on the opposite page. Long runs and bends lower water pressure slightly.

Hammer arresters (Step 3) prevent banging noise when you turn off a faucet.

Copper pipe is easily punctured or dented. Position it out of harm's way and install nailing plates to the studs to protect pipes against errant nails.

Hot water is always on the left, cold water on the right.

PRESTART CHECKLIST

☐ **TIME**
About half a day to run supply lines for a sink and toilet

☐ **TOOLS**
Drill, bit and bit extender, propane torch, fiber shield, tubing cutter, multiuse wire brush, groove-joint pliers, carpentry tools for installing braces

☐ **SKILLS**
Accurate measuring and drilling, working with copper pipe

☐ **PREP**
Install all or most of the drain and vent pipes; determine the supply routes

☐ **MATERIALS**
Copper pipe and fittings, flux, solder, damp rag

1 Consult the manufacturer's instructions to position pipes for the shower faucet, sink, and toilet. For example the shower faucet in this plan calls for vertical pipes 10 inches apart. Use a spade bit attached to a bit extender to drill holes in the center of the wall plate if possible.

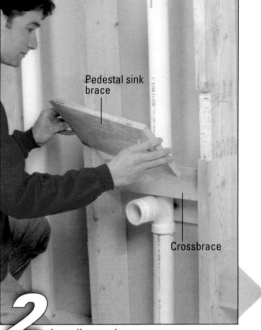

2 Install crossbraces so you can anchor the pipes firmly. Cut pieces of 2×4 or 1×4 to fit snugly between studs and attach them by drilling pilot holes and driving screws. If you plan to install a pedestal sink (page 188–189), attach a 2×6 or a ¾-inch plywood brace (shown) for its bracket.

Running and securing supply lines

A copper supply strap attaches to the face of the studs. Pipes fit into notches or holes, sized and spaced for correct placement. The pipes can be soldered onto the strap using the same techniques as for sweating fittings.

A drop-ear elbow makes the most secure attachment. If you use one the hammer arrester must be connected to a tee and an elbow just below the drop-ear elbow. Insert a brass threaded nipple into the elbow.

Hammer arrester

8–10"

19"

Toilet supply

8"

Pipe clamp

Toilet stub out

Cap

3 Tie into existing supply lines (page 141). Hot and cold stub outs are usually 8 to 10 inches apart and 19 to 23 inches above the floor; consult the manufacturer's instructions to be sure. A toilet stub out is usually 8 inches above the floor.

Dry-fit a complete assembly for the sink and the toilet. For each stub out use a tee fitting, a 6-inch length of pipe (which you will cut off later), and a cap to protect the pipe. Install a hammer arrester to each.

4 Sweat all the parts (pages 126–127). Anchor the pipes with at least one clamp—preferably two—at each stub out as shown.

Tap into shower supplies

45° elbow

Rather than running sink supply lines from below, you may want to run them horizontally from the shower. If the shower lines are ¾ inch, use reducer tees to tap into the lines. Use 45-degree elbows to snake one line past the other (in this case the hot past the vertical cold water line). If the sink is used at the same time as the shower, water temperature will change.

WHAT IF ...
Supply lines must run past drain or vent pipes?

45° elbow

Nailing plate

To run supplies around an obstruction such as a drain or vent pipe, use four 45-degree elbows. This arrangement makes for smoother water flow and less loss of water pressure than using 90-degree elbows.

Another option is to cut notches rather than holes and run supply pipes in front of the vent pipes. If you do this be sure to install protective nailing plates or the pipes could be punctured by a nail when the drywall is installed.

INSTALLING A BATHROOM VANITY SINK

Installing a bathroom sink in a vanity is simplified by the fact that the supply lines and the drain are all hidden within a cabinet. If the cabinet has no back, simply attach it to the wall so it encloses the plumbing. However if the cabinet has a back, measure and cut three holes for the two supply lines and the drain.

Choosing a cabinet and top

A high-quality vanity cabinet is made of hardwood to resist water damage. A less expensive cabinet made of laminated particleboard will quickly disintegrate if it gets wet.

A vanity top typically is a single piece comprised of the bowl, countertop, and backsplash. Acrylic or plastic vanity tops are inexpensive, but they scratch and stain more easily than other materials.

PRESTART CHECKLIST

☐ **TIME**
Two to three hours to install a basic cabinet and vanity top with faucet

☐ **TOOLS**
Drill, level, hammer, screwdriver, adjustable wrench, groove-joint pliers, basin wrench

☐ **SKILLS**
Installing a faucet, attaching a P-trap, connecting supply tubes, simple carpentry

☐ **PREP**
Shut off the water and remove the old sink

☐ **MATERIALS**
Vanity cabinet and top, faucet, P-trap, supply tubes that fit the stop valves, plumber's putty, wood shims, screws

1 The stop valves and drainpipe should be in place and close enough together to be enclosed by the cabinet. If your vanity cabinet has a back (many do not), remove the handles from the stop valves. Then measure and cut holes for the drain and the two supply pipes.

Stop valve
Drain

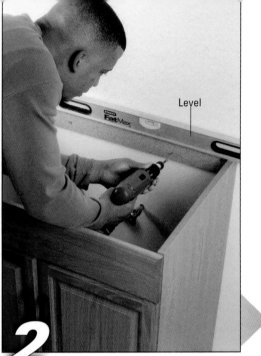

Level

2 Slide the cabinet into place and check it for level in both directions. If necessary slip shims under or behind the cabinet. Drive screws through the cabinet framing into wall studs to secure the cabinet.

VANITY SINK

Vanity top fitted with faucet, drain, and pop-up drain mechanism

Wall stud

2" fasteners

A vanity cabinet can be installed anywhere as long as the stop valves and drain line fit inside. A single-piece vanity top rests on top of the cabinet and is typically held in place by its own weight and a bead of caulk or adhesive applied to the top edge of the cabinet.

Labels on image:
Drain body
Clevis strap
Manufacturer's instructions

3 Set the vanity top upside down on a pair of sawhorses and install the plumbing. See pages 90–91 for installing the faucet, drain body, and pop-up assembly. Check the manufacturer's instructions for details.

4 Set the top onto the cabinet and check that it is centered. Remove it, apply caulk or adhesive along the top edge of the vanity, and reinstall the top.

Labels on image:
Supply tube
Trap

5 Connect the supply tubes to the stop valves. Connect the trap (pages 48–49).

Installing a drop-in sink

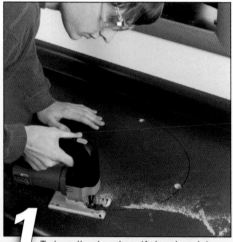

1 To install a drop-in self-rimming sink, first install a laminate countertop or, for a tile countertop, plywood and concrete backerboard. Use the template if provided or turn the sink upside down on the counter and trace its outline. Draw a line ¾ inch inside the first line. Cut this second line with a saber saw.

2 Plumb the sink (Step 3 above). Apply a bead of bathtub caulk or a rope of plumber's putty around the hole and set the sink. If the sink doesn't have mounting clips, apply a bead of silicone caulk instead of putty. Set the sink in, wipe away the excess caulk, and wait several hours before attaching the plumbing.

3 If your sink has mounting clips, slip several of them in place and turn them sideways so they grab the underside of the counter. Tighten the screws. Attach the supply lines and the drain trap.

CONNECTING A TOILET

Once the rough plumbing is completed, run electrical lines and install the lights, switches, receptacles, and a ceiling fan. Lay the finish flooring if you haven't already done so. Install cement backerboard on the walls that surround the tub/shower (pages 198–199) and moisture-resistant drywall (also called greenboard) on the other walls. Tile or apply prefab sheets to the tub/shower surround. Tape, prime, and paint the walls and the ceiling. You may want to install baseboard and trim, but often it's best to wait until the sink and toilet are installed to avoid bumps and nicks on the trim.

To install a stop valve for the toilet, follow the instructions on pages 118–119. Measure the length of the supply tube needed and confirm the connection dimensions.

PRESTART CHECKLIST

☐ **TIME**
Half a day

☐ **TOOLS**
Adjustable wrench, groove-joint pliers, torpedo level, screwdriver, drill

☐ **SKILLS**
Assembling plumbing parts, cementing PVC fittings

☐ **PREP**
Finish all the wiring, carpentry, and wall preparation; remove the drop cloth from the floor

☐ **MATERIALS**
Toilet, wax ring, toilet flange with bolts, supply tubes and decorative flanges, plumber's putty, silicone sealant, caulk, PVC primer and glue

Installing a toilet

PVC cement

PVC primer

Rag to temporarily seal drain

Toilet flange

1 Install finish flooring to within an inch of the drain hole. The toilet flange can rest on top of the finished floor or on top of the subflooring. Test-fit the flange, then prime and glue it so that you will be able to place the hold-down bolts on either side of the opening (Step 2). Remove the rag.

Tank

Spud gasket

3 Assemble the tank and the bowl of a new toilet following the manufacturer's instructions. A large spud gasket seals the opening below the flush-valve seat. Place a rubber washer under the head of each mounting bolt. Don't overtighten the nuts.

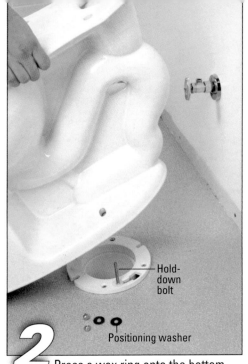

Hold-down bolt

Positioning washer

2 Press a wax ring onto the bottom of the toilet. Place the hold-down bolts in the flange and slip plastic positioning washers over them. Lower the bowl, threading the bolts through the holes in the bowl. Press down to set the bowl firmly. Slip on washers and nuts and gently tighten.

Toilet supply tube

Adjustable wrench

4 Attach a toilet supply tube by hand-tightening the nuts at the underside of the tank and the stop valve. Tighten a half turn or more with a wrench and open the stop valve. You may need to tighten the connection a bit further.

Pressure-assisted toilet

Actuator valve

Fill tube

Screen-type filter

1 Many people want more flushing power than modern 1.6-gallon toilets provide. A pressure-assisted toilet delivers a more forceful flush. It installs the same way as a standard toilet (pages 105–107).

2 Some manufacturers use a chain to link the flush handle to the actuator valve. Check that the chain is nearly taut; a chain that's too loose won't fully open the actuator valve and will interrupt the flush.

3 A screen filter at the base of the fill tube catches rust and minerals. Check it periodically by turning off the supply valve and detaching the supply tube. Pry out the filter with a bent paper clip and flush it with hot water. Reassemble and attach the tube.

HOW IT WORKS

2. Pressure forces central cylinder down, sealing tank outflow.

3. Air in tank is compressed, putting downward pressure on water.

4. When lever is turned, pressure is relieved above central cylinder. It rises, starting flush.

Lever

1. Water flows into the chamber.

Supply tube

5. Forced air pushes water out and into the bowl.

As the chamber is filled, household water pressure compresses air. The chamber holds the compressed air, primed for the next flush. When the flush lever is tripped, the central cylinder rises, releasing a rush of water into the toilet bowl.

How much will you save?

Old toilets use from 3 to 5 gallons per flush. Current federal regulations require toilets to use no more than 1.6 gallons per flush.

The first low-use toilets were no different from their older counterparts except they allowed less water into the tank. As a result people often had to flush two or more times to clear the bowl, sending water savings down the drain.

Newer 1.6-gallon toilets are better designed so water flows more smoothly and waste is more effectively flushed away. For maximum efficiency buy a power-assist toilet such as the one shown on this page.

If you have an older toilet and are tempted to decrease water consumption simply by placing a brick in the tank or some similar solution, see page 278.

INSTALLING A PEDESTAL SINK

A pedestal sink saves space in a bathroom but may require adding extra wall framing for support.

The project will probably require several days: On the first day install the framing and patch the wall. On the second day finish the patching and paint the wall. Install the sink on the third day. (If you have a tiled wall, consider cutting into the wall in the room behind the sink to install framing.)

A pedestal sink that actually sits on the pedestal makes the plumbing installation difficult and repairs nearly impossible. Buy a sink that mounts on a wall bracket and has a pedestal for looks only.

Supply lines that are close together can be hidden behind the pedestal. Otherwise let the plumbing show.

PRESTART CHECKLIST

☐ **TIME**
About 5 hours of work spread over a period of three days (see above)

☐ **TOOLS**
Drywall saw, drill, hammer, taping blade, sanding block, paintbrush, screwdriver, adjustable wrench, groove-joint pliers

☐ **SKILLS**
Installing a bathroom faucet with pop-up drain, connecting a trap, cutting drywall

☐ **PREP**
Locate studs behind the wall near the plumbing

☐ **MATERIALS**
Pedestal sink, bathroom faucet, supply tubes that fit the stop valves, plumber's putty, 2×6 or 2×8 piece, screws, drywall, joint compound, drywall tape, paint

1 Measure and mark the bracket height. To support the bracket cut a hole in the wall that spans two studs. Cut a piece of 2×6 or 2×8 to fit between the studs and attach it with screws. Drive the screws at an angle through the brace and into the studs.

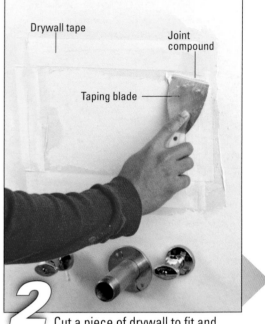

2 Cut a piece of drywall to fit and attach it to the brace with screws. Smooth pieces of drywall tape around the edges. Use a taping blade to cover the tape with joint compound. Allow the compound to dry, then sand until the patch is smooth. Paint the patch.

PEDESTAL SINK

Framing for bracket

Vent

Bracket

Stop valve

Trap

Pedestal

A pedestal sink is essentially a wall-hung sink with a decorative pedestal underneath. The bracket must attach to solid framing, usually a horizontal piece of 2× lumber. If the bracket happens to be over a stud, notch-cut one stud in order to install the brace.

3 Set the sink on top of the pedestal and against the wall. Hold the bracket in place and mark the position of the bracket. Install the bracket by driving screws through the wall into the 2× brace.

Bracket

4 Install the faucet and the drain body on the sink (pages 90–91). Lower the sink onto the bracket. Slide the pedestal in place to make sure the bracket is at the right height and adjust it if necessary. Hook the supply tubes to the stop valves and attach the drain.

5 Slide the pedestal under the sink. Stand back to determine if the pedestal looks level and sits squarely on the floor. Adjust it as needed. You may caulk the bottom of the pedestal or leave it uncaulked so it can be removed for cleaning.

Pedestal

WHAT IF …
You want a freestanding bowl sink?

Faucet unit

Umbrella drain

1 Drill two holes in the countertop, one for the drain and one for the faucet. There is no overflow, so use an umbrella drain (shown) that covers the drain but does not close it. Apply silicone sealant and anchor by tightening the nut from below.

Faucet unit

Nut with leveling screws

2 The faucet unit comes with flexible supply tubes already attached. Apply silicone sealant to the bottom of the faucet and drop the lines through the hole in the countertop. Anchor the faucet from below by tightening the nut and leveling screws.

Tailpiece

3 Wrap the threads of the stop valves with pipe-thread tape and attach the supply tubes. Make a tailpiece from a section of trap and attach it with a rubber washer and trap nut.

Hooking Up A Shower or Tub Faucet

Installing separate ¾-inch lines to supply the shower ensures good water pressure and protects from temperature changes when another faucet is turned on or the toilet tank refills. Tap into the cold and hot water lines as close to the water heater as possible.

Choose the tub or shower faucet before you run pipes. Follow the manufacturer's directions for plumbing the faucet.

If your faucet does not have integrated shutoff valves (see box, opposite), install shutoff valves in the lines to the valve.

Assuming an 18-inch-tall tub, position the faucet about 28 inches above the floor for a tub, about 48 inches for a shower. You may want to compromise and position it about 38 inches above the floor.

Prestart Checklist

☐ **Time**
About half a day to run supply lines and install a tub/shower faucet

☐ **Tools**
Drill, tubing cutter, multiuse wire brush, flame guard, propane torch, damp rag, groove-joint pliers

☐ **Skills**
Accurate measuring and drilling, working with copper pipe

☐ **Prep**
Tap into the hot and cold water lines and run ¾-inch pipe up into the room; if needed move a stud to make room for the plumbing behind the tub

☐ **Materials**
Tub/shower faucet, copper pipe and fittings, flux, solder, pipe-thread tape

Crossbrace

1× scrap stands for ½" backerboard plus ¼" tile.

1 Most faucets come with a plastic cover that protects the faucet and serves as a guide for the depth at which it must be set. To determine where to place the braces, consider the total thickness of the finished wall—often ½-inch-thick backerboard plus ¼-inch-thick tiles.

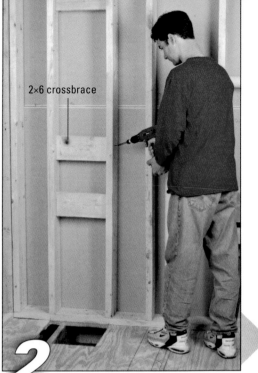

2×6 crossbrace

2 Determine how high you want to locate the spout (make sure it will clear the tub), faucet handles, and showerhead. Install a 2×6 brace for each. Anchor the braces with screws rather than nails so it's easier to move them if they need adjustment.

Tub/Shower Installation

A typical single-handle tub/shower faucet attaches with screws driven through its housing; use drop-ear elbows and pipe clamps to anchor the pipes for the shower arm and the spout.

Threaded drop ear

½" pipe

Hammer arrestor

Threaded adapter

½" tee

½" nipple

Reducer coupling

Faucet

½" nipple

¾" pipe

Threaded drop ear

¾" galvanized nipple

Hammer arrester

Tee

Reducer coupling

¾" pipe

3 Assemble all the pipes in a dry run. Install ¾-inch pipe up to the height of the faucet, add reducer couplings or elbows, and run short lengths of ½-inch pipe to the threaded adapters on the faucet. Add hammer arresters. Anchor the faucet according to manufacturer's directions.

Flame guard

Propane torch

Solder

4 Once you are sure of the connections, sweat all the fittings (pages 126–127). Start at the faucet, then move on to the shower arm and spout connections. Run ½-inch pipe up to the shower arm and down to the spout; attach drop-ear elbows at both spots.

Galvanized nipple

Pipe-thread tape

5 Finger-tighten a threaded nipple—either brass or galvanized—into both drop-ear elbows. Once the wallcovering is in place, remove them and install the shower arm and tub spout.

STANLEY PRO TIP

Add reinforcement to shower-arm drop ears

Drop-ear elbow

Pipe clamp

Whacking the showerhead with your elbow can bend or crack a drop-ear elbow. As an extra safeguard screw a pipe clamp just below the drop ear.

WHAT IF ...
You have other faucet setups?

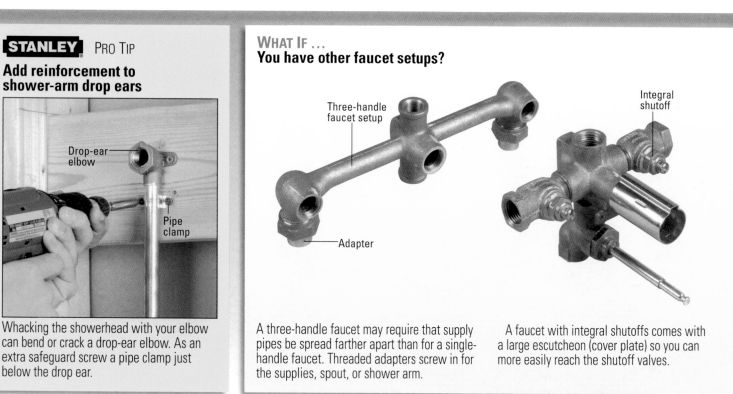

Three-handle faucet setup

Integral shutoff

Adapter

A three-handle faucet may require that supply pipes be spread farther apart than for a single-handle faucet. Threaded adapters screw in for the supplies, spout, or shower arm.

A faucet with integral shutoffs comes with a large escutcheon (cover plate) so you can more easily reach the shutoff valves.

INSTALLING A WHIRLPOOL TUB

Some whirlpool tubs or spas have a finished side or two, so framing and finishing the side panel are not required. Rectangular models install much like a standard tub (pages 165–167), except that a GFCI electrical receptacle is required. Triangular whirlpools fit into a corner.

If the whirlpool has an integral spout, follow the manufacturer's instructions for running supply lines to the unit.

Large whirlpools are heavy when filled with water, so you may need to strengthen the floor by adding joists. Check the whirlpool's instructions and local codes.

Ideally it's best to lay flooring after the tub is framed and installed but before tiling.

PRESTART CHECKLIST

☐ **TIME**
Two or three days to frame, install, and tile a whirlpool tub

☐ **TOOLS**
Carpentry tools, groove-joint pliers, PVC saw, wiring tools, tiling tools, putty knife, screwdriver, adjustable wrench

☐ **SKILLS**
Connecting PVC pipe, basic carpentry, basic wiring, installing tiles

☐ **PREP**
Measure the space carefully, taking into account the framing, backerboard, and tile thickness

☐ **MATERIALS**
Whirlpool tub, waste-and-overflow unit, lumber and screws for framing, GFCI receptacle, cable, breaker, cement backerboard with screws, mortar mix, tile, mastic, grout, caulk, spacers, pipe thread tape, rag

Ledger supports tub edge

2×4 frame

1 Build a frame following manufacturer's directions. It's especially important to get the height right. You may snug the whirlpool up against one, two, or three walls. Where you snug the tub against the wall, attach a 2×4 ledger as you would for a standard tub (page 165).

Where you will install tiles, plan the framing carefully, taking into account the thickness of the backerboard and tile (Steps 2 and 11). Most whirlpools require access to the plumbing at one end and the pump motor at the other end; check the manufacturer's directions.

WHIRLPOOL TUB INSTALLATION

Flange

Pump access panel framing

Mortar bed

Cement backerboard

Tiles

A whirlpool needs an extra access panel to reach the electric pump. A 2×4 frame is covered with backerboard, then tiled. The whirlpool's flange rests on tile, but its weight must be supported by a mortar bed.

2 Cut strips of cement backerboard to fit where needed on top of the framing. Backerboard pieces should overhang the framing by ½ inch. You also can cut the side backerboard pieces, but don't install them yet. Attach the backerboard using special backerboard screws.

3 Cut several spacers ⅛ inch thicker than the tiles you will install. (For ¼-inch-thick tiles, cut pieces of ⅜-inch plywood.) Set the spacers on top of the backerboard wherever there will be tile.

Set the whirlpool in place and see that it fits. Be sure the bottom of the tub is at the correct depth so it will rest on the mortar bed (Steps 7 and 8).

Installing a GFCI receptacle

Most whirlpools plug into a GFCI receptacle, though some are hardwired into an electrical box. For most models you will need a 15-amp circuit that supplies only the whirlpool. Check the manufacturer's instructions. Consult with an electrician if you are not sure how to run cable and install a new circuit. Use cable that meets

local codes: NM cable, armored cable, or conduit with wires running through it. Run cable from the service panel to the whirlpool. Strip the cable and clamp it to an electrical box (left).

Wire a GFCI receptacle (center), wrap the connections, secure the receptacle in the box, and attach a cover plate.

Shut off power to the service panel. Strip the cable and connect the hot wire to a new 15-amp circuit breaker. Connect the neutral and ground wires to the neutral and ground bus bars and snap the breaker into place. Restore power and test.

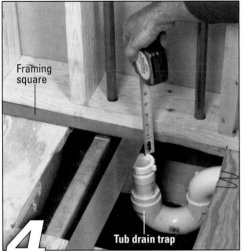

4 Check to make sure the drain trap is positioned at the correct height so the whirlpool waste-and-overflow unit will slide into it (Step 9). Plan how you will make this connection, either from the basement or crawlspace below or through the access panel (page 163).

Framing square

Tub drain trap

5 Assemble the waste-and-overflow unit. Some whirlpools come with a waste-and-overflow; if not you'll have to purchase a standard unit and add an extension (shown). Insert the shoe (cut to length if necessary) into the tee fitting.

Overflow

Drain flange

Extension

Shoe

Tee

6 Set the tub on two overturned buckets. Install the overflow by slipping in the plunger assembly, tightening the screws on the cover plate, and screwing the drain flange into the shoe (pages 162–163). Tighten the nuts on the drain extension.

Groove-joint pliers

Extension

Adding the tub hardware

1 Once the wall is finished, remove the temporary nipple (page 191). Wrap pipe-thread tape around the ends of the shower arm and screw it into place. Slip on the flange. Twist on the showerhead, then tighten with an adjustable wrench and groove-joint pliers. Protect the chrome with tape.

Flange

Shower arm

Showerhead

2 Following manufacturer's instructions slide the escutcheon over the faucet and screw it into place. It should seal against the tiles with a rubber gasket. Attach the faucet handle.

Escutcheon

3 Apply caulk around the spout hole. Choose a nipple of proper length for the spout and wrap pipe-thread tape around the threads on both ends. Thread the spout on by hand. Finish by wrapping the spout with a rag and tightening it with groove-joint pliers.

Tub caulk

Tub spout

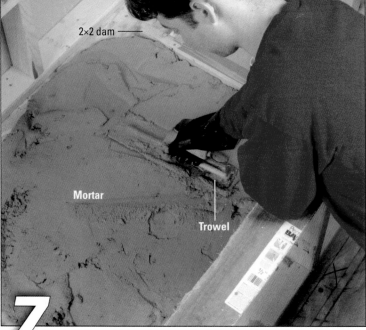

7 Test-fit the whirlpool to see that the waste-and-overflow unit will slip into the drain trap. Remove the whirlpool. Screw 2×2s to the floor around the drain hole to keep mortar out of the hole. In a bucket or wheelbarrow, mix water with dry mortar mix. The mortar should be just wet enough to be poured. Smooth enough mortar onto the floor to support the bottom of the whirlpool.

2×2 dam

Mortar

Trowel

8 Place spacers (Step 3) on the backerboard atop the side-panel frame. With a helper gently set the tub in place. Guide the waste-and-overflow into the drain trap but do not tighten the connection. Push down on the tub until the lip rests on the spacers but do not press hard. Allow the mortar to harden overnight.

Spacer

Mortar bed

9 Connect the waste-and-overflow to the drain and tighten the fittings (pages 162–163). Support the pump motor with pieces of lumber and attach it in place with screws. Plug the cord into the GFCI receptacle. Follow the manufacturer's instructions for testing the whirlpool.

GFCI receptacle

Pump motor

10 Install cement backerboard on all exposed sides. Drive backerboard screws every 6 inches or so. Wrap corners with fiberglass mesh tape.

Fiberglass mesh tape

Tile mastic

11 Apply thinset mortar using a notched trowel and set standard tiles on the side. When tiling the top edge, use bullnose caps for the outside corner for a finished look. After the thinset has dried, apply grout and clean the joints. Caulk the joint where the whirlpool rests on the tiles.

Bullnose cap tile

Thinset mortar

BUILDING A SHOWER ENCLOSURE

A new corner shower stall requires building one wall. In the middle of a wall, two new walls are required. If the walls do not go to the ceiling, the top ledge must be covered with tile or another moisture-resistant surface. The opening can have a door or a curtain rod.

A one-piece unit (page 198) is the simplest shower to install, though you have a limited choice of colors.

Buy a base that's at least 34 inches. Some bases must be set in thinset mortar or in a bed of sand, while others can simply be placed on the floor.

For details on how to run drain and supply lines, see pages 176-179.

PRESTART CHECKLIST

☐ **TIME**
Two or three days to install a base, plumbing, tiled walls, and a shower door

☐ **TOOLS**
Carpentry tools, drill, tools for plastic (page 128) and copper pipe (page 126), tiling tools, steel rod

☐ **SKILLS**
Working with plastic and copper pipe, framing a wall, installing tile

☐ **PREP**
Install a drainpipe with trap in the center of the base, as well as supply pipes, faucet, and shower riser

☐ **MATERIALS**
Shower base, PVC primer and cement, roofing felt, 2×4 studs, cement backerboard, backerboard screws, tiles, tile adhesive, grout, caulk, shower door

½" cement board

Tile adhesive

Ceramic tile

Showerhead riser

About 12"

About 76"

Shower faucet

Hot riser

Cold riser

About 50"

Shower base

Drain flange

P-trap

A shower drain should be installed at the center of the shower base. The flange should be level with the floor. Run the supply pipes after the framing is installed.

A. Installing the shower base

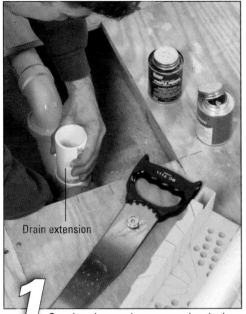

Drain extension

1 Set the shower base over the drain to make sure the drain is directly below the opening of the base. Remove the base and cut and cement an extension to the drainpipe. The extension should be flush with the floor.

Carpenter's level

Roofing felt

2 Place a layer or two of roofing felt to smooth any unevenness in the floor. (Some manufacturers require a bed of mortar or sand.) Set the shower base over the drain to confirm that the drain is positioned correctly. Check for level; shim with additional roofing felt as needed.

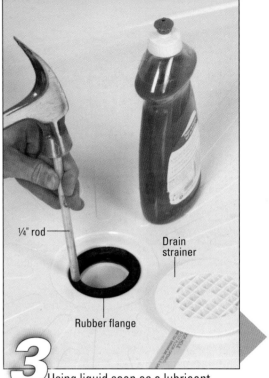

¼" rod

Drain strainer

Rubber flange

3 Using liquid soap as a lubricant, fit the rubber flange (provided with the shower base) over the drain extension and push it as far down as you can. Tap it all the way in place with a ¼-inch steel rod. Install the drain strainer.

REFRESHER COURSE
Installing a drain

Sanitary tee

Elbow

P trap

See pages 176–179 for instructions on running a new drain line. A shower drain should be connected directly to a trap. Drain lines must slope at a rate of ¼ inch per running foot and must be properly vented (pages 14–15).

WHAT IF …
The base uses a PVC flange?

Strainer

Drain body

Fiber gasket

Rubber gasket

Drain flange

Cement the drain flange to the drainpipe; the flange should be flush with the floor. Set the gaskets on top of the flange. Place the shower base over the drain hole. Check that the gaskets are still in place. Screw the drain body through the hole in the base and into the flange. Attach the strainer.

STANLEY PRO TIP
Hire a pro when installing a mortar-laid shower base

A mortar-laid, tiled shower base can be customized to whatever style, size, and color you want. With it you can achieve a truly custom look. However it is a major project in itself, requiring substantial prep work, including the services of a professional plumber.

Once the base of the shower is framed, a plumber should install the drain and join it to the CPE (heavy plastic) liner set inside the frame. A drain flange must be installed precisely so that water cannot seep under the liner. Then the area around the drain is filled with mortar, shaped so it slopes down toward the drain. When the mortar sets tiles are installed on top.

B. Framing the shower

2×4 stud wall

Doubled 2×4 stud at outside corners

Protect base with a drop cloth

Cement backerboard

1 With the shower base in place, build 2×4 walls for the sides. Remember that the studs will be covered with ½-inch-thick cement board, plus the tiles (usually about ⅜ inch thick). No studs should be farther apart than 16 inches. On the plumbing wall space the studs so you can position the shower faucet—a pair of studs spaced about a foot apart will accommodate most faucets. Install horizontal braces to support both the faucet and the showerhead arm. Some bases may require a ledger (page 165). Install the supply pipes and faucet, following instructions on pages 190–191.

2 Cut pieces of cement backerboard to fit. Cover all wood surfaces with the backerboard. Attach them to the studs with backerboard screws. Check that the wall surface is smooth and even because the tiles will follow any contours. Before tiling caulk the gap at the bottom.

One-piece shower units

Corner and rectangular shower stalls—made of acrylic fiberglass or polystyrene—are much easier to install than a custom-made enclosure. One-piece units are designed for new construction only because they are too large to fit through a door. Three-piece units are quickly assembled and are ideal for remodeling.

Two or three walls of these units must be installed against solid walls. A corner unit can simply be installed in any corner that is reasonably square. A rectangular or square unit requires an opening of the correct width and height.

Corner

Square

Rectangular

Ceramic tile

Grout float

3 Cover the backerboard with ceramic tile or with a prefab tub surround kit (pages 168–169). Consult a book on tiling for guidelines on selecting, laying out, and cutting tile. In general, tiling should be planned to minimize small pieces. Wherever a tile edge will be exposed, install a bullnose piece, which has one finished edge (page 195). Use a notched trowel to apply thinset mortar or organic tile adhesive and set the tiles. Use a tile-cutting hole saw for the faucet and showerhead stub outs. Once all the tiles are applied, allow the adhesive to set overnight.

4 Mix a batch of latex-reinforced grout and use a grout float to push the grout into the joints and scrape away most of the excess. Wipe several times with a damp sponge, working to create consistent grout lines. Allow to dry, and buff with a dry towel. Caulk all the inside corners.

CAULK THE EDGES OF THE STALL

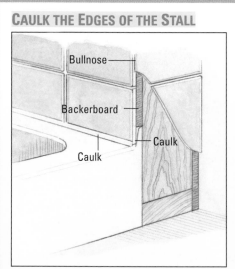

Bullnose

Backerboard

Caulk

Caulk

The bottom of a wall, where the tiles meet the shower base, must be installed correctly or water will seep behind the tiles and damage the studs. Install the backerboard to the top of the base's flange and fill the gap below with caulk. Apply tiles and a bead of caulk.

Installing a shower door

Jamb piece

Jamb piece anchored to stall

Hinge cap

Jamb insert (hinged)

Door

Measure the opening and select a door with a frame you can adjust to fit your unit. Follow manufacturer's instructions. In general you'll begin by cutting the jamb piece to size and installing a bottom track and seal. Each jamb is made of two interlocking pieces. One attaches to the stall with screws and anchors. When both jambs are installed, decide which way the door should swing and install the hinged insert with the clamps provided. Slide the door in place, cap, and add the door handle. Install the other jamb insert and adjust.

INSTALLING A LUXURY SHOWER

With the huge array of bathroom innovations, adding luxury to a shower can mean installing multiple shower jets, footbaths, waterfall showerheads, steam generators, sauna accommodations, heated towel bars, and more.

Power showers and shower towers (panels actually) are the most common, and although certainly more expensive than a single head on a flexible hose, they can definitely create the ambience necessary in a space for getting away from it all.

All these mood-altering improvements come with more technical differences than normal baths. To begin with, a multiple shower installation will usually call for larger piping—¾-inch pipe is the rule, installed from the source to the shower room—so you'll have enough water at all the showerheads. Multiple heads also require more piping, not just because you'll have more outlets, but because you need to balance the pressure so the water comes out at the same pressure and volume from all the the heads. (Without looping, water would just dribble out from the last head.)

Steam rooms need steam generators. Waterfalls and circulating baths require pumps, which can necessitate additional framing and plumbing too.

PRESTART CHECKLIST

☐ **TIME**
From one to two weeks, depending on the complexity of the installation

☐ **TOOLS**
Standard carpentry and plumbing tools

☐ **SKILLS**
Basic framing, electrical, and plumbing skills; professional assistance may be required for planning

1 For an existing shower room, remove sufficient drywall from the back of an adjoining wall to allow you to install blocking and framing for mounting the modular control units and shower fixtures. Hire a licensed electrician to mount and wire the GFCI outlet within the framing.

2 Using a manufacturer's template (or your own), drill the studs for the water lines. Install all fixtures. Run the water lines (with supply valves and water-hammer arrestors) from the fixtures to the valve location but do not connect them to the unit. Fasten the control unit to the framing in predrilled holes.

Installing pressure loops

Luxury shower installations with multiple showerheads will require both larger and additional water supply lines. Pressure loops—either within each fixture as shown here, or that tie all the heads together—are essential if you

Pressure balancing loop

want water coming from all the jets at equal force. Instead of the supply line terminating at each head, it continues to the next one that, in turn with the others, forms a continuous balanced loop.

3 Using your diagram showing which fixtures are supplied by each water line, identify any unused outlets in the valve and plug them. Wrap the plugs and all threaded pipe connections with 2 or 3 turns of teflon tape. Snug the connections, but do not over tighten them.

Outlet piping to shower fixtures

Unions

Hot and cold inlet piping

4 Connect the ¾-inch hot and cold supply lines to the outlets with unions. Make sure to connect the correct supply pipe to the correct outlet (they are color-coded and marked on the side of the valve body). Install the outlet piping on the appropriate outlets and secure all the piping to the framing.

5 Fasten the power supply unit to the framing in predrilled holes. Insert the power plug into the power receptacle on the valve unit body (inset, above right). Install the interface unit(s) if you haven't done so already, and connect them to the valve.

6 Plug in the power supply and make sure the valve unit door is sealed. Turn on the water supply valve, check for leaks, and make necessary adjustments. Turn on the main water supply and make sure the valve powers up and the indicator light is lit. Install an access door when finishing the drywall.

WHAT IF …
My unit requires a pump or heater?

A luxury shower model that requires a pump also requires special framing. Electrical power must be brought to their location too.

Depending on the pump's location and water exposure, you may also have to enclose the pump in a waterproof housing.

BUILDING A WET WALL

To build a new bathroom, half bath, shower unit, kitchen, or laundry room in your basement, you'll probably have to build a wet wall to enclose the pipes. This is an undertaking that sounds formidable, but the work is not complicated, just heavy. In many homes you will have to break out the concrete to expose the existing drain line. If drain stub ins are already in place, you won't have to remove the concrete.

You can save some money by tearing out the concrete with a sledgehammer (trim the edge neatly with a cold chisel) but you'll find a rented electric jackhammer well worth the expense. Be sure you have an easy way to remove the old concrete—trash bags won't work.

When you install the drain lines, slope them for proper flow; ¼ inch drop per foot is standard, but check your local codes. They may require a steeper fall.

1 Snap chalklines to mark the areas to remove. Using a sledgehammer and brick set or circular saw and masonry blade, score the lines. Break out the concrete with an electric jackhammer or sledgehammer. Dig a trench 2 inches deeper than the main drain.

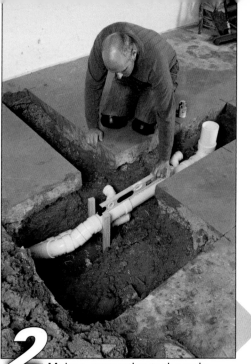

2 Make a connection to the main drain line (see below). Dry-fit and mark the new drain and vent lines and cut them to fit. Support the new lines with stakes to slope them properly.

PRESTART CHECKLIST

☐ **TIME**
About 2 days to frame and plumb an 8-foot wall

☐ **TOOLS**
Tape measure, chalk line, small sledgehammer and cold chisel, cordless drill, hammer, electric jackhammer or 12-pound sledgehammer, wheelbarrow, mixing hoe, level, reciprocating saw

☐ **SKILLS**
Measuring and marking, breaking concrete, installing PVC and copper pipe

☐ **MATERIALS**
PVC and copper pipe, stakes, protective plates, 2× lumber, PVC primer and cement, concrete mix

STANLEY PRO TIP

Building a branch drain

If you want a new bathroom in the basement but your chosen location is some distance from the existing main drain, you may have to install a branch line. This means breaking up the concrete and installing new lines and fittings as shown above. Before you tear into the floor, make sure you know exactly where the existing line runs.

Mark the position of the existing drain line and the proposed run of the branch line on the floor with a chalkline. Set the new shower and toilet in place to help you mark the exact location of the lines.

Score the lines with a masonry blade in your circular saw, then break up the concrete between the lines with a sledgehammer or rented electric jackhammer. After you get the first chunk out, dig out the soil as far as you can

under the remaining sections as you go—concrete is easier to break if there's nothing beneath it.

If you aren't sure of the nominal size of the existing line, measure it so you will know what size fittings to buy. Mark the position of the new fitting carefully on the old line. Cut the line with a chain cutter, reciprocating saw, or hacksaw.

Install the new fitting with no-hub connectors (pages 136–137) on both sides of the cutline. Adjust the fitting with a torpedo level to ensure the correct fall, then tighten the no-hub clamps.

Install the new drain line, then recheck the fall of the line over its length; adjust it at either end if necessary. Pour concrete into the excavated trench and finish the surface.

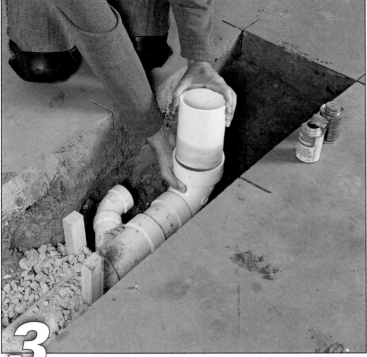

3 Cement the fittings to the pipe with solvent cement, keeping the fitting aligned. Recheck for proper drain slope and place aggregate around the line to hold it in position. After the line passes inspection from your local building department, backfill the trench with soil and concrete. Finish the concrete to match the floor.

4 Using the techniques on pages 176–181, frame a stud wall to enclose the drain and vent lines. Predrill holes in the studs for horizontal pipe runs. Assemble the remaining parts of the drain-waste-vent system. Connect the vent to the main stack.

5 Install shutoff valves on the supply lines closest to the new wet wall and extend copper supply lines to the wall using the techniques shown on pages 182–183. Install blocking or straps where necessary so the supply lines are supported properly and tack protective plates where the lines pass through the studs. Plug the lines to keep construction debris out. Leave the wallcovering off until the building inspector has approved the installation.

INSTALLING KITCHEN PLUMBING

Rough plumbing for a typical kitchen is much simpler than for a bathroom. Assuming there will be one sink and one dishwasher, only one drain line and one pair of supply pipes will be needed. All other connections—the drain and supply for the dishwasher, a supply line for an icemaker, and even a hot water dispenser or a water filter—are made with flexible tubing that does not run through walls.

The finish plumbing, however, can get complicated. The underside of a typical kitchen sink may look like a bewildering maze of tubes, appliances, and trap lines. This chapter eliminates the confusion by taking the project one step at a time.

The master plan

Remodeling a kitchen involves many operations. Usually the most efficient order of work is the following:

■ Cover sensitive surfaces and remove old cabinets, flooring, and wallcoverings.
■ Install the rough plumbing—the drain, vent, and supply lines.
■ Install electrical wiring and boxes and cut a hole for an exhaust fan if included.
■ Apply new drywall and patch any damaged walls. Prime and paint.
■ Install the flooring, then cover it with a protective drop cloth.

■ Install the wall and base cabinets, as well as the countertops.
■ Do the finish electrical work— lights, receptacles, and switches.
■ Install the sink, faucet, garbage disposer, dishwasher, and any other plumbing appliances.

For more help on remodeling tasks other than plumbing, see books in the Stanley series such as *Basic Wiring, Advanced Wiring, Basic Tiling,* and *Interior Walls.*

Rough plumbing for a kitchen is simple, but the finish installation calls for patient, methodical work.

CHAPTER PREVIEW

Planning a kitchen
page 206

Running drain lines
page 208

Extending supply lines
page 210

Preparing the cabinets
page 212

Installing an air admittance valve
page 214

Any horizontal run of the revent must be at least 6 inches above the "flood level" of the sink—the rim of the sink. In this case window framing is only a couple of inches above the countertop so a diagonal run of vent is needed. This prevents debris from settling in the vent should the sink back up.

If the drain line must travel more than 6 feet to reach the stack, you'll probably need to run the drain down through the floor and connect to the stack in the room below.

Hooking up the sink
page 216

Installing a garbage disposer
page 220

Adding a hot water dispenser
page 222

Adding an undersink filter
page 224

Hooking up an icemaker
page 225

Installing a dishwasher
page 226

You can dry-fit all or part of the drain and vent runs to accurately mark where to cut into the stack and where to route the lines. This allows you to double-check slope and the final location of the drain stub out too. Fasten the dry run in place with duct tape, then make the marks for cutting existing pipes and drilling holes in the framing.

PLANNING A KITCHEN

Many kitchen remodeling projects do not require new rough-in work. If the new sink is closer than 3 feet from an existing drain line, you can probably reach it by simply extending the trap. If supply lines need only to move over a few feet, you can probably attach a tee to one of the existing lines and route the new lines through cabinets, rather than inside walls. In this case you may not need a plumbing permit, but check with your local building department to be sure.

The plan shown here calls for the standard trio of kitchen plumbing appliances— a double-bowl sink, a garbage disposer, and a dishwasher. Other appliances, such as an undersink filter (page 155) or a hot water dispenser (pages 222–223), can be added without much trouble either during the initial installation or sometime later. A kettle-filler faucet (page 218), however, requires pipes that run through walls.

The drain and vent line
The sink trap connects to the sanitary tee of a 2-inch drain line. The ideal height of the tee varies depending on the depth of the sink. (If the tee is lower than the ideal height, you can simply extend the trap downward. If the tee is too high, you may need to install a new tee at a lower point.)

The drain line must be properly vented (pages 14–15). Often the kitchen drain is connected to a separate stack, smaller in diameter than the main stack, which extends up all the way out the roof. It's also possible to revent the drain line. Because kitchens are usually on the first floor, a revent line in a two-story house may need to travel up to the second floor or even to the attic.

Lots of grease gets poured down a kitchen sink. In many older homes the kitchen drainpipe leads to an outside catch basin, which can be accessed periodically in order to scoop out the grease. If your system has no catch basin (or grease trap), at least be sure there is an easily accessible cleanout. This plan calls for a cleanout just below the sanitary tee.

The supply lines
The hot water pipe supplies the faucet and the dishwasher; there should be a stop valve for each. The cold water pipe supplies the faucet as well as a line that runs to the icemaker; there is a stop valve for each.

KITCHEN PLUMBING OVERVIEW

The sink, cabinets, and countertop

The window above a kitchen sink is typically 42 inches high, so any vent lines must be installed to either side of the window. A standard base cabinet topped with a countertop is 36 inches high. A special "sink base" cabinet has no drawers or shelves to make room for the sink and the plumbing.

A hole must be cut in the countertop to accommodate the sink (page 213). You can do this yourself if the countertop is plastic laminate. If the top is granite or solid-surface, hire a pro to cut the top.

Usually the dishwasher is positioned next to the sink base to simplify running the drain and supply lines. (It is also the most convenient location for handling the dishes.) A 24-inch-wide opening in the cabinet houses a standard dishwasher.

Drawing a kitchen plan

On a piece of graph paper, draw a top view showing all the appliances, cabinets, electrical receptacles, and lights. Be precise, because every inch counts in a kitchen. A home center or kitchen supply source may have a computer program that will help you visualize possible layouts.

Kitchen designers often speak of a "work triangle," meaning that the sink, range, and refrigerator should all be within easy reach. This is easily accomplished in a kitchen that is U-shaped. If the kitchen is long and narrow, it's usually best to place one of the three elements on the wall opposite the other two. Make sure you can open the refrigerator without interfering with cooking or washing dishes.

Place the range at least 12 inches from the sink. And leave 36 inches of counterspace on either side of the sink for food preparation and draining dishes.

Most people prefer the sink to be placed in front of a window. The range should have a range hood above it, and the hood should vent to the outside.

If you plan to move or remove a wall, first check with a carpenter to make sure it's not load-bearing. If it is you may be able to install a beam in its place.

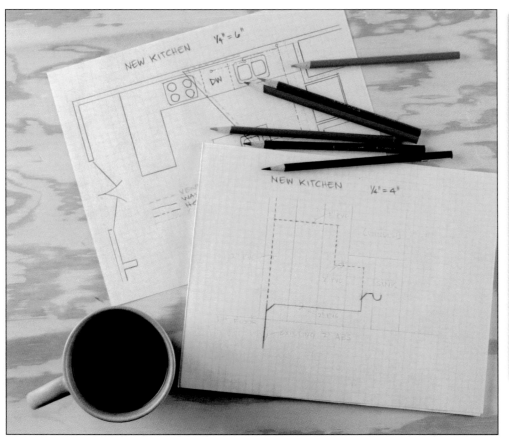

Make drawings (pages 40–41) to refine your plans and prepare for permit application. If you are tying into a drain-waste-vent (DWV) system with other fixtures, see the chart on page 37 to confirm drain and supply pipe sizes. Start with a floor plan (shown), then settle specifics with a DWV elevation.

Standard specs

Check local codes for all pipe sizes and other dimensions. Here are some standard specs:

Drain and vent pipes
Sink: 2-inch drain; 1½- or 2-inch vent
Stack: 2 inches or larger
Sink drain: 18 inches above floor

Supply pipes
Faucet: ½-inch pipe
Faucet stub outs: Locate them where they can be easily reached once the sink is installed.

Other fittings
Include stop valves on the hot water line for the dishwasher and sink. Include stop valves on the cold water supply for the sink and lines for other appliances such as an icemaker or hot water dispenser.

RUNNING DRAIN LINES

Draw a plan for a new drainpipe showing how it will be vented and where it will connect to the DWV system. Have your plan approved by a local plumbing inspector.

A kitchen usually does not have a 4-inch line that requires a thick wet wall as in a bathroom. Kitchen plumbing sometimes runs through an exterior wall, but pipes should be well insulated. In areas with cold winters, run supply pipes up from the basement through the floor rather than through the wall.

Remove all cabinets that are in the way. Completely cover all cabinets and flooring that you will reuse to protect them.

If wiring is in the way, **shut off the power to the circuit** and test to make sure power is off. You may want to remove a cable before working on the drain.

See pages 138–141 for ways to run pipes through walls and connect to existing pipes.

PRESTART CHECKLIST

☐ **TIME**
About a day to run a new drain line with a revent

☐ **TOOLS**
PVC saw or circular saw, level, layout square, drill with hole saw, reciprocating saw,

☐ **SKILLS**
Cutting and joining PVC pipe, running pipes through walls, connecting new pipe to old

☐ **PREP**
Clear the room of all obstructions; have your plans approved by an inspector

☐ **MATERIALS**
PVC pipe and fittings to suit local codes, PVC primer and cement, fitting for joining to the drainpipe, pipe straps

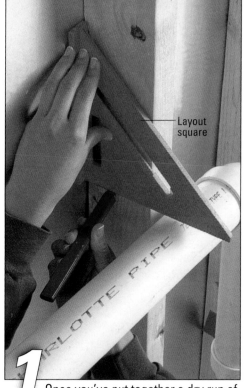

Layout square

1 Once you've put together a dry run of the drain and vent lines (page 205), mark for cutting holes in the framing. Using a layout square strike a line even with the top of the pipe. Then mark for the center of the pipe at the center of the stud.

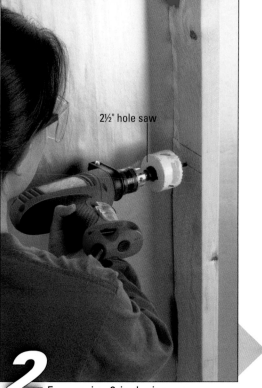

2½" hole saw

2 For running 2-inch pipe, use a 2½-inch hole saw to drill through the studs (see pages 176–181). When possible cut until the guide bit pierces the stud, then cut from the opposite side. Assemble the pipes in the wall, notching the studs where necessary.

INSTALLING A KITCHEN DRAIN-WASTE-VENT SYSTEM

No-hub coupling

Existing 3" pipe

45° elbow

Reducing Y

Sanitary tee with trap adapter

1½" trap

If you need to move a drain for remodeling, run 2-inch pipe for the vent and drain lines. The drain line, and perhaps the vent as well, must be sloped at ⅛ to ¼ inch per running foot. If you must tie into a main 3- or 4-inch drain line, use a reducing tee and a reducing Y.

3 Having used the dry run to mark the existing stack, add braces and pipe straps to stabilize the drain. If the stack is cast iron, see pages 136–137 for how to support it. Then cut away a section to make way for the new installation.

4 If the stack is ABS (shown in Step 3) or cast iron, use short lengths of PVC pipe and no-hub fittings to connect a sanitary tee for the vent and a Y-fitting and 45-degree street elbow for the drain. Then mark and cut a section of 2-inch PVC pipe to complete the stack.

5 Install a brace for the supply drop ears. Mark, prime, and cement (pages 128–129) the drain-vent system.

WHAT IF ...
You install a sink in an island?

A sink installed in a kitchen island poses a special problem because there is no easy way to tie into a vent. The solution is a loop vent. This is a complicated setup, so consult an inspector after you draw up your plans.

The drainpipe is run in the standard manner—a 1½-inch trap linking to a 2-inch sink drain that runs down to a 3- or 4-inch drainpipe by means of a sanitary tee.

The vent pipe first loops up as high as possible, then runs down and over to a suitable vent pipe run up a wall. Because some water will likely enter the vent pipe, it also must be connected to the drainpipe using a sanitary tee fitting.

EXTENDING SUPPLY LINES

In a typical kitchen setup, hot and cold supply lines emerge from the wall just below the sink faucet, where they are connected to stop valves. Supply pipes should run inside walls rather than through cabinets to keep them safe from harm.

Pipes under a sink are liable to get bumped; these pages show the most durable installation, using drop-ear elbows and galvanized nipples.

Half-inch rigid copper pipe is large enough for most kitchen installations. (For information on how to cut and join copper supply pipe, see pages 126–127.)

These pages show separate stop valves for the hot and cold faucet lines, the dishwasher, and an icemaker. If you want to add a water filter, hot-water dispenser, or other appliance, you may need additional stop valves. Saddle tee valves, which simply tap into a pipe, are easy to install but are prone to clogging.

PRESTART CHECKLIST

☐ **TIME**
Several hours to run copper supply lines through a floor or wall

☐ **TOOLS**
Drill, level, combination square, propane torch, groove-joint pliers, tubing cutter or hacksaw, fiber shield, C-clamps

☐ **SKILLS**
Cutting and joining copper pipe, running pipe through framing

☐ **PREP**
Install the drain line and carefully plan the location of the supply lines; shut off the water before beginning work

☐ **MATERIALS**
Copper pipe and fittings, flux, solder, galvanized nipples, stop valves, nailing plates, shims

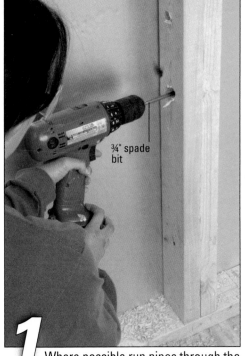

1 Where possible run pipes through the centers of studs. Use a level or other long straightedge to mark for straight runs from stud to stud and use a combination square to mark for the center of studs. Drill ¾-inch holes to accommodate ½-inch pipe.

¾" spade bit

45° elbow — Tee

45° street elbow

Existing supply line

2 **Shut off water** and drain the lines you will tap into. Cut the existing pipes and install new tee fittings (pages 126–127). If you must run around a pipe or other obstruction, use 45-degree elbows and street elbows.

STANLEY PRO TIP: **Stop valves**

Make sure each stop valve is the right size and type for both the pipe and the supply tube that it will attach to. A kitchen stop valve should have a ½-inch outlet.

If you will be joining to rigid copper pipe (rather than a galvanized nipple as shown opposite), buy a valve that sweats onto the pipe (page 126) or one that joins with compression fittings (upper right).

If the pipe rises vertically through the floor, use a straight stop valve (lower right), rather than an angle stop.

Compression-fitted stop valve

Threaded straight stop valve

3 Usually the most convenient location for stub outs is on each side of the drain trap adapter, as shown. However place them wherever they will be within easy reach but within 18 inches of the faucet inlets. At each stub out install a hammer arrester and a drop-ear elbow. Do a dry run (shown), then sweat the fittings and reattach the drop ears to the braces. Add nipples with caps; turn on the water and check for leaks.

Labels in image 3: 45° street elbow; Hammer arrester; Drop-ear elbow; ½" galvanized with cap; 90° street elbow; Tee; Drain trap adapter

4 Install the wallcovering, prime and paint the walls, and install the flooring. Install the kitchen base cabinets. Plumb and level them and attach them to each other (shown) and to the walls. If the sink base has a back, you'll need to drill holes for the stub outs.

Label in image 2: C-clamp

WHAT IF ...
Supply lines run beneath the floor?

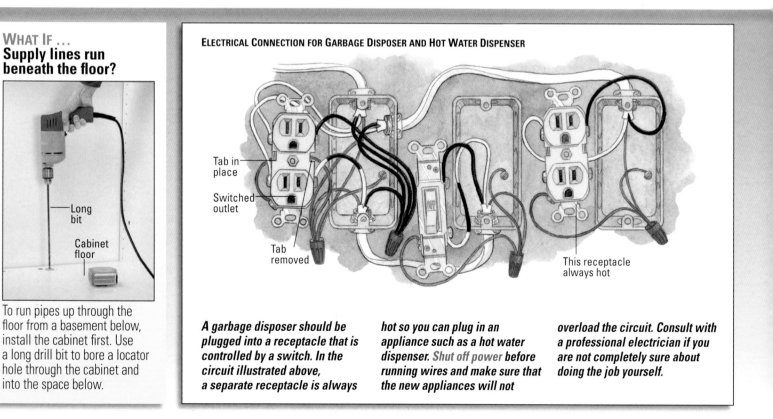

Labels: Long bit; Cabinet floor

To run pipes up through the floor from a basement below, install the cabinet first. Use a long drill bit to bore a locator hole through the cabinet and into the space below.

ELECTRICAL CONNECTION FOR GARBAGE DISPOSER AND HOT WATER DISPENSER

Labels: Tab in place; Switched outlet; Tab removed; This receptacle always hot

A garbage disposer should be plugged into a receptacle that is controlled by a switch. In the circuit illustrated above, a separate receptacle is always hot so you can plug in an appliance such as a hot water dispenser. Shut off power *before running wires and make sure that the new appliances will not* overload the circuit. Consult with a professional electrician if you are not completely sure about doing the job yourself.

PREPARING THE CABINETS

Once the drain and supply pipes have been installed and tested for leaks, run any electrical lines for receptacles and lights. Cover the walls with drywall and prime and paint. Install the finish flooring, then protect it with cardboard or heavy paper and a drop cloth.

Purchase the sink, garbage disposer, dishwasher, and any other appliances. Unpack them and check the manufacturer's literature for the installation requirements. In particular be sure about the dimensions of the opening for the dishwasher, as well as the size and location of the hole for its drain and supply lines.

A sink base cabinet has no drawers or shelves, providing room for all the appliances, tubes, and pipes that must fit inside it. Some sink bases are actual completed cabinets, while others consist of only the face and the floor.

Flange   Adjustable wrench

1 Shut off the water and drain the line. For each supply remove the cap from the nipple and slide on a flange to cover the hole at the wall. Wrap the nipple threads with pipe-thread tape and install a tee. Wrap

Teflon tape around the threads of two short nipples and screw them into the tee fitting. Screw stop valves onto the nipples. Turn the valve handles off and restore water pressure to test for leaks.

PRESTART CHECKLIST

☐ **TIME**
A day to install cabinets, plus several hours to run the wiring for the dishwasher

☐ **TOOLS**
Hammer, drill, level, groove-joint pliers, adjustable wrench, tape measure, screwdriver, hole saw

☐ **SKILLS**
Measuring, drilling, and sawing accurately to install cabinets that are level and properly spaced

☐ **PREP**
Run and test all the rough plumbing

☐ **MATERIALS**
Cabinets, shims, screws, tees, nipples, pipe-thread tape, stop valves, 14/2 armored cable

CABINET PREPARATION

For cabinets with backs precut holes before installation.

Hot supply

Cold supply

Trap adapter

Electrical cable

Hole for dishwasher drain and supply

To ease installation while avoiding unsightly gaps, be exact about the opening for a dishwasher. The cabinets on either side must be plumb. The dishwasher drain and supply lines run through a single hole in the cabinet.

2 The dishwasher opening should be 24¼ inches wide for most models; check manufacturer's instructions. If installing a cabinet to the other side of the dishwasher (shown above), level from the sink base cabinet, plumb, and fasten it in place.

14/2 armored cable

Cable connector

3 Run an electrical line for the dishwasher. Usually a 14/2 armored cable connected to a 15-amp circuit is sufficient, but check codes and the manufacturer's literature. Be certain that the dishwasher will not overload the circuit. **Hire an electrician if you are not sure of your wiring abilities.**

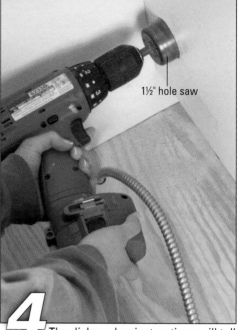

1½" hole saw

4 The dishwasher instructions will tell you the best place to drill a hole for running the drain and supply lines. Usually a single 1½-inch hole is sufficient.

STANLEY PRO TIP

Cutting countertop for a sink

Jigsaw

Cut along inner line

To cut a laminate countertop for a sink, place the sink upside down on top of the countertop, centered over the base cabinet. Apply wide masking tape to the approximate area and trace around the sink. Then draw another line ¾ inch inside the first line. Cut along the inner line using a jigsaw with a fine-cutting blade. The tape is easier to draw lines on and reduces chipping when cutting.

Choosing a sink

When it comes to sink materials, you generally get what you pay for. An inexpensive stainless-steel sink flexes when you push on it, scratches easily, and is difficult to keep clean. A higher-quality heavy-gauge (6- or 8-gauge) stainless-steel sink, such as one with a burnished finish, is a better choice. When choosing a stainless-steel sink, make sure the underside is well coated with sound-deadening insulation.

An enameled cast-iron sink comes in a variety of colors. It lasts much longer than an enameled steel sink. Acrylic sinks (like the one shown) have the look of enameled cast iron, and the higher-end models are nearly as durable. Both cast-iron and acrylic sinks have insulating properties so that water stays warm in them longer than it does in a stainless-steel sink.

Stainless steel

Heavy-gauge stainless steel

Cast iron

Acrylic

INSTALLING AN AIR ADMITTANCE VALVE

A common problem associated with plumbing remodeling is determining how to run new vent lines when access to the existing drain-waste-vent system is blocked by some structural element. Installing a new kitchen sink requires a new vent line, but if it is in an island installation, the vent can prove difficult.

Air admittance valves are gravity-operated devices that respond to the negative pressure of draining water and opens to let air in. Then gravity lets the valves close, keeping sewer gases out of the room. Depending on the valve and the size of the vent, AAVs can support one or multiple vent lines. Local codes govern use of AAVs in place of vents.

Air admittance valves are typically placed between the P-trap of a fixture and the drain line. They are usually mounted on one leg of a sanitary tee, the other of which goes to the drain. The unit must be located in accordance with local codes and manufacturer's instructions.

PRESTART CHECKLIST

☐ **TIME**
About an hour to cut and assemble five or six pipes and fittings

☐ **TOOLS**
PVC saw or backsaw, miter box or power mitersaw, deburring tool, felt-tip marker

☐ **SKILLS**
Sawing, measuring, working methodically

☐ **PREP**
Sketch drain/vent assembly; clear a path for the pipes

☐ **MATERIALS**
Primer and cement for your type and size of pipe, P-trap, air admittance valve, drain pipe

How does it work?

Air admittance valves are operated by gravity. When water and waste move down a drain line, negative air pressure is created behind them. This negative pressure in the pipe lifts the sealing washer and lets air in, which allows the waste to drain away freely. When the negative pressure ceases, the sealing washer falls back in place. Earlier versions of this device were spring operated. These units are still available but are not reliable and don't meet code in most localities.

1 Install PVC drain line, sanitary tee, and P-trap for sink. The appropriate coupling for the AAV (glued or threaded) attaches to the tee. AAV must be above the drain to the P-trap; manufacturer's instructions and local codes determine AAV height above the drain.

2 Using the appropriate plastic glue if necessary, install a glued AAV. Otherwise screw in the unit to the threaded collar.

3 Depending on local codes and the AAV model, completed installation should look something like this.

STANLEY PRO TIP

Reducing vent lines

One of the benefits of an air admittance valve is that it can serve as many as six fixtures (depending on local code allowances) as long as your DWV system employs at least one vertical vent stack that exits through the roof to the outside of the building. This reduces the number of potential leaks along the roofline and helps make the roof more attractive.

AAV

Drain

HOOKING UP THE SINK

Once you have cut the hole in the countertop (page 213), set the sink into the hole to make sure it will fit.

You can install the sink and then attach the faucet, garbage disposer, and drain from below. It's easier, though, to attach them first. Spread a drop cloth on the countertop and set the sink upside down with the faucet holes overhanging the edge. Or set the sink on two sawhorses, padded with rags or towels.

Enameled-steel (shown) and stainless-steel sinks clamp to the countertop with special clips that are usually included with the sink. Test to make sure that the clips will work on your countertop before you install the plumbing. A cast-iron sink is heavy enough that it needs no clips.

PRESTART CHECKLIST

☐ **TIME**
About half a day to install a sink with disposer and dishwasher connections

☐ **TOOLS**
Drill, screwdriver, groove-joint pliers, adjustable wrench, strainer wrench or spud wrench

☐ **SKILLS**
Connecting a trap, installing a faucet and garbage disposer

☐ **PREP**
Install the rough plumbing, a switched receptacle, and the cabinets

☐ **MATERIALS**
Sink, faucet, garbage disposer, appliance extension cord, wire nuts, trap assembly, s upply tubes, flexible copper line for dishwasher and icemaker supplies, drain hose (usually included with the dishwasher), air gap, plumber's putty, drop cloth

1 Install a standard basket strainer in one sink hole and the garbage disposer strainer in the other hole. Make sure you know which strainer goes to which hole. Place a rope of putty under the lip of the strainer body and hold it in place as you slip on the washers and tighten the nut.

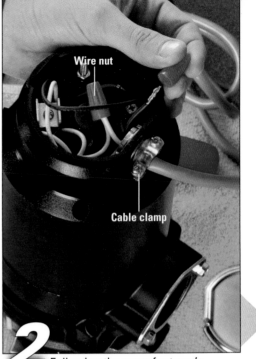

2 Following the manufacturer's instructions prepare the garbage disposer mounting hardware for installation. Open the electrical cover plate and hook up an appliance extension cord using wire nuts. Replace the cover plate.

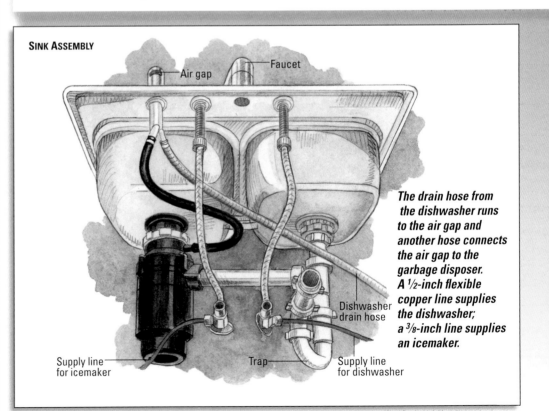

SINK ASSEMBLY

The drain hose from the dishwasher runs to the air gap and another hose connects the air gap to the garbage disposer. A ½-inch flexible copper line supplies the dishwasher; a ⅜-inch line supplies an icemaker.

Garbage
disposer

Mounting ring

Trap

Arm

Tailpiece

Groove-joint
pliers

⅝" drain hose

Inlet for
dishwasher
drain

Air gap

Mounting
nut

3 Slide the garbage disposer mounting ring over the flange. Then install the cushion mount, making sure the groove on the inside fits over the lip of the sink flange. Position the disposer over the flange; push down and twist until the disposer is fully anchored.

4 Assemble the drain trap. Begin by installing the tailpiece and the arm that attaches to the disposer. Cut pieces to size as needed, then install the trap. Set the sink in the hole to see whether the trap lines up with the trap adapter in the wall; you may need to trim a piece or add an extension.

5 Attach the air gap with a mounting nut. Run a ⅝-inch hose from the air gap to the disposer. Secure the hose with hose clamps. If the drain hose is easily disconnected from the dishwasher, attach it to the air gap now. Otherwise attach it when you install the dishwasher (pages 226–227).

ALTERNATE TRAP CONFIGURATIONS

Center tee

Side-mounted
tee

Side-
mounted
tee

Here are several possible ways to assemble traps. Local codes may require that each sink bowl have its own trap running to the drainpipe. Some codes do not allow you to connect the dishwasher drain hose to the garbage disposer; the hose must be clamped to a dishwasher tailpiece that is connected to the other bowl.

STANLEY PRO TIP

Assembling a trap

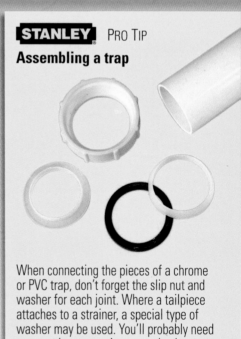

When connecting the pieces of a chrome or PVC trap, don't forget the slip nut and washer for each joint. Where a tailpiece attaches to a strainer, a special type of washer may be used. You'll probably need to cut at least one pipe; use a hacksaw or a fine-toothed saw (for PVC only) and a miter box.

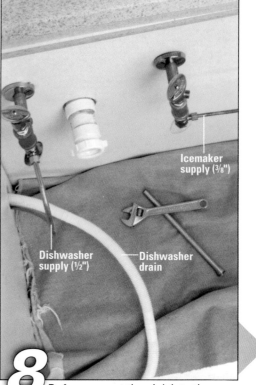

6 Install the faucet. If the faucet does not come with a plastic or rubber gasket, place a rope of putty under the faucet's flange to seal out water. Tighten the mounting hardware.

7 Screw flexible supply tubes onto the faucet inlets. Make sure their other ends are the right size to screw onto the stop valves. If the faucet has flexible copper inlets, use two adjustable wrenches to avoid kinking the inlets.

8 Before you set the sink into the hole, save yourself work later by hooking up as much plumbing as possible now. For instance attach the supply lines for the dishwasher (page 226) and icemaker.

Installing a kettle-filler faucet

A faucet like this makes it easy to fill a large kettle while it is on the stove or countertop. This model supplies only cold water, but other types have cold and hot handles.

It is important to install the faucet firmly in the wall. Run a cold water supply line up the wall. The last 2 feet or so should be strong pipe, such as galvanized steel or brass. Install a threaded tee and a hammer arrester. Anchor a 2×6 or larger brace behind the pipe and the tee and attach the pipe and the tee using two-hole pipe straps.

Along with the faucet buy a special inlet nipple, which has threads running along its length in the same direction. A locking nut with washers allows you to screw the inlet nipple to the faucet at just the right depth so you can screw the faucet into the tee fitting at maximum tightness against the wall.

9 Place a rope of plumber's putty, thick enough to seal at all points, around the bottom lip of the sink. Position at least some of the mounting clips in the channels and hold them upright, using dabs of putty. Turn the sink right side up and carefully lower it into the hole.

Mounting clip held by plumber's putty

Plumber's putty

10 From underneath turn the clips so they grab the underside of the countertop. There should be a clip every 8 inches or so. Tighten each clip with a screwdriver or a drill equipped with a screwdriver bit.

Mounting clip

11 Attach the trap to the trap adapter in the wall. Tighten all the connections with groove-joint pliers. To test, fill each bowl with water, then remove the stopper and watch for drips. Run the disposer with the water on and check for drips.

Installing a cast-iron sink

A cast-iron sink is very heavy, so have someone help you lift and position it. Apply a bead of silicone caulk around the hole. Carefully lower the sink into the opening. Avoid sliding it, which could compromise the caulk seal. Press down gently. Scrape away excess caulk with a plastic or wood scraper. Allow the caulk to set for several hours before attaching the plumbing.

Other sink installations

A flush-mounted or underhung sink makes for easier cleaning, but these styles require special countertop treatments.

Install a flush-mounted sink with its rim resting on plywood substrate. Install cement backerboard on the top up to the edge of the sink and cover it with tiles that partially overhang the sink flange.

Install and plumb an underhung sink after the substrate is installed. Then install tiles as shown, with cut pieces along the perimeter and bullnose trim pieces overlapping them.

Thinset mortar

Tile

Caulk

Cement backerboard

Plywood

flush-mounted sink

Bullnose tile

Cut tile

Thinset mortar

Plywood

Cement backerboard

Underhung sink

INSTALLING A GARBAGE DISPOSER

Replacing an existing disposer with one of the same size is simply a matter of disconnecting and reconnecting fittings. However if there is no existing disposer or if the new unit is a different size, you will need to reconfigure your sink trap.

A disposer must be plugged into a GFCI receptacle or directly wired to a junction box that is controlled by a switch. The switch is typically on the wall above the countertop. If the wiring does not exist under your sink, have an electrician do this work for you.

Local codes may regulate the use of disposers. Codes may require that a dishwasher drain hose be routed through an air gap before entering a disposer.

Installation, parts, and procedures vary considerably among disposer models. Follow the manufacturer's directions.

PRESTART CHECKLIST

☐ **TIME**
One to three hours, depending on changes to plumbing

☐ **TOOLS**
Screwdriver, wire strippers, groove-joint pliers

☐ **SKILLS**
Making simple electrical splices, installing a basket strainer

☐ **PREP**
Remove an existing disposer or part of the trap, and the strainer

☐ **MATERIALS**
Garbage disposer, cable clamps, appliance cord (thicker than normal extension cord) or armored cable ("whip"), wire nuts, plumber's putty, trap parts

1 Remove the electrical cover plate from the bottom of the disposer. Install a cable clamp and run an appliance cord through it. Strip the wire ends and splice the wires—black to black, white to white, ground (green) to ground. Cap each splice with a wire nut. Replace the cover plate.

2 Remove the old strainer (pages 52–53) and clean the area around the hole. Press a rope of plumber's putty around the underside of the disposer sink flange. Press the flange into place. Have a helper hold the flange in position while you perform the next step from below.

GARBAGE DISPOSER INSTALLATION

Once the sink flange and support ring are installed, the disposer can be installed by locking it onto the support ring and hooking up connections.

Support ring

Mounting ring

Cushion mount

Tailpiece

3 To install this type of mounting ring, slip on the fiber gasket and hand-tighten the support ring. Slide the mounting ring over the flange and install the cushion mount, making sure the groove on the inside fits over the lip of the sink flange. Scrape out any excess putty on the inside of the sink.

4 If the disposer is not too heavy and you can get into a comfortable position, simply lift the disposer up onto the mounting ring and twist it so it catches and is firmly anchored. If you have trouble doing this, construct a simple platform to help support the disposer.

5 To connect to the drain line, use the black elbow that comes with the disposer or discard the elbow and install a horizontal tailpiece, as shown. See pages 48–49 for tips on assembling a trap.

Attaching a dishwasher

Knockout hole

If you have a dishwasher, run its drain hose first to an air gap, then to the disposer's drain connection. Use a hose clamp to hold the hose firm.

USE THE BLACK ELBOW
Other disposer drain options

Double-bowl installation

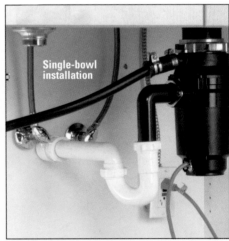

Single-bowl installation

Some local codes require that the drain line turn downward as soon as it leaves the disposer. Most disposers come with a black elbow designed to make this turn. If you have

a single-bowl sink, install the black elbow that comes with the disposer and run the drain line directly into a trap.

ADDING A HOT WATER DISPENSER

This handy appliance instantly provides water that's about 200 degrees. It plugs into a standard electrical receptacle. Copper tubing connects the dispenser to a cold water line, and hot water is delivered through a spout mounted on the sink ledge.

The dispenser requires an unswitched electrical receptacle near the sink. To supply a garbage disposer and a hot water dispenser from a single receptacle, have an electrician install a split GFCI receptacle.

Position the tank and the copper lines out of the way under the sink. Usually the rear wall is preferable to a side wall.

You can screw a saddle-tee valve into the pipe without shutting off the water to the pipe. However the valve is liable to get clogged. For a more trouble-free installation, shut off the water and drill a hole first (as shown in Step 1).

PRESTART CHECKLIST

☐ **TIME**
About an hour if there is an existing electrical receptacle and an available knockout hole on the sink

☐ **TOOLS**
Drill, adjustable wrench, basin wrench, groove-joint pliers, tubing bender, screwdriver, perhaps a hole saw

☐ **SKILLS**
Mounting a unit with screws, assembling appliance parts

☐ **PREP**
Clear out the cabinet below the sink; shut off water to a cold water line

☐ **MATERIALS**
Saddle-tee valve or stop valve, hot water dispenser

Cold water supply line

1 Shut off water to a cold water line; drain the line by opening a faucet at a lower level. Check the manufacturer's instructions for drilling a hole (typically about ⅛ inch) for the saddle-tee valve needle. Squirt a little multipurpose oil on the bit before drilling.

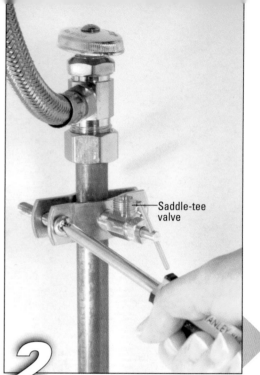

Saddle-tee valve

2 Position the two parts of a saddle-tee valve on the pipe, making sure the valve's point pokes into the hole. Tighten the screws. Turn the water back on and make sure the valve works and does not leak.

OVERVIEW OF HOT WATER DISPENSER INSTALLATION

Supply to heater
Supply tube
Vent tube
Hot water supply
Mounting bracket
Plastic supply tube
Saddle-tee valve
GFCI receptacle
Access panel

A hot water dispenser's tank mounts with a simple bracket. A copper tube runs from a cold water source to the spout, and two other copper lines run to the tank. A plastic vent tube connects with a clamp.

Knockout hole

3 Mount the spout first. Carefully slip the copper lines through the knockout hole. Have a helper hold the spout in position while you work from underneath. Slide on the washer and the mounting nut. Tighten the nut by hand. If that is not firm enough, use a basin wrench to tighten it further.

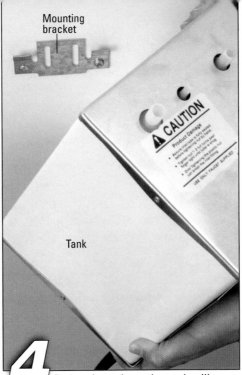

Mounting bracket

Tank

4 Determine where the tank will go; the copper lines must be able to reach it. Install the bracket with screws and slip the tank onto the bracket.

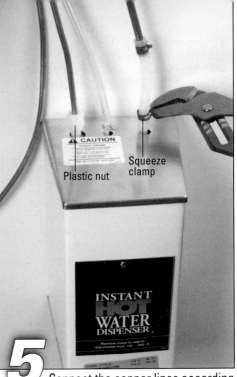

Plastic nut

Squeeze clamp

5 Connect the copper lines according to manufacturer's instructions. Bend the tubes carefully to avoid kinking; use a tubing bender to be safe (page 20). Copper tubes connect to the tank using a plastic nut and ferrule; plastic tubes are secured with squeeze clamps.

Other water connections

For a more secure supply connection, install a tee fitting in the cold water line and add a stop valve.

Another method is to replace a standard stop valve with one that has two outlets, one for the faucet and one for the hot water dispenser.

Maintaining a dispenser

Water that comes from this unit is nearly boiling, so keep young children away from the spout.

The tank gets hot too, so keep paper bags and other flammables away from it.

If you expect not to use the dispenser for a few days, unplug it to save energy.

If the unit gets clogged, shut off the saddle-tee or stop valve and disconnect the supply line. Hold the line over a bucket and slowly turn the water back on. If flow is slow the problem is probably the saddle-tee valve. Shut off the water and replace the valve.

If water drips from the spout when the unit is not in use, turn down the temperature. If that doesn't solve the problem, replace the spout.

No knockout on sink?

Drill a hole in a stainless-steel sink using a metal-cutting hole saw. In an acrylic sink use a standard hole saw.

ADDING AN UNDERSINK FILTER

A simple water filter can reduce the amount of sediment in water and improve its odor and taste.

Local water conditions vary, so check with a salesperson at a home center or hardware store to see which filter will work best for you. Most carbon-based units make water more palatable.

If your water is excessively hard, have a water softener company install and perhaps maintain a water softener.

The unit shown here purifies all the cold water that runs through a kitchen faucet. Also available is a unit that has its own faucet for a separate source of filtered drinking water.

For an easy-to-install alternative, consider a faucet-mounted water filter. Some purify all the water flowing through the spout, while others have a separate valve that allows you to choose filtered or unfiltered water. Both screw onto the faucet in place of the aerator.

PRESTART CHECKLIST

☐ **TIME**
An hour or two

☐ **TOOLS**
Adjustable wrench, drill, screwdriver, hacksaw or PVC saw, tubing cutter, groove-joint pliers

☐ **SKILLS**
Attaching with screws, cutting pipe, and making simple connections

☐ **PREP**
Add a tee and stop valve to the cold water supply; clear out the cabinet

☐ **MATERIALS**
Water purifier, perhaps extra parts for connecting

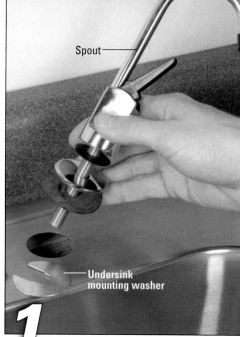

Spout

Undersink mounting washer

1 Mount the spout to the knockout hole in the sink. Have a helper center the spout while you work below to tighten the mounting nut.

2 **Shut off the water** to the cold water supply tube. Add a separate stop valve (page 118–119) or use one of the methods on page 223. Hold the filter in a convenient location and drive screws to attach it.

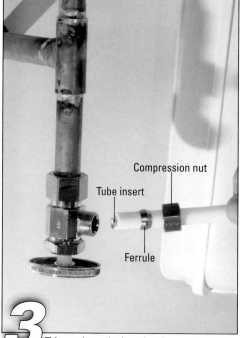

Compression nut

Tube insert

Ferrule

3 Trim to length the plastic supply tube for the filter. Poke the tube insert into the tube and slide on the compression nut and ferrule. Tighten the nut using a small adjustable wrench.

4 Connect the lines to the stop valve and spout according to the manufacturer's instructions. Compression fittings make these connections easy. Water will now run through the filter before reaching the spout.

HOOKING UP AN ICEMAKER

Most new refrigerators have icemakers, but installation is typically an added expense. If you are retrofitting an icemaker to an older fridge, you will need to tap into a cold water line to supply the icemaker. In either case doing it yourself is not difficult, as long as you work carefully with the copper tubing. If any kinks develop don't try to "fix" them—cut them off or use a new piece of tubing.

For ice that tastes extra nice, install a water filter (opposite) and run the icemaker line through it.

As an alternative to the saddle-tee valve, install a new stop valve or a stop valve with two outlets (page 223).

PRESTART CHECKLIST

☐ **TIME**
An hour or two for most installations

☐ **TOOLS**
Drill with long drill bit, screwdriver, adjustable wrench, tubing bender

☐ **SKILLS**
Drilling holes, cutting and running copper tubing, making simple connections

☐ **PREP**
Locate a nearby cold water pipe to tap

☐ **MATERIALS**
Copper tubing, saddle-tee valve

1 Behind the refrigerator drill a hole through the floor to a basement or crawlspace, or drill a horizontal hole to reach another room. Carefully unroll copper tubing and run it through the hole.

2 Install a saddle-tee valve on a cold water pipe (page 222) and hook the copper line to it by slipping on a ferrule and tightening a compression nut.

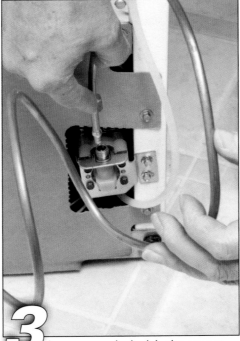

3 Leave enough slack in the copper line to allow you to slide out the refrigerator for cleaning. Connect the other end of the tubing to the icemaker connection on the refrigerator, using the same combination of a compression nut and a ferrule.

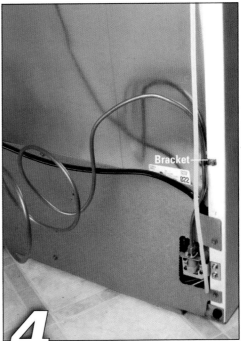

4 Moving the refrigerator for cleaning strains the compression fitting. Use one of the brackets provided with the refrigerator or the icemaker kit to firmly attach the copper tube to the fridge. Carefully bend the tubing into a coil as shown.

INSTALLING A DISHWASHER

Once you prepare the site, installing a dishwasher is easy. Make the opening the correct size and test-fit the dishwasher.

Run an electrical cable—armored or nonmetallic as required by code—to the space. Make sure it will not bump into the dishwasher's frame. A 14/2 cable is adequate for a 15-amp circuit. Make sure the dishwasher will not overload the circuit. Hire an electrician if you are unsure.

Most dishwashers come with a drain hose. The drain hose runs to an air gap mounted to a knockout hole in the sink (page 216). From there another length of hose runs to the garbage disposer. If there is no garbage disposer, it runs to a dishwasher tailpiece on the trap.

The water supply line is typically flexible copper, connected to its own shutoff valve. The cabinets on either side should be spaced according to manufacturer's instructions—usually 24¼ inches.

PRESTART CHECKLIST

☐ **TIME**
About an hour once the electrical and plumbing lines are run and the cabinets installed

☐ **TOOLS**
Tubing cutter, drill, screwdriver, adjustable wrench, wire strippers, groove-joint pliers

☐ **SKILLS**
Making simple plumbing and electrical connections

☐ **PREP**
Install the electrical and plumbing lines; install the cabinets and countertop

☐ **MATERIALS**
Dishwasher with drain hose, flexible copper supply line, hose clamps, air gap, electrical cable, wire nuts

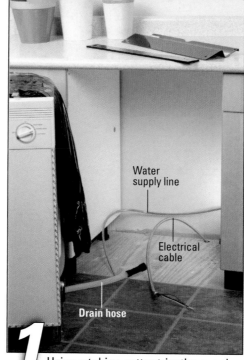

Water supply line
Electrical cable
Drain hose

1 Using a tubing cutter trim the supply tube to the needed length. Make sure the electrical cable is long enough to reach the junction box built into the dishwasher.

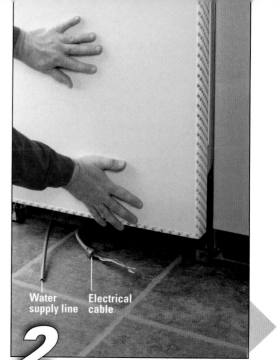

Water supply line
Electrical cable

2 Push the dishwasher into the opening. As you do so thread the drain line through the 1½-inch hole already cut in the cabinet. Make sure the lines do not become kinked or bent.

DISHWASHER CONNECTIONS

Three connections are needed for a dishwasher: An electrical cable supplies 120 volts of power; a drain line runs to the trap or garbage disposer; and a supply line, hooked to a stop valve under the sink, brings water to the dishwasher.

Electrical junction box

Drain hose

Stop valve

Drain outlet

Hot water hookup

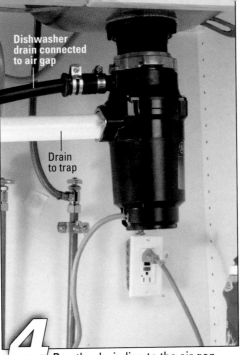

Dishwasher drain connected to air gap

Drain to trap

3 Slip a nut and ferrule onto the end of the supply line. Carefully bend the tubing and insert it into the supply inlet. Slide the ferrule down into the inlet and tighten the nut. Open the stop valve and check for leaks; you may need to tighten the nut further.

4 Run the drain line to the air gap, then to the garbage disposer or a tailpiece with a special dishwasher drain fitting. Slide a hose clamp onto the hose, slip the hose onto the fitting, slide the clamp over the fitting, and tighten the clamp.

5 Run the electrical cable through the cable clamp and tighten the clamp nuts to hold the cable firm. Strip and splice wires—black to black, white to white, and ground (green or copper) to ground. Cap each splice with a wire nut and install the electrical cover plate.

Anchoring and leveling the dishwasher

Adjustable leg

Groove-joint pliers

Slide the dishwasher in far enough so that only its decorative trim is visible. If the dishwasher won't go in far enough, pull it out and look for obstructions.

Stand back and check that the dishwasher looks straight in relation to the cabinets and the countertop. To raise or lower one or both sides, use groove-joint pliers to turn the feet at the bottom of the unit. Wiggle the dishwasher to test that it rests solidly on all four feet.

Once satisfied with the dishwasher's position, open the door and find the mounting tabs (usually on the top edge, sometimes on the sides). Drill pilot holes. To avoid drilling up through the countertop, wrap a piece of tape on the drill bit to mark the depth at which to stop. Drive short screws into the holes to anchor the dishwasher to the countertop.

Heating, Ventilation & Air-Conditioning

The heating, ventilation, and air-conditioning (HVAC) systems in homes are often called the comfort systems because their primary function is to regulate the temperature and humidity of your home. As a result they also have a lot to do with the health and safety of your home environment.

Heating starts with some kind of heat-generating device—a gas, oil, or electric furnace, or an alternative system such as a heat pump or solar panels. Whatever medium is heated—either air or water—is circulated through pipes or ducts to radiators, vents, or other convectors, which release the heat into the various rooms of your home. The heating unit, convection system, and dispersing units are all part of the heating system in your home. So are the thermostats.

Ventilation has to do with the quality of the air in your home. A properly vented home ensures the regular transfer of fresh air into your living environment, and the ventilation system helps regulate the temperature and humidity too. Proper ventilation also gives you the confidence that dangerous gases, such as carbon monoxide, radon, and other airborne chemicals from construction materials, are vented to the outside. Ceiling fans, bath and kitchen exhaust fans, air exchangers, and windows, doors, and vents are all part of the ventilation system in your house.

An air-conditioning system works in a manner opposite to that of a heating system. Instead of adding heat to an environment, it removes it, stores it in a refrigerant, and disperses it into the outdoors. A central air-conditioning system (including a large evaporative cooler) does this for the whole house. Window air-conditioners are designed to keep smaller spaces comfortable. A heat pump does both jobs, removing heat in the summer and adding it during colder months. Like the heating system the air-conditioning system includes the compressor and refrigeration unit, plus the convection and dispersal elements.

Maintaining the major components of your HVAC system is for the pros, but there are many tasks that will help keep the systems operating properly and are quite within the reach of the average homeowner.

A well-tuned HVAC system makes your home comfortable, safe, and healthy.

CHAPTER PREVIEW

Installing a whole-house humidifier
page 230

Maintaining a whole-house humidifier
page 232

Repairs to old radiators
page 234

Installing convectors
page 236

Regular maintenance of your HVAC system keeps its components operating at maximum efficiency and saves you money.

Installing underfloor hydronic heating
page 238

Reducing heating costs
page 240

INSTALLING A WHOLE-HOUSE HUMIDIFIER

Whole-house humidifiers are typically attached to the main stack of a forced air furnace. They add evaporated moisture to the air by running the air past an absorbent element mounted around a revolving drum or a stationary evaporative element or plates.

Whatever medium is used for evaporation, the unit draws its water from a nearby hot or cold water pipe and transfers it to the medium through a drip tray or other device. Most systems rely on a humidistat and a float valve to regulate the humidity and keep the water at a prescribed level.

Some humidifiers are installed in the return-air duct and add moisture to the air before it is heated. Others employ a bypass duct to move heated air through the humidifier and reintroduce it to the air going to the house. Installing either system involves cutting a hole in the venting using templates provided by the manufacturer. Be sure to shut off the furnace before installing the humidifier.

1 Using the manufacturer's template and instructions, mark out the hole for the humidifier with a felt-tip marker. Drill a starter hole in a corner of the outline and cut the hole with aviation snips. Position the mounting plate, drill screw holes, and attach the mounting plate with sheet metal screws.

2 Refer to the manufacturer's specification sheet for the location of the humidistat (most are attached on the cold air plenum). Mark the outline for this unit and cut the hole in the plenum.

PRESTART CHECKLIST

☐ **TIME**
About two hours to mark templates, cut holes, and install the humifier

☐ **TOOLS**
Felt-tip marker, cordless drill and bit, aviation snips, screwdriver, wire strippers wrenches

☐ **SKILLS**
Cutting sheet metal, drilling

☐ **PREP**
Shut off furnace

☐ **MATERIALS**
Humidifier unit, vent pipe, sheet metal screws, wire nuts

3 Install the humidistat mounting plate and attach the unit. Connect the humidistat to the furnace controls following the instructions. If the unit requires a step-down transformer and you haven't yet run the wiring, **shut the power off,** install the transformer, and wire the humidistat.

4 Using the correct-size wire nuts, connect the leads from the humidistat to the solenoid valve on the humidifier. Insert the wire ends into the nuts (do not twist the ends of the wires) and turn the nuts until they're tight.

5 If local codes allow tapping water lines directly, install a saddle valve on the hot (preferably) water line and run the water line to the humidifier, fastening it with the compression fitting. If saddle valves are not allowed, turn the water off, cut the water line, and install a T-fitting (page 141).

WHAT IF ...
My model requires a bypass vent ?

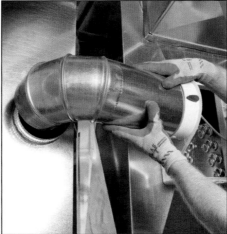

If your humidifier requires a bypass vent, use the template to mark the hole for a 6-inch bypass pipe. Drill a starter hole and cut the vent hole with aviation snips. Install a round collar in the hole, securing it with sheet metal screws. Measure the distance between the humidifier air inlet and the collar and cut the vent pipe to length. Install elbows on both ends of the vent pipe and fasten the assembly to the collar and humidifier air intake.

Hooking up the water supply

Turn off the water. Place the rubber gasket over the self-piercing tip and back the tip off about 1/16 inch from the bottom of the gasket. Assemble the straps on both sides of the pipe and tighten the nuts. Turn the self-piercing valve fully clockwise and install the water line to the humidifier. Turn on the water and check for leaks.

MAINTAINING A WHOLE-HOUSE HUMIDIFIER

Inspect the evaporative elements in either a drum style and pad or plate style humidifier once a month during the heating season and replace them yearly.
The evaporative elements will pick up minerals from the water, and their constant exposure to hot air will dry them, reducing their capacity to absorb and hold water.

Drip style humidifiers require less cleaning because the flow of water over their surfaces helps prevent mineral deposits and mold from forming. Drum style units need more attention because the drum is more likely to develop mold growth. If the evaporative element is serviceable and not caked with minerals, you can wash it in a mild dishsoap solution. Rinse it well and replace it.

PRESTART CHECKLIST

☐ **TIME**
About a half hour or less to replace the evaporative unit, more if scale cleaning is required

☐ **TOOLS**
Wrenches, screwdriver, old kitchen knife

☐ **SKILLS**
Removing access plate, replacing simple evaporative units

☐ **PREP**
Turn off furnace power and humidifier water supply

☐ **MATERIALS**
Replacement evaporator units, pipe cleaner

Maintaining a evaporative disc humidifier

1 Loosen the retaining nuts or remove the clips holding the humidifier cover and remove the cover. Lift the disc assembly by grasping the housing on both sides. You may have to jockey it a bit to remove it.

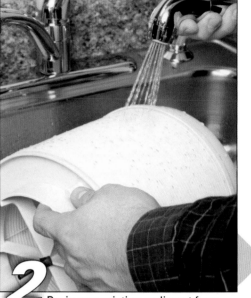

2 Drain any existing sediment from the basin and soak the disk wheel in vinegar or a cleaning solution approved for plastic. Rinse the disk wheel.

Maintaining a humidifier with evaporator elements or plates

1 To remove an evaporator element, slide your fingers under the unit and lift it out. If it's heavily scaled pry it out gently with an old kitchen knife—hardened mineral scales can be sharp. Remove the distribution tray if present.

2 Clean any mineral scale or deposits from the distribution tray with an old kitchen knife or flat-tip screwdriver.

3 The float assembly should be adjusted so that the water just covers the submerged discs. Don't lift the installed float against the stop or damage to the float seal can occur. Secure the float adjustment nut with a $^9/_{16}$" wrench.

4 Using the tabs as indicators, lower the disk wheel into the V-guides on the inlet and motor plates. Make sure that the inlet end of the axle is seated in the bearing at the bottom of the V-guide and that the gear on the other end of the axle is engaged with the moter gear.

5 Connect the plastic water line to the valve and float. Use the plastic compression fitting and insert on the valve end of the plastic line and insert the brass expander in the float end. Tighten both fittings securely.

3 Twist the evaporator element gently to pop off any mineral scales and wash it to remove loose particles. If the element crumbles it's time for a new one. The same holds true for evaporative plates.

4 Disconnect the drain hose and run a pipe cleaner up and down in the humidifier orifice to clean it. Flush the drain hose with water and reinstall.

Repairs To Old Radiators

Many older homes are heated with steam or hot water radiators. Newer homes may have convectors (pages 236–237). You can make minor repairs to radiators, but leave problems with a boiler or piping to a heating professional.

A steam radiator has a small air vent near the top that emits bursts of steam when the radiator heats. Steam systems cycle between hot and cold. Most are connected to only one pipe at the floor, but some have two. You can dismantle and service a steam radiator valve if the boiler is off. It can be difficult to work on, however, because the high heat tends to seize up the pipe joints.

Hot water radiators are connected to two pipes at the floor. They maintain a constant warmth, rather than cycling between hot and cold. Before you dismantle a hot water radiator valve, you must drain the system.

Prestart Checklist

☐ **Time**
About two hours, plus time for finding the parts

☐ **Tools**
Groove-joint pliers, pipe wrench, screwdriver

☐ **Skills**
Familiarity with your system

☐ **Prep**
Turn down the thermostat so the boiler will not come on while you work

☐ **Materials**
Radiator valve replacement parts or a new valve, strand packing, pipe-thread tape

Installing a new valve

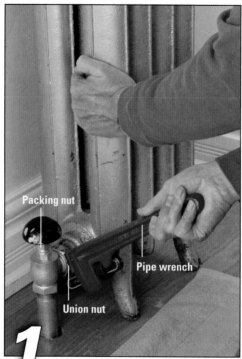

1 If water leaks from beneath the handle, turn down the thermostat and wait for the radiator to cool. Tighten the packing nut (just under the handle) using groove-joint pliers and tighten the larger union nut using a pipe wrench. If this does not solve the problem, move on to the next step.

2 With a hot water system, water must be drained from the radiator. Turn down the thermostat. Attach a hose to the boiler's drain valve; open the valve to drain the system into a nearby floor drain. Open the bleeder valves (opposite, below) of all radiators, starting at the top floor.

IDENTIFYING HOT WATER AND STEAM RADIATORS

In a steam system steam quickly heats the radiator when the boiler fires. In a hot water system, heated water continually circulates through the radiators.

Hot water radiator

One-pipe steam radiator

Two-pipe steam radiator

Strand packing

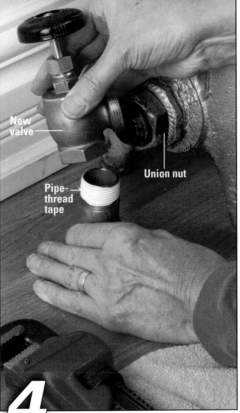

New valve

Pipe-thread tape

Union nut

Setscrew

Replacement handle

3 Unscrew the packing nut and remove the stem, first by unscrewing and then by pulling it out. If the leak originates just under the handle, wrap the stem with strand packing and reinstall. If the leak is lower or if this does not solve the problem, replace the valve (Step 4).

4 Unscrew the union nut that attaches the valve to the radiator, then unscrew the valve from the pipe. Take the old valve to a plumbing and heating supply store to find an exact replacement; look carefully to be sure it will fit. You also may need to replace the short pipe that emerges from the radiator.

If a handle is cracked or loose, remove the top screw and pull off the old handle. If the stem's threads are in good shape, buy a replacement handle that has the same size screw. If the stem is damaged, buy a "fits-all" handle, which clamps onto the stem with a setscrew.

Repairs to radiators

Adjustable air vent

Bleeder valve

Bleeder key

Aluminum sheet

A steam radiator valve must be turned either all the way on or all the way off. An adjustable air vent makes it possible to turn the heat up or down. Turn down the thermostat and use pliers to unscrew the old air vent. Buy a compatible adjustable unit. Wrap the threads with pipe-thread tape and screw the new unit in place.

If a hot water radiator is not heating enough, air may be trapped inside. Turn the thermostat up and wait for the radiator to get warm. Hold a cup under the bleeder valve and open it with a bleeder key, long-nose pliers, or screwdriver. Spluttering water or hissing air may come out. Once water flows in a steady stream, tighten the valve.

To improve a radiator's performance, move furniture and other obstructions out of the way. Air should flow freely under and above the radiator. A sheet of aluminum or reflective insulation placed behind the radiator directs more heat into the room.

INSTALLING CONVECTORS

An older radiator can be unattractive and take up a lot of space. Buying a radiator cover will improve appearances. Check the phone book or ask a plumbing and heating store for companies that custom-make metal units to fit all sizes of radiators. However if you want more space in a room and you have a hot water (not steam) system, you may be able to replace your radiator with a convector.

The steps shown at right can be used to add a convector to an existing heating system. Consult with a heating contractor to be sure you install a unit of the right size.

A convector is surprisingly simple and lightweight. The system usually has a copper pipe surrounded by thin aluminum fins. When the boiler heats the water running through the pipe, the fins direct the heat away from the pipe.

A convector's cover may appear to be merely decorative, but it is actually precisely sized to produce convection; cool air enters below the fins, and warm air comes out the top. Keep obstructions at least a foot away from a convector.

1 Drain the system (page 234, Step 2). Unscrew the union nuts at each end of the old radiator and remove the radiator. From below remove the plumbing leading from the old radiator to the heat pipe. These old pipes may be difficult to detach.

Back panel

Chisel

Backsaw

2 Using a fine-tooth saw like a backsaw (shown) and a chisel, cut the baseboard molding to accommodate the convector. Attach the convector back panel to the wall with screws driven into studs.

PRESTART CHECKLIST

☐ **TIME**
One day to replace a radiator with a convector

☐ **TOOLS**
Pipe wrenches, groove-joint pliers, screwdriver, drill, carpentry tools, propane torch

☐ **SKILLS**
Connecting copper to steel pipe, basic carpentry skills

☐ **PREP**
Consult with a heating expert to determine convector size

☐ **MATERIALS**
New convector, copper pipe, dielectric unions, valves as needed

THREE TYPES OF CONVECTOR SYSTEMS

One-pipe system

Loop system

Two-pipe system

In a one-pipe or two-pipe system, individual convectors can have separate heat-control valves. In a series loop system, individual valves are not possible. Many homes have zoned heating, two or three separate heating loops, each controlled by a separate thermostat.

3 Temporarily mount the convector onto the back panel and mark the location of the floor holes. Drill holes wide enough so that the pipes will be at least ½ inch from any wood surfaces.

4 From below install plumbing to reach the convectors. Use a dielectric union to make the transition from steel to copper. If needed a flexible connector easily makes complicated turns.

5 Mount the convector onto the back plate and sweat the joints (pages 126–127) at each end. Install the end caps and the front panel of the convector unit.

Maintaining convectors

If a convector has a bleed valve, bleed air from it using the method shown on page 235. A balance or heat-control valve may have a handle, or you may need a screwdriver to open and close it. When the slot is parallel to the pipe, the valve is open; when the slot is perpendicular, the valve is closed.

If fins are bent, the convector will radiate heat less efficiently. Straighten the fins using two putty knives, pliers, or a fin comb.

If a convector makes a humming or grating sound, the fins may be rubbing against a support bracket. Slip a piece of plastic between the fins and the bracket to dampen the sound.

INSTALLING UNDERFLOOR HYDRONIC HEATING

Hydronic tubing is relatively easy to install. The real work lies in the planning. Plan your system room by room, using grid paper to draw the tube spacing and locations of the manifold stations (the place where each circuit begins). Have a professional design the layout based on your plans.

PEX tubing comes in different diameters. Make sure the flow of water through the pipes is sufficient for the room you're heating. For example ½-inch tubing needs a manifold station every 300 feet; ⅝-inch tubing needs one every 450 feet.

Space the tubing lines closer along exterior walls. This increases the heat output in the coldest areas of the room. Provide access panels to manifold stations so you can make repairs easily.

1 Plan the system so you can locate the holes for the PEX tubing as close as possible to the subfloor and to the end of the joists. Using a drill and hole saw or Forstner bit ¼ inch larger than the tubing (a spade bit will wear out quickly), drill all the holes in the joists before you begin threading the tubing.

2 Lay a coil of tubing on the floor at one end of the room. Walk the end of the tubing down the length of the room and thread the tubing through the first joist. Have a helper unwind the tubing from the coil and push the tubing through the holes as you walk it down the bays between the joists. Untwist the tubing from the roll so it does not kink as you thread it through the holes.

PRESTART CHECKLIST

☐ **TIME**
A day to run underfloor PEX lines

☐ **TOOLS**
Drill, hole saw, staple gun, PEX cutter and crimping tool

☐ **SKILLS**
Connecting PEX tubing, basic carpentry skills

☐ **PREP**
Determine tubing size and arrangement under floor

☐ **MATERIALS**
PEX tubing, fittings as needed

Hydronic thin-slab installation

CONCRETE THIN-SLAB

Polyethylene moisture barrier — PEX tubing — Floor tile — Concrete — Subfloor — Insulation — Joists — Plastic mounting clip

Burying a hydronic system in 2 inches of concrete results in a heavier load than most wood-frame floors can handle. Even thin slabs, which are perfect for installing radiant heat in an addition to your home, may not be suitable

GYPSUM THIN-SLAB

Waterproofing/membrane — First gypsum coat — Second gypsum coat — Finished floor tile — Subfloor — Insulation — Joists

in existing construction. They add 15 to 18 pounds per square foot. Thin slabs also raise the floor level, which requires raising base cabinets and toilet flanges, and shortens the floor-to-sill distances of windows.

Installing an above-floor hydronic system

3 Staple the diffusion plates to the subfloor, spacing the plates and tubing as directed by the manufacturer. One-coil systems are generally centered between the joists. If you're working with a system that has a return line, label the inflow and outflow lines and <u>connect the lines to a boiler.</u>

Cut ¾-inch plywood or 1× sleepers to a width that will space the tubing consistent with the manufacturer's specifications. Make sure the ends of the tubing will bend without crimping. Mark the locations of the sleepers on the subfloor and fasten the first two with 1½-inch decking screws. Dry-lay a run of tubing to make sure it won't crimp, then fasten the remaining sleepers. If using a diffusion-plate system, snap and fasten the plates between the sleepers and press the tubing into the recesses of the plates. Cover the installation with plywood or thinset as recommended by the manufacturer.

CONNECT THE LINES TO A BOILER
Supplying hot water to hydronic systems

Although building codes in some localities may allow water heaters to be used for small hydronic systems, most systems require a hot water boiler or geothermal heat pump. Boiler manufacturers generally make models with and without a self-contained water heater for home use. When planning a hydronic system, make sure the output of the boiler or heat pump meets the heat-load requirements of the room.

Using precut underlayment

Avoid having to cut and fasten sleepers by using plywood underlayment with channels precut in its surface. Fasten the panels to the subfloor, snap in the diffusion plates (if required), and press the tubing into the channels. Cover the installation with the proper substrate.

REDUCING HEATING COSTS

If you're an average homeowner, more than 50 percent of your energy costs go to heat and cool your house. Obviously anything you can do to reduce your energy use will take a bite out of your monthly gas or electric bills.

There are a number of ways to save money on heating costs. The most expensive, of course, is to completely upgrade your system with new equipment that employs energy-saving technologies. The second is to add supplemental heating sources that are energy efficient. But for starters you can do a lot to reduce your energy consumption by sealing up the drafty places in your home and changing the way you use your appliances.

Start with insulation around your doors and windows. Seal the spaces around hose bibs and air-conditioner lines from the outside condenser. Set up reflectors behind radiators on exterior walls. They come in styles to match different interior designs.

Vacuum warm-air registers, baseboard heaters, and radiators as needed. Make sure furniture doesn't block the circulation of the heat. Install a ceiling fan to move cool air in the summer and warm air in the winter. This simple addition helps equalize the temperature in the room, reducing hot and cold spots, and you can change the thermostat setting about 4 degrees without noticing any difference in comfort. Install a programmable thermostat that adjusts the temperature according to your schedule. Seal all joints on heat ducts with mastic (do not use duct tape, it deteriorates).

Changing the way you use energy also will save money. Wash only full loads of dishes and clothes. Rinse handwashed dishes all at once rather than individually. Take short showers instead of baths. Lower the thermostat on your hot water heater to 120 degrees. For further information do an Internet search for "reducing home heating costs."

Seal transitions

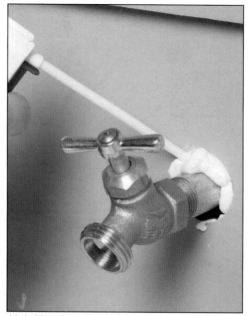

Air infiltration to and from the outside is a major cause of heat loss. Seal the openings around hose bibs, dryer vents, and any other openings to the outdoors. Use polyurethane foam. You can sand it down and paint it when it's dry.

Replace/clean filters

Cleaning furnace filters may not rank high on your list of maintenance priorities, but clean filters allow your furnace to run more efficiently, thus reducing heating costs. Clean or replace filters once a month during the heating system. Use a vacuum to clean nondisposable elements.

STANLEY PRO TIP

Install a drainwater heat recovery (DHR) system

Every time you're done using a volume of hot water, it's not just the water that goes down the drain, it's also the heat. A drainwater heat recovery (DHR) system is designed to capture that heat.

Cool water flows through a coiled copper pipe that encircles the drainpipe. As hot water goes down the drainpipe, it heats the water in the coils, which is then recirculated to the water heater. The fact that this water is preheated means that the water heater does not have to raise the temperature quite as much to provide hot water.

Insulate hot-water pipes

Foam insulation for pipe comes in tubes with a self-adhering seal applied down the tube. Cut the insulation to length, pry the slit open, and push the tube onto hot water pipes. Reclose the self-stick edges.

Install heat traps

Heat traps are small one-way valves that allow water to flow into the water heater but prevent unwanted hot water migration out of the tank. Inside the valves small balls float or sink into a seat, which stops convection. The valves are designed specifically for hot and cold water connections.

On-demand water heater

On-demand water heaters (pages 156–157) deliver hot water instantly but reduce heating costs because they employ a system that heats only the water you use. That way you don't use energy keeping a large volume of water at a constant temperature.

Insulate your water heater

1 Water heater insulation jackets are sold in kits that come with belts to help make their installation easy and neat. Make cuts from the edge of the top insulation member so you can slide it to fit around the piping. Cut circles for the piping. Tape the cut section closed after the top has been installed. Fold the corners or the top down and tape them to the sides of the tank.

2 Run the blanket around the tank in such a way that the ends don't meet over the access panels to the burner or electric cathode. Fasten the belts in place, making sure the lower belt does not cross the access panel. If your insulation blanket does not come with belts, run tape around the top and bottom of the blanket, then tape the vertical seam.

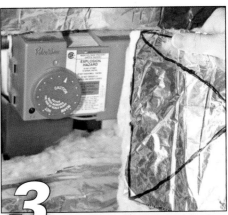

3 Push on the blanket to locate the four corners of the access panel and make small "X" cuts at the corners. Cut a rectangular hole in the blanket between the Xs to provide easy access to the panel.

UTILITY ROOM & BASEMENT UPGRADES

Plumbing improvements in utility areas and basements can be relatively easy compared with other areas of the house. Often there are no walls that have to be removed to run new lines—and you won't have to disturb oft-used rooms while completing the project.

Water treatment
The high mineral content of local water can lead to staining, soap scum buildup, and a reduction in the ability of soap and detergent to get things clean. Such signs indicate that your household water needs softening. Water softeners are pricey and are often rented by the month, but if you install your own it can pay for itself in two to three years.

Basement plumbing
Architects have equated a basement with digging a well and then trying to keep the

You can make improvements in utility rooms and basements quickly and easily.

CHAPTER PREVIEW

Installing a sump pump
page 244

Installing a water softener
page 246

Installing an upflush toilet
page 249

Setting up a laundry room
page 252

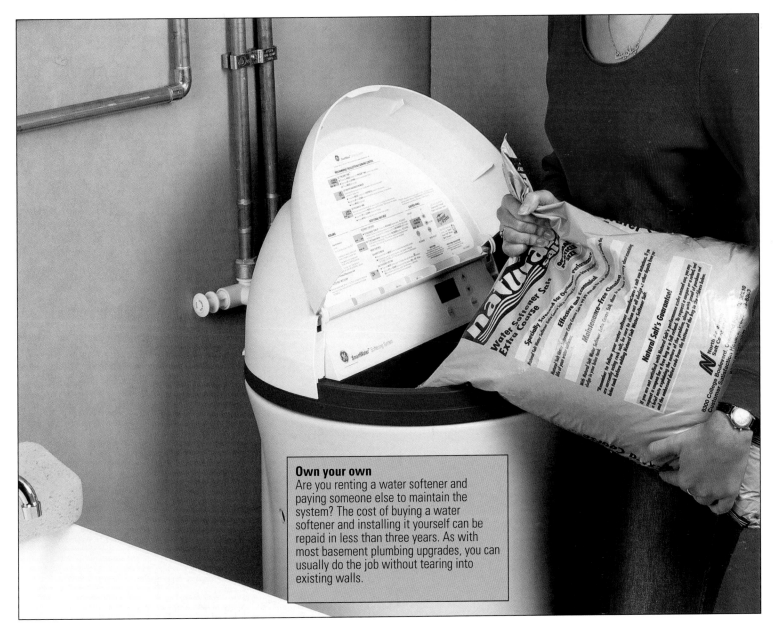

Own your own
Are you renting a water softener and paying someone else to maintain the system? The cost of buying a water softener and installing it yourself can be repaid in less than three years. As with most basement plumbing upgrades, you can usually do the job without tearing into existing walls.

water out. If your basement floods after heavy rainfall, you may want to install a sump pump. Digging a hole for the reservoir is the difficult part; you'll have to chop through a concrete floor and dig into hard-packed clay, gravel, and sand. But once the reservoir is in place, the plumbing is relatively easy.

If the main drain line is too high for a bathroom in the basement—or you don't want to break into the concrete floor to trench for drain lines—consider an upflush toilet unit. Once the drain and vent connections are made, these units are surprisingly easy to install and typically use standard toilets. Most units allow you to hook up sink and tub/shower drains as well. Once the bathroom is framed out and flooring and walls are added, the unit will be hidden.

Adding a laundry area involves running hot and cold supply lines to the washer and tapping into a drain stack. A nearby utility sink is handy for heavy-duty cleanup. The same techniques apply whether a laundry is upstairs or down.

Upgrades such as this water softener installation can be ideal projects for homeowners; they rarely disrupt the use of other rooms and systems while they are under construction.

INSTALLING A SUMP PUMP

If your basement floods or becomes damp during wet periods, first try directing rainwater away from the house by changing your gutter downspouts. If that does not solve the problem, a sump pump may be the solution.

There are two basic kinds of sump pump installations. If you have no drainpipes under the basement designed specifically for handling rainwater, then dig a hole at a low point of the basement and install a perforated pit liner (you may have to perforate it yourself using a ⅜-inch spade bit). Water under the basement will slowly percolate into the liner.

If your house has rainwater drainpipes, it probably also has a pit already dug for a sump pump, with a drainpipe running into it. Purchase a nonperforated pit liner and cut a hole for the drainpipe.

A wise add-on is a rechargeable battery backup unit, which will power the pump if a heavy storm causes a power outage. A pump-failure alarm is also a good idea.

PRESTART CHECKLIST

☐ **TIME**
About half a day

☐ **TOOLS**
Sledgehammer or electric jackhammer, cold chisel, drill, masonry bit, spade bit, hole saw, PVC saw, torpedo level, screwdriver, groove-joint pliers

☐ **SKILLS**
Basic carpentry skills, cutting and joining PVC drainpipe

☐ **PREP**
Locate a low spot where the pump won't take up usable space; if necessary install a GFCI receptacle

☐ **MATERIALS**
Sump pump, pit liner, PVC pipe, primer, cement, check valve

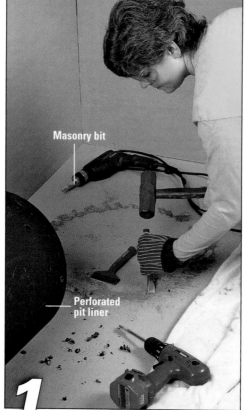

1 Use the pit liner to mark for cutting a hole in the basement floor. Using a masonry bit drill a series of holes along the perimeter. (A concrete basement floor is usually 3 inches thick.) Chip out the concrete with a sledgehammer and cold chisel or an electric jackhammer (pages 21–22).

2 Dig the hole deep enough for the pit liner and set the pit liner in place. Make sure the liner is resting solidly on the ground so it can support the pump. Attach a PVC standpipe to the unit, using the adapter parts supplied by the manufacturer.

SUMP PUMP INSTALLATION

Liner lid — Concrete — Stand pipe — Float switch — Power cord — Switch cord — Perforated liner — Liner lid — Concrete — Stand pipe — Float switch — Drainage pipe

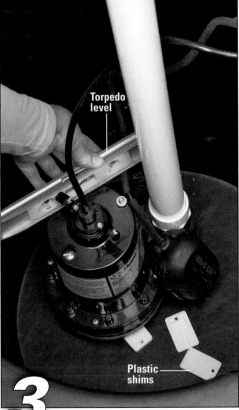

Torpedo level

Plastic shims

3 Set the pump on the bottom of the liner. It should be near the center so the float won't touch the side of the liner. Check to make sure the pump is level; place plastic shims if necessary. Place the lid on the liner.

Check valve

4 Just above the level of the floor, install a check valve, which ensures that water does not flow back into the pump. Run PVC pipe up and toward the exit point. Clamp the electrical wires to the side of the pipes. Plug the unit into a GFCI receptacle.

5 Cut a hole through the rim joist for the pipe to exit the house. Run PVC pipe out of the house and extend it so it carries water at least 6 feet from the house. Water that is discharged near the house will seep back into the basement.

Pedestal sump pump

A pedestal-type sump pump has its motor above the water and is not waterproof. It is recommended for a basement that needs frequent draining; its float can be adjusted. This type is less expensive than a submersible but is also noisier.

Ejector pump for graywater

If your drain lines are above floor level and you want to install a utility sink, the simplest solution is a graywater sump box. It must be connected to the house's drain and vent lines.

To provide drainage for a toilet as well, install an upflush unit (pages 249–251).

Sump box

INSTALLING A WATER SOFTENER

Hard water contains large amounts of minerals such as iron, calcium, and magnesium. Telltale signs include reddish stains, white mineral buildup in pipes and fittings, reduced cleaning ability of soap and detergent, and soap scum buildup. Hard water also can damage faucets and appliances.

A water softener captures minerals and periodically flushes them away. The more often it flushes, the more often you need to change the salt. The most efficient softener is one that flushes according to the amount of water used or the amount of minerals detected, rather than one that uses a timer.

Softened water contains sodium, sometimes at levels undesirable for people with high blood pressure. You can install a bypass line for drinking water, drink bottled water, or install a whole-house filter.

PRESTART CHECKLIST

☐ **TIME**
A day to install a water softener

☐ **TOOLS**
Groove-joint pliers, screwdriver, tubing cutter, propane torch, flux brush, sandpaper, wire reaming brush

☐ **SKILLS**
Cutting and joining copper or steel pipe

☐ **PREP**
Plan to install the softener where water enters the house

☐ **MATERIALS**
Water softener, flux, solder

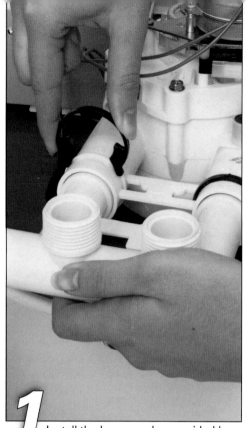

1 Install the bypass valve provided by the manufacturer. Lubricate the O-rings, push the valve into the ports, and slip on the clips.

Bypass valve

2 Shut off gas or electricity to the water heater and turn off the water supply at the main shutoff valve. Open faucets on the lowest floor to drain the line. Provide a stable, level surface near the main water line for the softener to rest on so it's easily accessible. Position the unit.

STANDARD WATER SOFTENER INSTALLATION

Soft water

Union

Installation parts, supplied by maker

Bypass valve

To install a water softener, break into the main supply line with elbows. To provide a hard-water supply to a hose bib, break into the line upstream from the water softener.

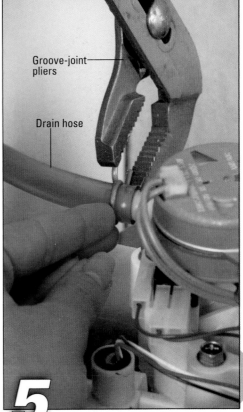

Groove-joint pliers

Drain hose

3 Break into the main supply line (page 141) and install elbows. Make sure that hard water will enter the inlet and soft water will exit via the outlet. If the main supply pipe is larger than ¾ inch, use reducer elbows. Local codes may require that you install three valves (below).

4 Install pipes leading down toward the bypass valve. Install the connecting parts supplied by the manufacturer and attach them by soldering a coupler on each line. Do all the soldering before installing any plastic parts.

5 Connect the drain hose to the softener unit using the clamp provided. The drain hose must end at a point at least 1½ inches above a drain, and it must be clamped firmly in place. Also connect the brine tank's overflow line.

THREE-VALVE INSTALLATION

Hard water to hose bib

Hard water

Soft water

Shutoff valve

A three-valve installation allows you to shut off water at several points and is required by some local codes. The shutoffs allow you to bypass the water softener so you can easily turn off the water to it when making repairs.

WHAT IF ...
There is no drain nearby?

Where there is no nearby drain, run the drain tube to a utility sink. Firmly attach it, making sure the tube end is 1½ inches above the highest point to which water could rise. If the hose end were to become immersed, wastewater could back up into the softener.

GFCI receptacle

Transformer

6 If your electrical system is grounded to the cold water pipe, the water softener will interrupt the path to ground. Install the jumper strip supplied with the unit (shown) or use grounding clamps and an 8-gauge or heavier copper wire. If you're unsure how the house is grounded, call an electrician.

Jumper strip

7 Carefully follow the manufacturer's instructions for expelling air from the water softener. Usually this involves running water past the softener with the valve on "bypass," then pulling the valve out to the "service" position, which runs water through the softener and expels air.

8 Check for leaks in all the pipes. Attach the transformer to the wires for the unit. Plug the softener into a GFCI electrical receptacle. Open the softener's lid and follow the manufacturer's directions for filling with water and salt.

Program the softener

Many water softeners have programmable controls that allow you to adjust the hardness of the water as well as the time when the recharging takes place.

To find the hardness level recommended in your area, consult with your building department or call the manufacturer for a water testing kit. If you find that the water is too hard or too soft, adjust accordingly.

Set the softener to recharge when your water use is low; while the unit is recharging, water in the house will be hard.

Maintaining a water softener

If the water shows signs of becoming hard, the softener's line might be clogged. With the valve set to "bypass," disassemble the nozzle and venturi housing. Remove the screen filter and clear any debris by soaking the parts in clean water and brushing them with a toothbrush.

Sometimes the salt becomes crusty and forms a "bridge," either on top or at the bottom. Stir the brine with a broom handle or piece of wood; make sure the handle reaches the bottom. Break apart any congealed salt. A salt bridge may be caused by high humidity or by using the wrong kind of salt.

INSTALLING AN UPFLUSH TOILET

Installing a new bathroom in a basement can be a major undertaking. The concrete floor must be broken into and drainpipes installed, then new concrete must be poured.

An upflushing unit makes the job much easier. Instead of using gravity to drain, it has an electric pump that efficiently discharges waste up and away. A GFCI receptacle must be installed nearby.

Upflushing units usually are installed under or near the toilet. Most can serve a sink and a tub as well.

Some upflushing units, especially those installed in the '70s and '80s, were unreliable and needed frequent repairs. Newer units are more dependable. Ask a plumbing supplier about the track record of the model you are considering.

Plan plumbing for the entire bathroom. Run exposed pipes or hide the pipes in walls. Make sure the unit's pump is powerful enough to send wastewater the required distance to the house's drain.

PRESTART CHECKLIST

☐ **TIME**
   A day

☐ **TOOLS**
   Level, adjustable wrench, PVC saw, deburring tool, screwdriver, carpentry tools

☐ **SKILLS**
   Planning and running drain and vent lines, basic carpentry skills

☐ **PREP**
   Purchase a unit, draw a plan, and consult with a plumbing inspector to make sure the plumbing will meet code

☐ **MATERIALS**
   Upflushing unit, PVC pipe and fittings, primer, cement, toilet

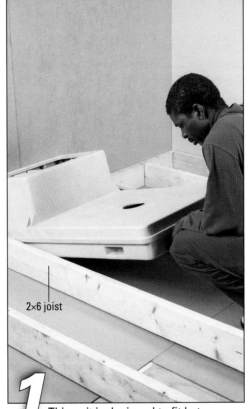

2×6 joist

1 This unit is designed to fit between 2×6 joists. It must rest on a stable, fairly level surface. If necessary build a simple 2×2 frame, mix and pour sand-mix hydraulic concrete, and set the unit in the concrete. Level in both directions. Allow the concrete to cure before proceeding.

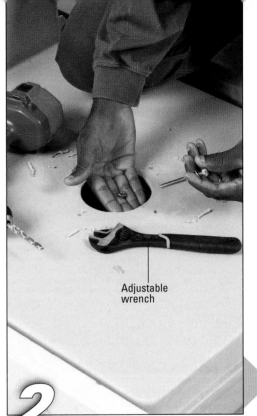

Adjustable wrench

2 Prepare the unit for the toilet: Install the iron support flange. Make sure that the toilet mounting bolts are in the correct positions and are long enough for mounting the toilet.

UPFLUSH TANK AND PUMP

Backflow device

3" PVC vent

2" PVC discharge tube

Float switch

Pump

Float

An upflushing unit has a heavy-duty pump activated by a float and switch. When the lower portion of the tank fills, the pump turns on, forcing waste up through the 2-inch drain. A 3-inch vent is required. Make sure the vent and drain conform to local plumbing codes.

Float switch
Discharge tube
Float
Pump

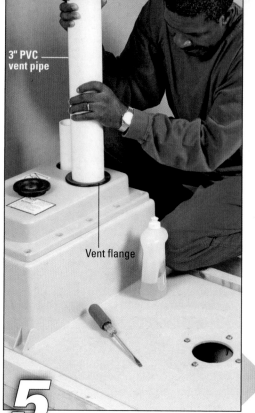

3" PVC vent pipe
Vent flange

3 Assemble the float switch. Install the discharge pipe. Place the pump in the tank and mount the float switch. Before sealing the unit make sure the pump works. Attach a garden hose to a water supply and run it into the flange hole.

4 Connect the discharge to a drainpipe leading to a bucket or floor drain. Tape the temporary drainpipe joints—the pump is forceful. Plug the unit into a GFCI receptacle. Slowly fill the tank with water. The pump should come on and discharge water once it reaches the correct level.

5 Insert the rubber flange provided and insert 3-inch PVC vent pipe to the unit. (It's a tight fit; liquid soap helps.) Run the vent to the main stack (pages 176–181). Be sure to configure the vent and drain in a code-approved manner.

WHAT IF ...
A toilet must be placed well below the sewer line?

A macerating toilet is useful if a bathroom will be well below the sewer line (as much as 12 feet) or if pipes must travel a long distance (up to 150 feet) before connecting with the main sewer line.

A macerating toilet has a rotating blade that grinds waste before pumping it away. Macerating units have smaller discharge and drainpipes. The flush cycle normally takes 15 to 18 seconds.

A macerating unit must be connected to a horizontal outlet toilet. Some manufacturers combine a toilet and pump. You can choose between stand-alone macerating toilets and units with connections for a tub/shower and a sink. (With either type the tub/shower must be raised to facilitate drainage.)

Discharge tube
Horizontal outlet toilet
Sink and tub waste
Macerator

Backflow device

6 Connect the discharge pipe to the backflow device to ensure that wastewater will not flow back into the unit. (Be sure to install it correct-end up—it is clearly marked.) Connect a 2-inch PVC drainpipe to the discharge unit and run it toward the house's drain in a code-approved manner.

7 Connect the drain and vent pipes to the house's system (pages 140–141). Plug the unit into a GFCI receptacle within reach from the access panel. Install the supply line. Install the subfloor and walls, being careful not to puncture the tank with any fasteners.

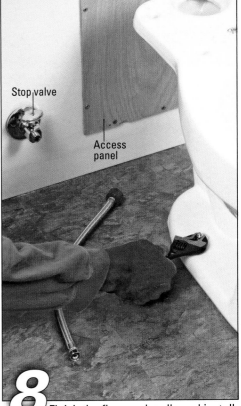

Stop valve

Access panel

8 Finish the floor and walls and install the access panel. Install the toilet onto a wax ring where the bowl rests on the upflush unit (pages 105–107). Connect the toilet to a cold water supply line with a stop valve.

WHAT IF ...
Other fixtures will be connected?

Additional plumbing fixtures—usually a tub/shower and a sink—can be connected to an upflush unit. Drainpipes for these fixtures must flow down to the upflush unit.

This does not pose a problem for the sink, because its drain is usually 16 inches above the floor. The tub, however, usually must be raised so the drain line can flow down to the upflush unit. One solution is to rest the tub on a shallow platform made of 2×4s and plywood. Vent pipes must be run in the standard manner (pages 176–181).

Most manufacturers supply an extra flange for hooking up a tub/shower and sink drain to the tank. Follow the manufacturer's specifications exactly for cutting the access hole for the drain.

2" sink drain

2" tub drain

Tub/shower platform

Trap

Tank

Trap

Trap

SETTING UP A LAUNDRY ROOM

A washing machine needs hot and cold water and a drain. Install washing machine valves, which look like outdoor hose bibs but point straight down.

The washer drain hose hooks to a sink or a standpipe. The drain for either of these must slope down at a rate of ¼ inch per running foot.

Many washing machines are self-leveling. Grab the machine by its control panel at the top rear, pull forward to slightly tilt the machine, and let it drop back solidly on all four feet. Adjust the front legs to make sure the machine is level in both directions.

PRESTART CHECKLIST

☐ **TIME**
About half a day

☐ **TOOLS**
Screwdriver, groove-joint pliers, propane torch, hacksaw, tubing cutter

☐ **SKILLS**
Working with copper and PVC pipe

☐ **PREP**
Locate supply and drain lines

☐ **MATERIALS**
Utility sink, washing machine, solder, flux, PVC primer and glue, trap, pipe, fittings

1 **Shut off water** to the supply pipes and drain the lines. To tap into a copper supply pipe, cut the pipe with a tubing cutter to install a tee fitting.

Mini tubing cutter

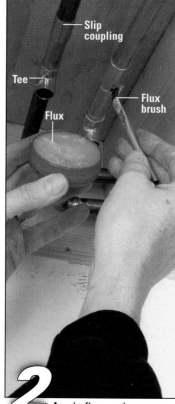

Slip coupling
Tee
Flux
Flux brush

2 Apply flux and sweat the tee fitting in place (pages 110–111). If there is not enough movement in the pipe, a piece of pipe and a slip coupling (shown above) may be necessary. Or try a compression fitting (page 111).

Tee for washer supply
Wood scrap keeps cookie sheet away from wall.
Solder
Supply stub out
Cookie sheet as scorch guard

3 Add lengths of pipe to reach the laundry tub, including tees to run pipes to the washer. At the end of each supply pipe, sweat on a brass supply stub out. Anchor the stub outs to the wall with masonry screws.

LAUNDRY ROOM OVERVIEW

Supply pipes branch off to provide both the utility sink and the washing machine with hot and cold water. The machine's drain hose clips to the side of the utility sink, which has a P-trap that connects to a house drain line.

Supply pipe

Washer drain hose

P-trap

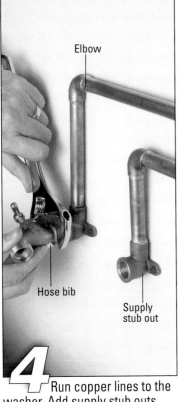

Elbow

Hose bib

Supply stub out

4 Run copper lines to the washer. Add supply stub outs and anchor them to the wall with masonry screws. Apply pipe-thread tape and hand-twist each hose bib into its stub out, then tighten it with a wrench.

5 Install stop valves (pages 118–119) on the sink stub outs. A plastic utility sink is inexpensive and easy to assemble. Install a faucet onto the sink and connect supply tubes to the stop valves.

Adapter

6 Tap into a drain line with a tee fitting and run a drainpipe (sloped at ¼ inch per foot) to the sink. Glue an adapter to the pipe end and attach the trap.

Washing machine supply line

Washing machine drain hose

7 Set the washing machine in place and level it. Screw the machine's supply lines to the valves and tighten with pliers. Drape the drain hose over the side of the utility sink and clamp it firmly in place.

WHAT IF ...
You extend steel pipe?

To tap into galvanized steel lines, cut and remove a section of pipe. Replace the section with a combination of lengths of threaded pipe, nipples, a tee fitting, and a union to suit your situation. Extend the supply line from the tee and attach a stop valve. (See pages 134–135 for more about working with steel pipe.)

Tee

Nipple

Union

Making a direct drain connection

Where there is no room for a utility sink, install a standpipe for the washer drain. The pipe must be large enough to insert the washing machine's drain hose into it, and the top must be above the machine's water level.

WASHING MACHINE SUPPLY BOX

Single-lever stop valve

Hole for drain hose

If your walls are not finished (the studs are exposed) or if you are able to run pipes through walls, install a washing machine supply box for a neater look. It controls hot and cold water with one valve and provides an outlet for a drain hose.

INSTALLING OUTDOOR PROJECTS

Running a water supply out of the house and to the yard is in some ways easier than interior plumbing: Pipes that are exposed or run in trenches are usually easier to install than pipes run through walls and floors. And most outdoor projects call for supply lines only—no drain and vent lines.

Because outdoor plumbing is not protected as well as interior plumbing, you must take care to keep it from harm. Local codes set standards to make outdoor plumbing safe. Use only pipes and valves designed for outdoor use. Bury pipes deep enough so they will not be disturbed by normal gardening activity. Draw a map showing pipe locations so you can avoid hitting them if you do any digging later. Where pipes are exposed clamp them firmly to stable structures.

Winterizing

If you have freezing winters, make sure you can drain all the lines in the fall. Run supply pipes at a consistent slope so water cannot collect in low spots. Install valves, faucets, or sprinkler heads designed for draining. Or plan to open the system and blow compressed air through the pipes.

Some outdoor work—digging trenches by hand for instance—is physically demanding. Unless you are used to such work, go at an easy pace and take plenty of breaks. Consider renting a machine or hiring laborers to make the job easier.

This chapter describes projects that are not difficult, especially if you have basic plumbing skills taught elsewhere in this book. All the installations make outdoor living more enjoyable and hassle-free. An outdoor kitchen equipped with running water means fewer trips to the kitchen. A window box drip irrigation system keeps flowers blooming on the hottest days and eliminates the chore of daily watering. And adding a new hose bib or two can make watering and other outdoor chores easier.

The techniques in these projects can be used for other outdoor installations, such as fountains, pools, or spas.

CHAPTER PREVIEW

Basic plumbing skills and a few special materials will get most outdoor plumbing jobs done.

Plumbing for an outdoor kitchen
page 256

Adding microsprinklers
page 258

Installing a hose bib
page 260

Installing an irrigation system
page 262

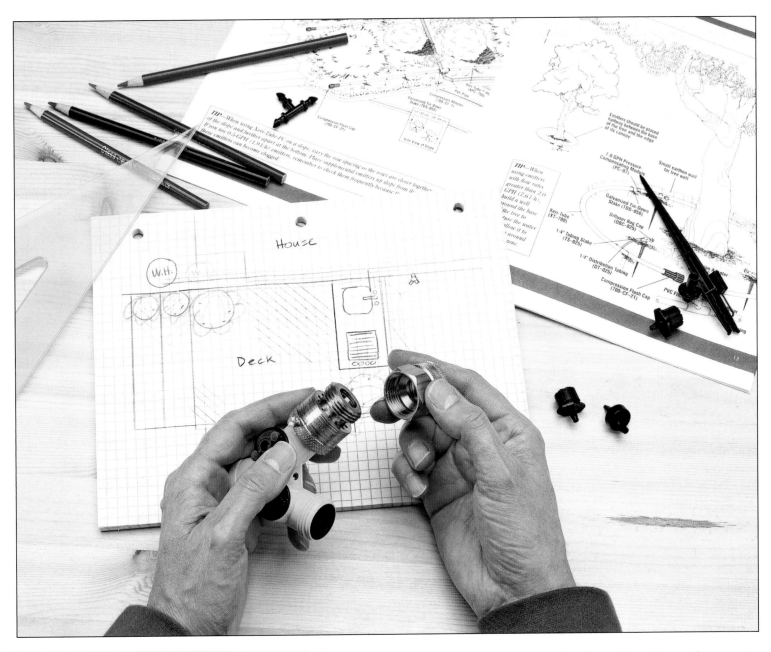

By combining several outdoor projects into one plan, you can choose the best locations for extending supply lines from the house and avoid having to add connections later. A simple scale drawing helps when checking local codes, buying materials, and locating any underground hazards. Before you dig ask your utility companies to mark the locations of gas, electric, communication, and water lines.

Installing a pond with a fountain
page 268

Maintaining swimming pools
page 272

Installing eco-friendly systems
page 274

PLUMBING FOR AN OUTDOOR KITCHEN

Most decks and patios have a grill. Adding a small sink with a faucet helps with food preparation and reduces trips in and out of the house. And a gas barbecue unit that's built into a tiled countertop gives the cook plenty of convenient cooking and preparation space.

Construct the cabinets and countertops to resist weather. Unless you live in a very dry climate, provide an awning or some other shelter from rain so the outdoor kitchen is at least partially protected.

If you have freezing winters, install plumbing that can be drained in the fall. Be sure you can shut off water from inside the house. The drain line shown here runs to a simple dry well and needs no venting. It is acceptable for the graywater that a prep sink produces.

PRESTART CHECKLIST

☐ **TIME**
A day to run plumbing and a gas line for a sink and barbecue

☐ **TOOLS**
Groove-joint pliers, screwdriver, level, shovel, posthole digger, hole saw, tools for joining copper and plastic pipe

☐ **SKILLS**
Installing PVC drain pipe, installing a sink, running supply lines

☐ **PREP**
Plan the location for your sink and barbecue; build the cabinet

☐ **MATERIALS**
Sink, gas-fired barbecue, supply pipes and fittings, drain pipes and fittings, trap, garbage can, gravel

Type L copper pipe

2-hole clamp

Shutoff valve with drain plug

1 From inside the house run supply pipe designed for outdoor use (pages 126–127, 134–135). Slope the pipes slightly to help them drain. Install shutoff valves with drain plugs at the lowest point. Attach the pipes firmly with two-hole clamps every 4 feet or less.

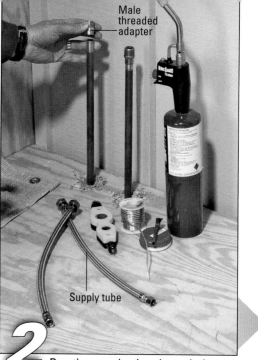

Male threaded adapter

Supply tube

2 Run the supply pipe through the house wall and to the outdoor kitchen routing up through the bottom of the sink/grill base cabinet. Sweat male threaded adapters to connect with the supply tubes for the sink.

PLUMBING FOR AN OUTDOOR KITCHEN

Gas valve

Flexible gas line

Drip leg

Hot water supply

Trap seals off any odors from dry well

Cold water supply

Dry well

A basic outdoor kitchen has a cabinet and countertop, topped with a sink supplied with hot and cold water. The drain runs into a dry well.

Gas shutoff valve

10" drip leg

PVC drain with adapter

Corrugated supply line to barbecue

3 Install the PVC drainpipe and adapter for the sink trap. To supply a barbecue with natural gas, run pipe that is code-approved for exposed outdoor gas lines in your region (page 135). Some barbecues may require a gas regulator. Install the sink and trap.

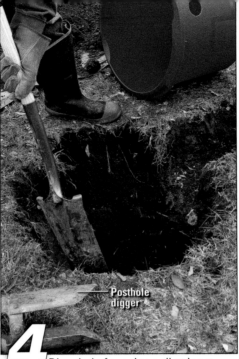

Posthole digger

4 Dig a hole for a dry well at least 10 feet from the patio or deck (check local codes). Dig a trench to it that slopes down and away from the house. Run the drain line—1½-inch PVC probably will be acceptable—in the trench. Check that it slopes at a rate of at least ¼ inch per foot.

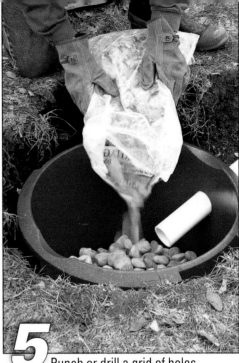

5 Punch or drill a grid of holes, about ½ inch wide, in a garbage can. Set the can in the hole; its top should be 2 inches below grade. Mark where the pipe will enter and cut a hole for the pipe. Set the can back in the ground, install the pipe into the hole, and fill the can with coarse gravel.

WHAT IF ...
The outdoor kitchen is a long way from the house?

As an alternative to bringing hot water all the way from the house, install a hot water dispenser. This simple plug-in unit fits easily in the cabinet. With it you need only run a cold water line outdoors; a saddle tee and branch line run to the dispenser. It is designed to supply nearly boiling-hot water, but you can turn the thermostat down to 140 degrees, which is within the range of normal hot tap water.

See pages 222–223 for installation instructions. You will have to run 120-volt GFCI-protected electrical line to the unit; use only outdoor cable.

STANLEY PRO TIP
Using the drain

Wastewater in this system simply runs into the ground, so be careful what goes down the drain.

■ Keep a record of the dry well's location so you can find it easily if you ever need to dig it up.
■ Keep the strainer in the sink's drain hole so no solid material can pass down the drain.
■ Avoid pouring oil or grease down the drain; they can clog the system.
■ Use biodegradable dishsoap to minimize damage to plants near the dry well.
■ Unless the soil is very dry, avoid running water for prolonged periods.
■ If you live in an area with freezing winters, dismantle the trap in the fall and drain any remaining water.

Choosing the right materials

Codes for outdoor plumbing vary widely from area to area (and even from one town to a neighboring town), so check with your local building department before buying any pipes and fittings.

Among the options for supply pipes, PEX and CPVC are easy to run. If you install copper pipe, choose Type L or K, which are thicker and stronger than Type M.

PVC is the standard choice for drainpipe. You may want to run perforated drainpipe underground; this will allow some water to percolate out along the way to the dry well.

Gas pipe options include aluminum composite pipe (page 133), and certain types of copper, green-coated steel, galvanized steel, and schedule 80 PVC (which is stronger than standard schedule 40).

ADDING MICRO-SPRINKLERS

Microsprinkler systems for containers and small planting areas are often referred to as "drip" irrigation. Many of these components spray or bubble water like larger systems designed for lawns and gardens. Correctly installed, these systems make it easy to deliver the right amount of water to plants.

A backflow prevention device keeps irrigation water out of your household water supply. A filter prevents tiny openings from getting clogged. Water is carried to the vicinity by ¾-inch supply hose, and ¼-inch distribution tubing delivers it to the containers. You may want to add a timer to turn the water on and off automatically.

If you intend to bury water lines or install a larger system, check local codes and discuss your plan with an inspector.

PRESTART CHECKLIST

☐ **TIME**
Several hours to connect a simple watering system for five or six containers

☐ **TOOLS**
Groove-joint pliers, screwdriver, tubing cutter, hole punch, hammer

☐ **SKILLS**
Making simple plumbing connections

☐ **PREP**
Draw up your proposed system and show it to an irrigation retailer or mail in a form to a sprinkler manufacturer

☐ **MATERIALS**
Microemitters and sprayers, ¾-inch supply hose, ¼-inch distribution tubing, connectors, caps, stakes, clips, clamps

1 To connect to a hose bib, start with a dual shutoff Y-connector so you can still connect a standard hose. Add an antisiphon device to prevent backflow and a filter. Connect the ¾-inch supply hose with a compression fitting.

Antisiphon device • Y-connector • Filter

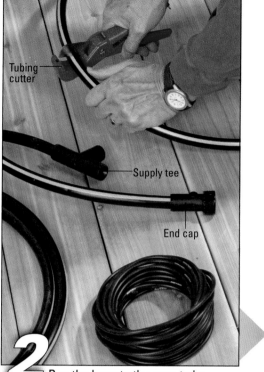

2 Run the hose to the area to be watered and route it past the containers using push-in compression tees, elbows, and couplings. Cut the hose with a tubing cutter. Install an end cap at the end of the run.

Tubing cutter • Supply tee • End cap

CHOOSING COMPONENTS

¼" distribution tubing • Multioutlet • Clamp-type stake • Stake • ¼" connector • ¼" tee • In-line drip emitter • End-line emitter • ½" tee • Sprayer head • End cap • ¾" supply hose

Once you've drawn up a plan (page 262), you can choose among components like these to finetune your system.

Tubing cutter
Distribution tubing
Supply hose
Hole punch

3 To connect ¼-inch distribution tubing to the supply hose, first poke the hose with a hole punch. Push a connector into the hole and slip the tubing onto the connector. If you make a mistake or change your mind, push a "goof plug" into the hole you no longer want to use.

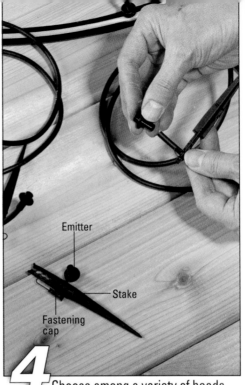
Emitter
Stake
Fastening cap

4 Choose among a variety of heads, such as bubblers and sprayers. In most cases the head slips onto the end of the tubing and the tubing connects to a stake that is driven into the soil. Some heads have adjustable sprays.

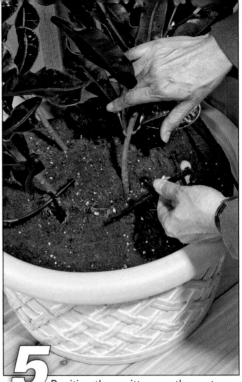

5 Position the emitters so the water sprays midway between the leaf canopy and the soil. Turn the water on and reposition the heads for the best watering. Use plastic clips to hold the supply and distribution tubing in place.

MICROSPRINKLER SYSTEM FOR CONTAINERS

Distribution tube

Supply hose

Route the supply hose and the tubing so they will be at least partially hidden. Once the hose is installed, you can finetune the positions of the distribution tubing and the heads.

INSTALLING A HOSE BIB

A conveniently located hose bib (sometimes called a "sill cock") can save you from having to stretch a garden hose around the house. The most difficult part of installing a hose is breaking into a cold water supply pipe and installing a tee fitting. The type shown has an extended stem so the freeze-sensitive valve is indoors. Instructions on these pages include installing a shutoff valve so you can turn water off from the inside as well as the outside.

If you live in an area with freezing winters and the hose bib pipe will enter a heated space, buy a long-stem, frost-free hose bib (below right), which shuts water off inside rather than outside. If you live in a warm climate, simply connect pipe to a standard hose bib.

If the hose bib will attach to a sprinkler system, install a hose bib with an antisiphon device, which prevents water from backing up into the house and possibly contaminating your household water.

PRESTART CHECKLIST

☐ **TIME**
An hour or two to tap into a supply line and install a hose bib

☐ **TOOLS**
Tools for working with pipe, carpenter's square, drill, spade bit, screwdriver, caulk gun

☐ **SKILLS**
Working with supply pipe

☐ **PREP**
Find a location that's convenient for attaching hoses and close to a cold water pipe

☐ **MATERIALS**
Hose bib, silicone caulk, deck screws, pipe and fittings, flux, solder, pipe-thread tape

Cold supply

Spade bit large enough to accommodate hose bib

Rim joist

1 At a point slightly higher than the cold water pipe you will tap into, drill a locator hole with a long, thin bit. Bore through the rim joist, sheathing, and siding. To avoid splintering the wood, drill partway from the indoors out, then finish by drilling from the outside in.

Gasket

Hose bib

2 From the outside slip on the plastic gasket and push the hose bib through the hole. Apply silicone caulk around the hole and attach the hose bib by driving two deck screws that are coated to resist rusting.

FROST-FREE HOSE BIB INSTALLATION

Adapter

Shutoff valve

Nipple

Extended stem

Siding

Frost-free hose bib

Hose bib stem valve

Plan for all the pieces you will need to install a hose bib. In this case a short nipple connects the hose bib to the shutoff valve. The valve connects to the supply line with a sweated copper adapter.

3 Hold a carpenter's square or straight board alongside the hose bib location and mark the cold water pipe for the location of the tee fitting. **Shut off the water.** Cut into the pipe and install the fitting.

4 Dry-fit a nipple and an elbow to the tee. Dry-fit an adapter, a nipple, and a shutoff. (A dielectric fitting is not needed if the bib is chrome-plated brass.) Make sure the hose bib slopes so it drains when turned off. Place the final nipple in the valve and mark it for cutting.

5 Remove the inner parts of the shutoff valve. Protect the framing with a heat-proof fiber shield and sweat all the joints (pages 126–127).

Galvanized-pipe connections

To break into a galvanized pipe, cut the supply pipe with a hacksaw or reciprocating saw equipped with a metal-cutting blade (pages 134–135) and remove pipe back to the nearest joint. Add sections of threaded pipe to reach the location of the hose bib.

Install a union and tee fitting and add a nipple and elbow to reach the level of the hose bib. (Build in a slight incline away from the hose bib.) Drill a locator hole and bore a 1⅛-inch hole (Step 1, opposite). Add nipples and a union to reach a coupler attached to the hose bib.

If the supply line does not already have a stop valve in the near vicinity, add one between the union and the coupling.

INSTALLING AN IRRIGATION SYSTEM

A home irrigation system can solve a number of landscaping and other problems in a single installation.

First it can save you the time and trouble of having to tend sprinklers and drag hoses around the yard at preappointed times.

Second by matching the watering needs of your landscape to your schedule, climate, and plantings, it will save you money wasted by inefficient manual watering. Your savings will increase even more if you're in the habit of leaving the soakers and sprinklers on all night.

Installing an irrigation system requires some manual labor, but it's not backbreaking stuff, especially if you don't rush it. You probably can't get the whole thing done in one weekend anyway, so you might as well take your time. Furthermore modern technology has made assembly of the system itself—the valves, fitttings, piping, and spray heads—even easier, further simplifying the job.

There's one aspect, however, you won't be able to avoid, and that's planning your system.

Planning starts when you begin to map your irrigation system—making a careful sketch of your yard, designating trees, shrubs, sidewalks, fences, slopes, sunny and shaded areas, and all permanent structures and planting beds, along with dimensions between them and a brief description of what's planted where. That information will help your supplier determine what kind of sprinkler head will meet the specific watering needs of each area. Your map will also need to show where the manifold (connection/distribution point) will be, usually in an inconspicuous spot close to the water line (below).

Your supplier also will need to know something about the water pressure at your house, and most will loan you a gauge you can use to measure it. (If not, see page 264 for ways to measure flow and pressure yourself.) Water pressure and flow rate matter because you can't have more than 60 to 75 percent of the total pressure going into an irrigation system. If you need more heads than this general rule allows, you can establish subsystems, each with their own dedicated valve, programmed so they water at different times.

And when it comes to timers, you'll find that manual timers, though inexpensive, require more attention than you may want to give to a system you intended to do the work for you. Automatic timers irrigate your landscape right on schedule, even when you're not there.

When you begin installation, your sketch will prove invaluable. You'll still need to lay down mason's lines to guide your excavation, but your irrigation map will show you where to start and stop and how many heads to install along a given line and at what intervals.

You'll notice that each sprinkler head is designed for a specific watering need. Many are adjustable to allow targeted spot-watering without watering inorganic objects such as sidewalks, driveways, or the house.

PRESTART CHECKLIST

☐ **TIME**
Four days to a week to excavate and install, more for large or complicated systems

☐ **TOOLS**
Shovel, wrenches, screwdriver, tape measure, PVC cutter, mason's line, marking paint

☐ **SKILLS**
Excavating; assembling PVC pipe, fittings, spray heads

☐ **PREP**
Sketch plan and consult with irrigation supplier

☐ **MATERIALS**
PVC pipe, fittings, glue, spray heads

MAPPING YOUR IRRIGATION PLAN

Make a detailed sketch of your entire landscape, noting the location and dimensions of all permanent structures and features, as well as the exact distances between them. Note, too, the length and width of the perimeter. Indicate the areas you intend to irrigate and list the species of grass in the yard, as well as the kind of plantings in each area. Take this map to your irrigation supply dealer for a consultation about the kinds of spray heads you need, the type and diameter of the piping, and an analysis of the cost.

Pop-up lawn heads

Shrub spray heads

Dedicated valve

Bubblers along front edge

When your order is delivered, gather all the parts onsite and compare what you have on hand with your irrigation plan. Make sure everything is there. If something is missing go back to the supplier to get it before starting your excavation.

Pop-up style sprinkler heads are installed just below ground level so mowers or foot traffic won't damage them. The best ones are adjustable. Shrub sprinklers are taller for use in flower and shrub beds. When selecting the proper height to install, keep in mind the mature size of the plants.

Valves

Electronic control valve

Antisiphon valve

PVC risers

Existing hose bib

Supply pipe

Tee-fitting

Shutoff valve

Spray heads

Rotating spray head

Pop-up head

Bubbler

Spray head

Spray head on flexible riser

Typical couplings

Select sprinkler heads based on the coverage needed for a given area. Large areas need one style, corners need another, and areas under shrubs need still another type. Don't put a shrub head or spray head on a riser anywhere a person would trip on it.

Installing the system

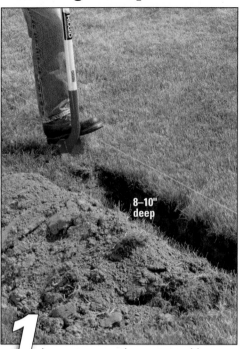

1 Lay out your entire system with stakes and mason's lines. Use the lines as a guide or mark the ground with upside-down paint and move the lines out of your way. Excavate to a depth of 8 to 10 inches (but consult your retailer for depth in a cold climate). Save the sod to re-cover the trench.

8–10" deep

Anti-siphon valve

Irrigation system shutoff valve

2 Connect piping to the main water supply pipe, then install a control valve and antisiphon valve at least 6 inches above ground level. When you assemble the lines and heads in the trench, start here and work from this location outward.

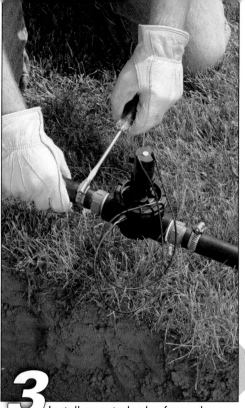

3 Install a control valve for each circuit in the system. Some types are made to be wired to the timer. Manual control valves are less expensive but less convenient by a large margin. If budget allows get the low-voltage models. Make sure the covers of all the valve boxes are at ground level.

Checking your water pressure

Purchase an inexpensive pressure gauge with a hose fitting at a home center. Screw it tightly to an outdoor hose bib. Make sure all other faucets in and outside are off, then open this one fully. Make note of the pressure. Take repeated readings at other hose bibs and use the lowest to calculate your system pressure.

Checking the flow rate

Insert the end of a garden hose in an empty gallon milk jug. Turn the valve on all the way and time how long it takes the bottle to fill. Divide the container size (in gallons) by the time (in seconds) it takes to fill it. Multiply it by 60 seconds. The resulting number is the flow rate in gallons per minute (GPM). (Multiply that number by 60 if you need to determine gallons per hour.)

What If …
My irrigation line ties to an interior water line?

Mark the location of the pipe carefully on the outside wall. Cut the appropriate size hole in the outside surface of the foundation. Insert a straight piece of PVC pipe through the hole and mark its location on the inside line. **Shut the water off,** install a tee fitting on the inside line, and connect the exterior water line to the tee. Seal the hole around the pipe with polyurethane foam.

4 Lay out the pieces on the ground in the order they will be installed. Cut pipe to length and dry-assemble the pieces outside of the trench in sections. Lay a section in the trench to make sure it fits. Then disassemble, glue (or clamp), and reassemble. Mark spray head locations clearly.

5 Take periodic measurements as you're excavating and assembling. Spray heads must be level with each other or gravity will favor one over the other and prevent pop-ups from operating properly.

6 Clamp-on spray head fittings install easily where you need them. Some spray head fittings employ a self-piercing tip that screws into the fitting to punch a hole in the line.

WHAT IF ...
My soil needs amendments?

Soil types and conditions will affect the efficiency of your irrigation far more than you might think. Sandy soils absorb water more quickly than clay soils. If you supply more water than the soil can absorb, the excess water will simply run off.

In all cases you simply want the best growing medium for whatever you have planted in a specific location. Although most soils are not perfect for growing, you can amend them (usually with organic matter) to improve their ability to nurture your plants. Garden centers carry amendments appropriate to the condition of your soil and your planting plans—generally a mix of well-rotted manure, compost, and soil conditioners.

Add any amendments before excavating your irrigation lines. Spread the organic amendments over the soil. Then mix the amendments into the soil thoroughly, using a rototiller. As a last step distribute the amended soils over the area evenly.

Installing the system *continued*

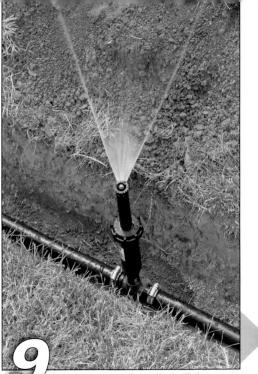

7 Wherever the flow of water will change directions, install the appropriate fitting—either a tee fitting, four-way cross, or elbow. If using glued pipe make sure the surfaces of the joints are clean before gluing. If using clamped fittings do not overtighten the clamps.

8 When you reach a spray head location, install the head specified by your irrigation map. Install lawn heads just above ground level but lower than mower blades. Cut the risers for shrub heads long enough to position the head above the foliage.

9 Once you have installed all the spray heads, but before you hook up the system permanently, attach a hose and flush out the system. Make sure all heads are operating properly and provide the coverage required.

Water supply options

MILD CLIMATES
Outdoor faucet
Irrigation line shutoff valve
To control valves

COLD CLIMATES
To control valves
Irrigation line shutoff valve
Compression tee
Drain cap
House service line
Water meter

In climates where winter weather doesn't bring freezing temperatures, tapping your irrigation system into an outside water line makes an easy installation, especially because you won't have to cut any existing water lines. Unscrew the outdoor faucet and install a tee fitting whose outlet diameter matches the size of your shutoff valve piping. Install nipples on either side of the shutoff valve that will put the connecting elbow exactly at the bottom of the trench.

In cold climates the best location for the irrigation service is indoors, close to the water meter. Cut the water line between the water meter and the house service line and install a tee fittting and shutoff valve that will service the irrigation line. Note the drain cap at the bottom of the line before it goes into the irrrigation field. This allows you to drain the system before winter freezes.

10 Connect the control valve and antisiphon valve wires, following the manufacturer's instructions. One of the advantages of low-voltage wiring is that you can lay it directly in the trench. It doesn't require separate conduit. Seal the connections to keep out moisture.

11 Mount the timer at its location and finish wiring the control valves and the power source of the timer. Program the timer to water the various zones of your system at the times of your choice.

12 Cover the valves with the manufacturer's covers, then backfill the trench in soil layers of about 2 inches, tamping the soil gently as you go. Do not disturb the orientation of the spray heads. Re-cover the trench with sod.

Spray patterns and overlap

Install **lawn heads** so they recede to ground level when not activated but pop up high enough that their spray pattern rises above the grass.

Different spray heads exhibit patterns for various irrigation purposes. No matter what kind of spray heads are installed in a given area, make sure you have enough heads installed so their patterns overlap. Failure to overlap will cause dry spots in the irrigated field.

Shrub heads should be installed on risers that put their spray pattern above the foliage.

Bubblers let water out just above ground level.

INSTALLING A POND WITH A FOUNTAIN

No matter what style of landscape you have—or are considering—there's a style of pond and fountain that will complement it. Installing your own pond and fountain may seem like a formidable task, and it does involve some physical labor, but building a pond is well within the reach of most homeowners. Besides, much of the physical labor makes an excellent excuse for a pond-building party. Before you get the shovels out, however, you'll need to do some planning.

Location

Where you put the pond will depend on a number of factors. First consider the general terrain. You'll want to stay away from slopes, unless you plan to turn them into waterfalls. Soil conditions matter too. Rocky soil will make excavation difficult and may call for an aboveground pond. Sandy soil may not be stable and could require a preformed liner. Clay, though difficult to dig, holds its shape and is excellent for flexible liners. How the sun hits your location will affect fish, plantings, and even how you use the pond.

And while you'll want easy access to this water feature, you may want it somewhat hidden from view so it provides a private retreat. How you want to use the pond will have as much to do with its location as any other feature. On an entirely practical level, however, the installation of a fountain in conjunction with the pond means you'll either have to locate it fairly close to an existing power source or bring the electric power to it in underground conduit.

Design

Because flexible liners fold into and follow the shape of the excavation, you can design the shape of your pond in whatever contour you want. Even if you decide to install a preformed liner, you'll find modern designs can match most every expectation. You'll want to consider the scale of your pond, of course, making sure it does not overpower the size of your yard or otherwise look insignificant in a large space. And as much as possible you want to choose edging that makes this artificial creation look as if nature put it there without your help.

Plants and Fish

Plants add color, shape, and texture to a pond and make it fit more naturally into the landscape. If you want plants your pond location needs to get four or more hours of sunlight each day—and you need to be willing to tend to them. Fish also add movement, color, and a touch of the exotic to a pond, and they help control the mosquito population. They also require extra care and, in cold climates, the ability to overwinter them in another location.

All of these factors will affect your design, something best done with a sketch on paper. If you don't have a site plan of your landcape, you can make your own, showing all the permanent features of your yard including the general shape of your house, as well as the location of trees, sheds, and planting beds. Experiment with general shapes that seem pleasing in the location you are planning. If you're thinking about plants and fish, you'll have to do some research about depths and incorporate that into your final design.

PRESTART CHECKLIST

☐ **TIME**
Two days to a week, depending on the soil type, pond size, and liner type

☐ **TOOLS**
Old hose or rope, upside-down paint, spade, level, long 2×4, tamper, masonry trowel

☐ **SKILLS**
Excavation; ability to use level; basic plumbing, wiring, and assembly skills

☐ **PREP**
Consult with a landscape designer if necessary

☐ **MATERIALS**
Flexible or preformed liner, sand, submersible pump, water and electrical line

In addition to the visual appeal of the fountain design itself, fountains add sparkle and the pleasant, relaxing sound of falling or splashing water to a pond or outdoor water feature.

1 Lay out the shape of your pond on the grass, using an old garden hose or heavy rope, according to your final design plan. When the contour is right, spray the hose with upside-down marking paint (from your hardware store). This will give you an excavation outline.

2 Cut the sod along the painted line with a spade, pushing in the spade at least 2 inches deep. Slice the sod in foot-wide strips. Then working from one edge of the pond outline and with your spade at a low angle, slice the sod roots from the soil. Roll up the sod and set it in the shade.

3 Excavate the main body of the pond and outline a shelf about a foot wider, again using the hose or rope and the marking paint so its shape conforms to the pond. Dig a shelf about a foot deep all around the pond, using a level on a straight 2×4 to keep the height of the shelf consistent.

Choosing a location

As much as any other consideration, how you want to use your pond will affect where you choose to put it.

For example if you want to enjoy the sights and sounds of your pond as part of the experience of your outdoor deck or patio, or if you want to see it through the windows from inside the house, then place your pond close to the edge of the deck or patio.

But if your pond will serve as a private retreat, you'll want to put it farther from the house, connecting it to the rest of the landscape with a rock or flagstone path. Hiding it behind existing trees or shrubs will increase its seclusion and create a pleasant visual surprise at the end of the walkway. A remote location, of course, will require the additional expense of installing longer power lines for the fountain pump.

4 Strip away the sod along the top edge to create a recess for border materials.

5 Remove stones and roots that could puncture the liner. Tamp a 1- or 2-inch layer of wet sand on the horizontal surfaces. This sand will act as a cushion for the liner. As an alternative you can spread commercial underlayment material available at your pond supplier.

6 Spread the liner in the sun for about an hour to make it more pliable. Then pull it into the excavation. Drape it loosely across the excavation, overlapping the pleats to make it fit. Work from the bottom up, pushing it into the corners.

WHAT IF ...
The pond is at the bottom of a slope?

Locating a pond at the bottom of a slope is not a good idea. Rainwater runoff will flow into the pond, muddying it, perhaps harming your fish, and upsetting the eco-balance required for your plants.

In addition the runoff can easily get under the liner at the edges and run to the bottom, causing the liner to bubble up with the trapped water.

If you must choose a low-lying location, give the runoff a place to go by installing a French drain. A French drain is perforated pipe in a gravel-filled trench (right). The drain can discharge to the surface farther down the slope or into a dry well.

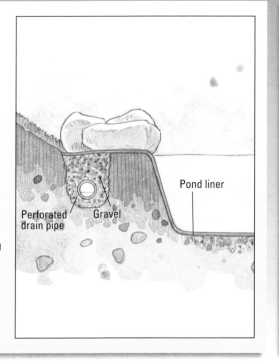

Perforated drain pipe

Gravel

Pond liner

STANLEY PRO TIP
Loosening compacted soil

If you're excavating clay or compacted soil, make your job easier by loosening it with a rototiller before taking the spade to it. Don't loosen the edge where the ledge will be.

7 Continue working the liner into the contours of your pond and settle it with a few inches of water. Pleat the outer edges of the liner and use stones to hold it in place.
If you're not installing a fountain, proceed to Step 8. Otherwise install the fountain (below), then proceed to Step 8.

8 Fill the pond with water. Finish-trim the edges of the liner with heavy scissors.

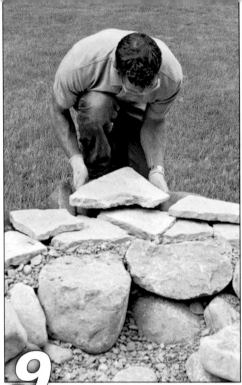

9 Add edging rocks, stones, and other natural fill material to cover the liner and make it invisible.

Installing a fountain

1 Drain the pond if you are adding a fountain to an existing pond. Assemble the fountain riser to the pump outlet and other parts required by the manufacturer. Set the fountain pump and riser on a block or flat stone so sediment from the bottom of the pond won't block its intake.

2 Assemble the fountain and set it on a block. Adjust the riser until the fountain head will just clear the intended water level. Hold a 2×4 on the edge of the pond to help determine the water level.

3 Install an outdoor GFCI outlet with conduit buried to a level specified by local codes. Arrange the electrical cord along the bottom of the pond and thread the cord between the border rocks so it stays hidden. Fill the pond and plug in the cord.

MAINTAINING SWIMMING POOLS

Simply described, a swimming pool is just a big tub with a water supply and a few mechanical pieces of equipment—a pump, filter, pipes, and perhaps a heater—between. Seems easy enough to maintain, right?

The mechanical aspects of pool equipment, however, can make the prospect of maintenance seem daunting. But there are many tasks—starting with cleaning the pool basket and filters, and even doing some routine maintenance on the pump—that are simple. If you perform them regularly, you'll get years of trouble-free enjoyment from your pool.

Debris is the main enemy of pool parts, and your filter is the main line of defense against it. You'll probably find one of three kinds of filters in your pool system, and cleaning each kind requires slightly different steps.

A **sand filter** is just a big canister of special sand whose sharp edges separate debris particles from the water.

A **cartridge filter** employs a pleated filter element that screens out dirt on its surface. It begins as a clean slate, filtering out larger particles. When those particles clog the pores, finer particles are screened out.

A **diatomaceous earth** (DE) filter uses a porous powder whose particles act like sponges, trapping debris but allowing water to pass through.

Before you clean any filter, you have to know when to do it. Although different manufacturers will list requirements specific to their filters, it's usually time for a cleaning when the pressure gauge on the filter reads 10 psi above its normal operating level.

For routine maintenance clean sand and DE filters by backflushing water through them. Replace sand every three to five years and DE every three to four months. Clean a cartridge filter by flushing it with water from a garden hose. Soak it in a cleaning solution. Keep a replacement on hand so you can rotate filters without downtime.

Cleaning a skimmer basket

You'll find the skimmer basket under a cover on the pool deck. It's designed to trap floating debris and needs to be emptied often—daily during heavy use. A clogged skimmer basket will make the rest of the mechanical pool components work harder.

Backflushing a sand filter

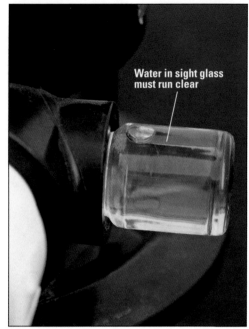

Water in sight glass must run clear

Most filter bodies will contain instructions for backwashing the filter. Look for a multiport valve on the top or body of the filter. If present its various functions will be noted on the dial sections. Turn off the pump, rotate the dial to "backwash," and turn the pump on for about 10 minutes.

How a swimming pool pump operates

Discharge port

Intake port

Impeller

Pump motor

Filter basket

A swimming pool pump operates in a similar manner to all impeller-driven pumps. An electric motor spins an impeller disk on which are mounted curved vanes. The rotation of the vanes causes negative pressure in the water line that draws water from the intake source and pushes it toward the pool through the discharge port.

Cleaning a diatomaceous earth (DE) filter

Servicing the pump motor

1 At the beginning of each season, disassemble your DE filter and clean the grids. **Shut off the circuit breaker to the pump and bleed the system at the pressure relief valve before removing the top.** Remove the top and pull out the filter grid.

2 Set the grid section with the pipe down so water can drain out. Use a garden hose nozzle with a narrow spray to wash away the DE sludge on the surface of each section. Spray until both sides are fairly clean. Reassemble the grids and recharge, following the manufacturer's instructions.

Shut off power to the pump and remove it from the water lines. Remove the bolts holding the motor to the housing and pull the motor free. Most manufacturers sell the motor separately, so you can replace it without purchasing the whole pump. Be sure to get a new gasket before reassembling.

WHAT IF ...
There is turbulence in the basket cover?

If the pressure in the system falls due to leaks in the pump lines, the leak will draw air, which will show up as turbulence in the pump basket cover.

One of the first places to look for leaks is the gasket on the basket cover. Turn the pump off and inspect the gasket. If you see signs of flattening, shiny spots on the gasket, or broken areas (no matter how small), replace the gasket before you operate the pump. Pumps are made to push water, not air, and air in the system will shorten the life of a pump dramatically. Do not try to compensate for a damaged gasket by overtightening the cover fasteners.

If the cover gasket is sound, follow the piping and look for a cracked PVC joint on the intake side of the system.

No air in the system, no turbulence

Air in the system causes bubbles and turbulence under the basket cover.

INSTALLING ECO-FRIENDLY SYSTEMS

Rising energy costs, increased concern about global warming and its relation to the consumption of fossil fuels, and the gradual but certain reduction in available resources have fueled an intense interest in the use of new Earth-friendly technologies.

Alternative systems for heating and cooling and for water conservation are not yet the norm. but their increased appearance in residential construction and remodeling has gradually reduced costs. Installation of such systems makes not only philosophical but financial sense as they become more affordable.

The technologies shown here make use of such eco-friendly developments. Their initial costs may still prove somewhat higher than traditional methods, but when properly designed and installed, they will pay for themselves—all in the long run, and some in the short term too.

Why ground loop?

About 6 feet underground on most of the planet, the temperature is a relatively constant 45 to 70 degrees all year. Geothermal heat pumps capture the heat from the warmer earth and transfer it to the home in the winter. In the summer they take heat from inside and discharge it into the cooler ground.

A closed loop system is a continuous series of pipes containing an antifreeze solution. Once the heat is captured in the pipes, it passes through a heat exchanger, which concentrates it and then distributes it through the home through ducts.

The systems are generally low-maintenance and require only a small amount of electricity to power the compressor and heat pump. Most systems will result in a 25 to 50 percent reduction in monthly energy bills.

To minimize leaks systems employ pipe up to 500 feet long. Joints are heat-fused and pressure-tested. Closed loop systems are often warranted for 50 years.

Installing a ground-loop heat pump

Heat-pump technology has been around for some time, and most older systems relied on the exchange of warm and cold air, using the temperature differential between indoor and outdoor air to warm a home in the winter and cool it in the summer. A ground-loop heat pump is based on the same principle, capturing the relatively constant temperature of the subsurface ground and using it as a heat sink to cool interior areas in the summer and warm them in the winter. The major cost savings of a geothermal system is the absence of a fuel like natural gas or electricity to heat or cool the air.

WHAT IF ...
Yard space is limited?

Ground-loop heat pumps require a substantial amount of piping in order to work efficiently. If horizontal yard space is limited, the piping can be buried vertically in holes drilled to depths of several hundred feet.

Vertical installations are more costly than their horizontal counterparts, but the energy savings are the same. Thus the payback from a vertical system would be spread over a longer period of time.

All heat-pump systems must be sized correctly, and sizing will vary with climate and the energy efficiency of the home. In horizontal installations several hundred feet of trenches are dug with a backhoe or trencher. Piping is then laid in the trench and the trench is backfilled.

Ground loop piping can be laid in straight runs, but modified "slinky" layouts are becoming the norm in residential systems. Slinky-coil loops are a more economic and spacesaving configuration. The coils are laid in overlapping loops in the bottom of a wide trench.

Before you install

Although a ground-loop system is a proven energy-saving technology, like all home improvements it requires a little research to make sure it's right for your home. The energy savings of an alternative technology, of course, are relative to the cost of fossil fuels in the local area.

At the low end of local electrical rates (10¢ per kilowatt-hour), costs for geothermal heat are competitive with fossil fuel heating, and on the cooling side are slightly cheaper than conventional air-conditioning. In some areas costs for geothermal heating and cooling can actually be more than those for fossil fuel heating and electric-cooling.

Even in such circumstances, however, there are additional reasons to consider a ground-loop heat pump. These systems don't produce carbon monoxide and other gases, don't require storage of toxic fuels, and don't need chimney maintenance. In addition heating, cooling, and some water heating come as a package deal and with the leading manufacturers you get top-of-the-line equipment. You also don't have to put up with the noise and aesthetic problems associated with standard outdoor compressors.

Installing a graywater diversion system

The term "graywater" refers to wastewater from bathtubs, showers, washing machines, and sinks. It is distinguished from "blackwater," or wastewater from sewage systems (although in some localities water from kitchen sinks, garbage disposers, and dishwashers is also considered blackwater because of its high concentrations of organic waste).

What's useful about graywater is that you can divert it with ancillary drain systems and use it for irrigation. A graywater diversion system thus takes water that has already served one useful purpose and reuses it for another, saving freshwater. Filtered graywater is usually used for subsurface irrigation of nonedible landscape plants. It conserves treated tap water and may benefit plants because of its concentration of nitrogen and phosphorus. Even filtered, graywater is not safe to drink.

A graywater system employs the same traps and vents as a standard drain-waste-vent (DWV) system, but the drains from the fixtures terminate in an irrigation system (right), not in a sewage system. Installing a diversion system means more than simply running separate PVC lines to an irrigation field, however. Graywater needs to pass through a filter because if left unfiltered, it rapidly becomes a base for bacteria and pathogen development. The system will also require a tank to hold the sudden influx of water from indoor use, as well as a pump to push the water through the irrigation system (graywater is not pressurized like tap water). In addition it is useful to install a diversion valve so the water can empty into the normal waste-removal lines when necessary.

Although graywater diversion can prove to be a valuable conservation technique, it is not necessarily free from safety regulations. Many states do not allow it, and most of those that do require approved permits.

Use of graywater near a domestic well may be prohibited, for example, as well as discharging it under the root level of the soil (which constitutes a leach field). Check with your local health department before installing such a system.

To vent through roof

Outlet from pump

To tank and pump

Diverter valve

To toilet drain

To septic or sewer

Install a three-way diversion valve

Though not required by all local codes, a graywater system should include a three-way diversion valve so that if blockage, plugging, or backup of the system occurs, graywater can be directed into the sewage collection system or onsite wastewater treatment and disposal system.

Graywater pump and filter

Where permitted by local codes, a graywater system should include a surge tank, pump, and filter.

You can construct your own system using a pump and sand filter designed for swimming pools.

If the mechanical components of your system are below ground level, you should house them in a concrete or metal structure large enough to give you easy access to the parts for inspection, operation (like backflushing the filter) and routine maintenance. An 8- to 12-foot corrugated galvanized steel culvert form makes an excellent enclosure.

GRAYWATER PUMP HOUSING

Graywater from house

Galvanized culvert form

Overflow pipe (to leach field where codes permit)

Backwash line from filter to overflow line

Filtered graywater to irrigation area

Pump (activated by float in surge tank) forces graywater through filter.

Installing a solar hot water heating system

Solar water heaters can be a cost-effective alternative to heating water for your home. In a flat-plate collector system, sunlight heats a liquid in a closed piping system and transfers that heat through a heat exchanger to the water in your home. In integral collector-storage (ICS) systems, water is heated by the sun in black tanks and is then passed to a conventional water heater. ICS systems should not be used in hard-freeze climates. Systems are also classified as active, which have circulating pumps (that circulate either the water or the heat transfer fluid), and passive, which don't.

Passive solar water heating systems typically cost less than active systems, but they're usually not as efficient.

However passive systems can be more reliable and may last longer.

In two-tank systems the solar water heater preheats water before it enters the conventional water heater. In one-tank systems the backup heater is combined with the solar storage in one tank.

Cold water line

Solar collector

Hot water line

Back up heater and solar water storage unit

In an integral collector-storage system, water passes directly through the solar collector and is preheated before going to a conventional gas or electric water heater. In a one-tank system, both the backup heater and solar storage are housed in one tank.

Harvesting rainwater

To harvest rainwater for irrigation purposes and thus conserve domestic water supplies, you need four elements: a collection system (usually the roof), a conveyance system (usually downspouts and gutters), a storage device (usually a barrel of some sort), and a distribution system (some form of piping and soaker hoses). You can make your own system or purchase commercial units. Shown below are some of the requirements of a harvesting system. Rainwater is not potable and may contain harmful chemicals leached from the roofing materials.

A storage tank can be almost any kind of watertight barrel but should include a valve for controlling the outlet flow to soaker hoses.

Whether homemade or commercial the tank needs to have an overflow outlet, which also can be used to connect two tanks.

The storage unit should have some kind of screen to keep out leaves and debris and help control mosquitoes.

You can cut off your downspout so it drains directly in your tank or buy a commercial device made specifically for diverting rainwater.

Water-saving techniques

Although Earth's total water volume is constant—because water goes through a continuous cycle of precipitation, infiltration, runoff, evaporation, and transpiration by plants—climate changes and shifts in population can cause dramatic reductions in surface and groundwater resources, the source of most of our water for daily use. In addition most of the world's water is contained in its oceans and is not potable. In reality only 1 percent of Earth's water is available for human use; the rest is in saltwater oceans, glaciers, and polar ice caps.

Water conservation makes good sense for a whole host of reasons. It reduces demand—which allows aquifers as well as rivers and streams to remain at adequate levels and flow—and helps sustain fragile ecosystems. Perhaps most importantly water conservation reduces our overdraw from groundwater resources. Besides, on a monthly basis conservation saves you money.

There are many water-saving practices you can employ in your home. Some of the simplest and most effective are shown here. More information can be found by a quick Internet search for "water conservation in the home."

In the meantime take a quick inventory of your home. Here are the five most common water-wasting culprits.

■ Leaks. Check your appliances and irrigation systems for leaks.

■ Old toilets. These are the largest water user inside your home. New models save water and work effectively.

■ Outdated washing machines. Clothes washers are the second-largest water user in your home. New models use 35 to 50 percent less water and 50 percent less energy per load.

■ Plants. Select plants that are appropriate for your local climate conditions.

■ Unnecessary irrigation. Most garden water is wasted by watering when the plants don't need water. If you are watering by hand or hose, set your oven timer or other reminder to move the water promptly.

Install flow restrictors

To install a flow restrictor on a sink faucet, remove the aerator and clean off mineral deposits with an old toothbrush. If removal damages the aerator, replace it. Insert a flow restrictor screen in the aerator and reattach it. Installing a restrictor in a showerhead follows a similar procedure.

Control water level

All wash loads are not the same size, and all do not require the same amount of water. Resetting the load-size control on your washing machine takes just a second but can save gallons and dollars in a short time.

STANLEY PRO TIP

Installing toilet-tank reducers

Low-flow toilets have been available since the 1990s advent of water-conservation laws. It was clear that the old style tank using up to 7 gallons was a water waster, but early low-flow designs resulted in clogged lines and sabotaged conservation intentions by requiring double flushing.

In the meantime do-it-yourself solutions such as bricks, toilet dams, and water-filled bottles—all aimed at reducing the volume in the tank—took hold and are hanging on.

University studies have shown such solutions aren't really solutions at all. That's because they change only the volume of water used and not other aspects of toilet design. In short most of these devices don't work as well as they promise, and with many localities offering rebates on improved low-flow units, it pays to toss out the bricks and bottles and go low-flow.

Touchless faucets turn the water on and off using electronic sensors or motion detectors. They save water because it flows only when you need it. A similar and less costly device is a pedal-activated valve, which is easily installed and equally effective at controlling water use.

Maintain irrigation control

Installing an irrigation system (pages 262–267) and managing it electronically can pay for itself in reduced water costs. Even the simplest timers can reduce overwatering, and new weather-based controllers evaluate weather conditions and automatically water your landscape only when nature won't.

Capture the cool water

Depending on the temperature setting of your hot water heater and its distance to a faucet, it can take from several seconds to almost a minute for hot water to reach a faucet. Capture the cold water that flows in the meantime and use it to water indoor plants.

Install a hot water recirculation system

Hot water recirculation systems take the wait out of running the hot water until it's hot. They're a great water-saving device because they keep gallons of cool or cold water from going unused and down the drain. In these systems a recirculating pump rapidly pulls the cooler water in the line back to the water heater, which causes hot water to flow from the heater.

Some models are activated by a push button near the fixture. Others are controlled by a thermostatic sensor, and still others are run by motion sensors.

Thermostatic systems automatically turn on the pump whenever the water temperature drops below a certain point. They make sure hot water is present immediately when you turn on the faucet.

GLOSSARY

For terms not included here, or for more information about those that are, refer to the index on pages 283–288.

ABS: One of the first plastic drainpipes used in homes. ABS (acrylonitrile-butadiene-styrene) is now forbidden in many municipalities in favor of PVC drainpipe.

Access panel: A removable panel in a wall or ceiling that permits repair or replacement of concealed items such as faucet bodies.

Adapter: A fitting that makes it possible to go from male endings to female endings or vice versa. Transition adapters allow for joining different kinds of pipe together in the same run. Trap adapters help connect drain lines to a sink or lavatory trap.

Aerator: A device screwed to the spout outlet of most lavatories and sinks that mixes air with the water, resulting in less water splash and smoother flow.

Air chamber: A short, enclosed tube on water lines that provides a cushion of air to control sudden surges in water pressure that sometimes result in noisy pipes.

Auger: A flexible metal cable fished into traps and drain lines to dislodge clogs.

Ballcock: The assembly inside a toilet tank that when activated releases water into the bowl to start the flushing action, then prepares the toilet for subsequent flushes. Also called a flush valve.

Basin wrench: A special plumbing tool with a long shaft to reach into small spaces to loosen or tighten hold-down nuts.

Basket strainer: A drain fitting on kitchen sinks that prevents debris from flowing into the drain. It can be rotated so the sink can be filled.

Buffalo box: A type of whole-house shutoff where the valve is in a plastic or concrete box set in the ground.

Capillary action: The action that occurs when a liquid is drawn into a thin space between two solid surfaces, such as when molten solder is drawn into and around a copper pipe joint.

Catch basin: An underground grease catchment connected to a drain. Catch basins are commonly bypassed or abandoned.

Cleanout: A removable plug in a trap or a drainpipe that allows easier access to blockages inside.

Closet bend: The elbow-shape fitting beneath a toilet that carries waste to the main drain.

Codes: See Uniform Plumbing Code.

Compression fitting: A brass or plastic fitting used to join pipe by tightening two nuts that force a ringlike ferrule into the fitting to assure a tight seal.

Coupling: A copper, galvanized steel, plastic, or brass fitting used to connect two lengths of pipe in a straight run.

CPVC: Heat-resistant and as strong as PVC, CPVC (chlorinated polyvinyl-chloride) is approved by many municipalities for indoor supply lines.

Dielectric fitting: This fitting joins copper and steel pipe. By means of a specially designed plastic washer, it insulates the pipes from an otherwise corrosive chemical reaction. See Transition fitting.

Diverter: A valve on a faucet that changes the flow of water from a faucet spout to a hand sprayer or, on a tub/shower faucet, from the tub spout to the showerhead.

Drain-waste-vent (DWV) system: The network of pipes and fittings that carries liquid and solid wastes out of a building and to a public sewer, septic tank, or cesspool, and allows for the passage of sewer gases to the outside.

Drum trap: Found in older homes this cylindrical trap is built into the floor and covered with a brass, chrome-plated, or expandable cap.

Elbow: A fitting used to change the direction of a water supply line. Also known as an ell. Bends do the same thing with drain-waste-vent lines.

Fall: A word used to express the slope of drain lines to ensure proper waste drainage. Minimum fall per foot is 1/4 inch.

Fitting: Any connector (except a valve) that lets you join pipes of similar or dissimilar size or material in straight runs or at an angle.

Fixture: Any of several devices that provide a supply of water or sanitary disposal of liquid or solid wastes. Tubs, showers, sinks, lavatories, and toilets are examples.

Fixture drain: The drainpipe and trap leading from a fixture to the main drain.

Flow restrictor: A device found in some showerheads to restrict the flow of water and thus reduce water use.

Flux: A stiff jelly brushed or smeared on the surfaces of copper and brass pipes and fittings before joining them to assist in the cleaning and bonding processes.

Hammer arrester: A shock-absorbing device that provides a cushion of air to prevent water hammer.

Hose bib: A threaded faucet onto which a hose can be attached; also called a sill cock or a bibcock.

I.D.: The abbreviation for inside diameter. All plumbing pipes are sized according to their inside diameter. See also O.D.

Increaser: A fitting used to enlarge a vent stack as it passes through the roof.

Knockout: A partially cut hole in a sink that may be punched open to allow addition of a fixture such as a sprayer.

Loop vent: A vent installation for a kitchen island that loops as high as possible under the island and connects to a stack by means of a vent line that runs under the floor.

Main drain: That portion of the drainage system between the fixture drains and the sewer drain. See also Fixture drain and Sewer drain.

Nipple: A 12-inch or shorter pipe with threads on both ends that is used to join fittings.

No-hub fitting: A neoprene gasket with a stainless-steel band that tightens to join PVC drainpipe to ABS or cast-iron pipe.

Nominal size: The designated dimension of a pipe or fitting. It varies slightly from the actual size.

O.D.: The abbreviation for outside diameter. See also I.D.

O-ring: A round rubber washer used to create a watertight seal, chiefly around valve stems.

Packing: A plastic or metallic cordlike material used chiefly around faucet stems. When compressed it results in a watertight seal.

PE: Flexible PE (polyethylene) supply pipe is the newest type of plastic pipe. Many codes restrict its use.

PEX pipe: Cross-linked polyethylene plastic tubing. Where approved by local code, it may be used for radiant floor heating and hot and cold supply lines.

Pipe joint compound: A material applied to pipe threads to ensure a watertight or airtight seal. Also called pipe dope.

Pipe-thread tape: A synthetic pipe-thread wrapping that seals a joint.

Plumber's putty: A doughlike material used as a sealer. Often a bead of it is placed around the underside of toilets and deck-mount sinks and lavatories.

Plunger: A suction-action tool used to dislodge obstructions from drain lines. Also called a force cup.

PSI: The abbreviation for pounds per square inch. Water pressure is rated by PSIs.

PVC: Polyvinyl-chloride (PVC) pipe is the most commonly accepted type of plastic drainpipe. PVC is sometimes also used for supply pipes, but most codes no longer allow it for hot water supply lines because heat causes it to shrink, weakening joints.

Reducer: A fitting with different size openings at either end used to go from a larger to a smaller pipe.

Revent: A pipe that connects a fixture drainpipe to a main or secondary vent stack.

Riser: A pipe supplying water to a location or a supply tube running from a pipe to a sink or toilet.

Rough-in: The early stages of a plumbing project during which supply and drain-waste-vent lines are run to their destinations. All work done after the rough-in is finish work.

Run: Any length of pipe or pipes and fittings going in a straight line.

Saddle-tee valve: A fitting used to tap into a water line without having to cut the line apart. Some local codes prohibit its use.

Sanitary fitting: Any of several connectors used to join drain-waste-vent lines. Their design helps direct waste downward.

Sanitary sewer: Underground drainage network that carries liquid and solid wastes to a treatment plant.

Seat grinder: Specialized tool used to smooth the seat of a faucet valve.

Self-rimming sink: Common type of kitchen or bathroom sink that includes a formed lip that rests on the countertop, holding the sink in place.

Septic tank: A reservoir that collects and separates liquid and solid wastes, then digests the organic material and passes the liquid waste onto a drainage field.

Sewer drain: That part of the drainage system that carries liquid and solid wastes from a dwelling to a sanitary sewer, septic tank, or cesspool.

Shock absorber: A device that provides a cushion of air to prevent water hammer.

Snake: A flexible metal cable fished into traps and drain lines to dislodge clogs; also called an auger.

Soil stack: A vertical drainpipe that carries waste toward the sewer drain. The main soil stack is the largest vertical drain line of a building into which liquid and solid wastes from branch drains flow. See also Vent stack.

Soldering: A technique used to produce watertight joints between various types of metal pipes and fittings. Solder, when reduced to molten form by heat, fills the void between two metal surfaces and joins them.

Standpipe: A special pipe that connects a washing machine drain hose to the drain system.

Stop valve: A device installed in a water supply line, usually near a fixture, that lets you shut off the water supply to one fixture without interrupting service to the rest of the system. Stop valves are built into some tub/shower faucets.

Storm sewer: An underground drainage network designed to collect and carry away water coming into it from storm drains. See also sanitary sewer.

GLOSSARY *continued*

Stub out: A brass drop-ear elbow that has one threaded opening and two holes that can be screwed tightly against a wall. Some can be sweated; some have threaded ends.

Sweating: A technique used to produce watertight joints between copper pipe and fittings. A pipe and fitting are cleaned, coated with flux, and pushed together. When the fitting is heated to the proper temperature with a torch, solder is drawn into the joint by capillary action to make the seal.

Tailpiece: That part of a fixture drain that runs from the drain outlet to the trap.

Tee: A T-shape fitting used to tap into a length of pipe at a 90-degree angle to begin a branch line.

Transition fitting: Any one of several fittings that joins pipe made of dissimilar materials, such as copper and plastic, plastic and cast iron, or galvanized steel and copper.

Trap: Part of a fixture drain required by code that creates a water seal to prevent sewer gases from penetrating a home's interior.

Uniform Plumbing Code: A nationally recognized set of guidelines prescribing safe plumbing practices. Local codes take precedence over it.

Union: A fitting used in runs of threaded pipe to facilitate disconnecting the line (without having to cut it).

Vent: The vertical or sloping horizontal portion of a drain line that permits sewer gases to rise out of the house. Every fixture in a house must be vented.

Vent stack: The upper portion of a vertical drain line, which discharges gases to the outside. The main vent stack is the portion of the main vertical drain line above the highest fixture connected to it.

Water hammer: A loud noise caused by a sudden stop in the flow of water, which causes pipes to repeatedly hit up against a nearby framing member.

Water supply system: The network of pipes and fittings that transports water under pressure to fixtures and other water-using equipment and appliances.

Wet wall: A strategically placed cavity (usually a 2×6 wall) in which the main drain/vent stack and a cluster of supply and drain-waste-vent lines are housed.

Y: A Y-shape drainage fitting that serves as the starting point for a branch drain supplying one or more fixtures.

METRIC CONVERSIONS

U.S. UNITS TO METRIC EQUIVALENTS			METRIC EQUIVALENTS TO U.S. UNITS		
To Convert From	**Multiply by**	**To Get**	**To Convert From**	**Multiply by**	**To Get**
Inches	25.4	Millimeters	Millimeters	0.0394	Inches
Inches	2.54	Centimeters	Centimeters	0.3937	Inches
Feet	30.48	Centimeters	Centimeters	0.0328	Feet
Feet	0.3048	Meters	Meters	3.2808	Feet
Yards	0.9144	Meters	Meters	1.0936	Yards
Square inches	6.4516	Square centimeters	Square centimeters	0.1550	Square inches
Square feet	0.0929	Square meters	Square meters	10.764	Square feet
Square yards	0.8361	Square meters	Square meters	1.1960	Square yards
Acres	0.4047	Hectares	Hectares	2.4711	Acres
Cubic inches	16.387	Cubic centimeters	Cubic centimeters	0.0610	Cubic inches
Cubic feet	0.0283	Cubic meters	Cubic meters	35.315	Cubic feet
Cubic feet	28.316	Liters	Liters	0.0353	Cubic feet
Cubic yards	0.7646	Cubic meters	Cubic meters	1.308	Cubic yards
Cubic yards	764.55	Liters	Liters	0.0013	Cubic yards

To convert from degrees Fahrenheit (F) to degrees Celsius (C), first subtract 32, then multiply by $\frac{5}{9}$.

To convert from degrees Celsius to degrees Fahrenheit, multiply by $\frac{9}{5}$, then add 32.

INDEX

KNOWLEDGE IS THE BEST TOOL

FREE DVD INSIDE WIRING BOOK!

STANLEY COMPLETE
WIRING
EXPANDED EDITION! FREE DVD INSIDE!
UPGRADES FOR YOUR HOME
■ TROUBLESHOOTING AND REPAIRS
■ STEP-BY-STEP INSTRUCTIONS

STANLEY COMPLETE
BATHS
■ PLANNING & DESIGN
■ PLUMBING & LIGHTING
■ FLOORING, FRAMING, CABINETS, COUNTERTOPS

STANLEY COMPLETE
Tiling
■ STEP-BY-STEP INSTRUCTIONS
■ FLOORS, WALLS & COUNTERTOPS
■ DECORATIVE PROJECTS

CONSTRUCT   REJUVENATE   PLAN & REPAIR   ENHANCE   MAINTAIN

LOOK FOR THESE EXCITING
HOME IMPROVEMENT TITLES
WHEREVER BOOKS ARE SOLD

STANLEY ®
MAKE SOMETHING GREAT™